EATING WELL

EATING WELL

AN INTERNATIONAL
COLLECTION OF RECIPES,
FOOD LORE, FACTS, AND
TIPS FROM ONE OF THE
WORLD'S BEST-KNOWN
TV CHEFS

BURT WOLF

Illustrated by Burt Wolf

A JENNIFER LANG BOOK

DOUBLEDAY

New York London Toronto Sydney Auckland

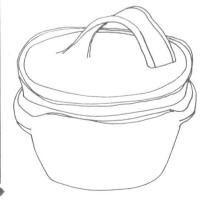

PUBLISHED BY DOUBLEDAY

a division of Bantam Doubleday Dell Publishing Group, Inc.

666 Fifth Avenue, New York, New York 10025

DOUBLEDAY and the portrayal of an anchor with a dolphin are trademarks of Doubleday, a division of Bantam Doubleday Dell Publishing Group, Inc.

Library of Congress Cataloging-in-Publication Data
Wolf, Burton.
    Eating well : an international collection of recipes, food lore, facts, and tips from one of the best-known TV chefs / by Burt Wolf.
      p. cm.
    1. Cookery, International.   I. Title.
TX725.A1W583   1992
641.59—dc20   92-5455
                                                CIP

ISBN 0-385-42404-3
Copyright © 1992 by Burt Wolf

BOOK DESIGN BY CAROL MALCOLM-RUSSO

This book is dedicated with love,

respect, and admiration to

EMILY ARONSON

For the past eighteen years, she has been

the Executive Producer of all of my television reports

and the best parts of my life.

She deserves at least half the credit for my work . . .

and none of the blame.

ACKNOWLEDGMENTS

To make fifty-two television shows, each a half hour in length, and to make all of them on location around the world is a complicated task. Not a single moment of production took place within the controlled environment of a studio. Everything in "Eating Well" was taped on location, from the Norwegian salmon farms floating out in the Atlantic Ocean to the Chinese steam basket weavers in the mountains of Taiwan.

The "Eating Well" television programs and this companion book are the result of the work of over two thousand talented men and women, cooks, restaurateurs, hoteliers, farmers, fishermen, cattlemen, government representatives, businessmen, helicopter pilots, airline employees, celebrities in entertainment and sports, producers, camera operators, lighting directors, sound engineers, television and print editors, research assistants, public relations experts, advertising agencies, and dozens of other crafts people who helped get the job done. I thank each of them and hope that they know I will not forget the contributions that they made to this work.

There are, however, a number of organizations and individuals that I would like to mention by name, because their contributions run throughout the undertaking.

TELEVISION PRODUCTION TEAM

Emily Aronson, Executive Producer
Caroline McCool, Senior Producer
John Holland, Associate Producer
David Dean, Senior Editor
Drew Crossman, Kevin Moran, Editors
Joel Jason, Katy Keck, Mary Lynn Mondich,
    Recipe Adaption and Development
Panavideo, On-Line Editing
Merry Aronson, Public Relations Advisor
Ted Aronson, Financial Advisor
Jeanne and Zola Aronson, Lighting Advisors
Andrew Wolf, Camera Operator
Stephen Wolf, Special Effects Coordinator
James Wolf, Special Projects

THE PROCTER & GAMBLE COMPANY

supplied the primary funding for the project and was represented by an extraordinary group of people who supported the project from the beginning:

Carol Boyd
Gibby Carey
Jim Connell
Billy Cyr
Andy Demar
Betsy Dunne
John Finocharo
Betty Gabbard
Terry Heinicher
Jurgen Hintz
Harry Kangis

Beth Kaplan
Kip Knight
Marc Lefar
Charles Lieppe
John Lilly
Bob Norrish
Maria Puoti
Jim Stengal
Mark Upson
Kathy Willis

CABLE NEWS NETWORK

John Barbera
Tom Johnson
Tom Knott
Burt Reinhart
Jay Suber
Ted Turner

WINN-DIXIE

Mr. A. Dano Davis, Chairman of the Board/CEO
Mr. James Kufeldt, President
Mr. C. H. McKellar, Executive Vice President
Mr. G. E. Clerc, Vice President/Director of Advertising

Senior Vice Presidents and Regional Directors:
Mr. T. E. McDonald
Mr. Howard Hess
Mr. E. T. Walters
Mr. Charles E. Winge

Vice Presidents and Division Managers for each division:

Atlanta	J. R. Pownall
Charlotte	B. B. Tripp
Greenville	T. N. Alexander
Jacksonville	W. C. Calkins
Louisville	Dennis L. Whitford
Miami	R. J. Ehster
Montgomery	H. E. Miller
New Orleans	R. A. Sevin
Orlando	Dan LaFever
Raleigh	John W. Critchlow
Tampa	D. L. Kimsey
Texas	Larry Sadlowski

GREY ADVERTISING

John Fox
Ken Levy
Tony Pugliese
Hy Rosen

THE WILLIAM COOK AGENCY

Laura Benton
Glyn Denton
Carson Eddings
Pam Kennedy
Marty Lynch
Dick Matthews
JoAnn Nolan
Pat Ovard
Jim Radcliff
Mike Russell

IN ADDITION

William G. Barry
Bill Dreher
Toby Feinstein
Kenneth Jackier
Judith Kern
Dan Klayman
Joel Kleiman
Jonathan Korn
Michael LaBonia
Jenifer Harvey Lang
Dario & Gabriella Mariotti
May Mendez
Mykal
Rosemary O'Brien
Larry Ossias
Janet Pappas
Lynn Prime
Virginia Shields
Dawn Smith
Ira Tumpowski

The American Dietetic Association

And at the core of every project, our legal counsel, confidant, and loyal friend, Raymond Merritt of Willkie, Farr & Gallagher.

CONTENTS

INTRODUCTION

Why is there a handle on my teacup in Tulsa, but not in Tokyo? Why do I eat with a fork in Paris, but not in Peking? Why is it appropriate to have a biscuit, berries, and cream at breakfast, while the exact same ingredients reassembled into strawberry short-cake are unsuitable in the morning? What made a high-fat diet essential for survival in the past and a killer today? For some reason that I cannot explain, questions like these, about how and why people eat and drink the way they do, have fascinated me for over 30 years, and I have spent most of those decades researching and reporting on our consuming passions.

In 1989, I began videotaping a series of fifty-two television programs that take a look at the history, folklore, food habits, and recipes of various cities around the world. I wanted to understand why the people in these towns eat the way they do, to discover some of their best-tasting foods and recipes, and adapt them for use in the average home kitchen. I also began evaluating the information being presented by scientists on the relationship of food to health and incorporating the most reliable nutritional rec-ommendations into the specific recipes. This book contains the information presented in the first twenty-six episodes of that series, which is called "Burt Wolf/Eating Well."

I have chosen recipes that reflect the cooking of the communities I have studied, but I have made a great effort to avoid ingredients that are hard to come by as well as techniques that are difficult to perform. I like recipes that are simple, easy, and worth the time, effort, and money.

I hope this book gives you as much pleasure in its use as it gave me in its preparation; and if the text leads you to join me on your local educational television station when it is broadcasting "Eating Well" . . . all the better.

BURT WOLF
NEW YORK CITY MARCH 1992

SOUPS AND STEWS

SOUPS

STEWS, CHILIES, AND CHOWDERS

BLACK BEAN SOUP
ZARAGOZANA RESTAURANT ◆ OLD SAN JUAN, PUERTO RICO

MAKES 12 SERVINGS

1 pound dried black beans
10 cups chicken stock
4 tablespoons unsalted
  butter
2 ribs celery, finely
  chopped
2 medium onions, finely
  chopped
1 clove garlic, crushed
1½ tablespoons all-purpose
  flour
1 bay leaf
Freshly ground black
  pepper
Salt
½ cup Madeira wine
  (optional)

GARNISHES
Lemon slices
Chopped onion
Chopped tomato
Cooked rice

White adobe walls, solid wooden beams, and terra-cotta tiles give the restaurant La Zaragozana the feeling of Old Spain and the kitchen specializes in the classic foods of Spain, Cuba, and Puerto Rico. The restaurant's most famous recipe is for a traditional black bean soup.

1. Wash the beans. Place in a large pot and add cold water to cover. Let soak overnight, or boil the beans in 6 to 8 cups of hot water for 2 minutes, then set aside for 1 hour.

2. Drain the beans and place them in a large pot. Add the chicken stock and bring to a boil. Reduce the heat to low, and simmer for 1½ hours, adding more water if necessary.

3. In another pot, melt the butter over moderate heat. Add the celery, onions, and garlic and sauté until softened, but not browned, 8 to 10 minutes.

4. Stir in the flour and cook, stirring constantly, for 1 minute.

5. Stir the vegetable mixture into the beans. Add the bay leaf and pepper to taste. Cover and simmer, stirring occasionally, over low heat for 2 to 3 hours. Check occasionally, and add water if the beans are not completely covered with liquid.

6. Remove and discard the bay leaf. Add salt to taste. Puree the soup through a food mill, food processor, or blender until smooth.

7. Return the soup to the pot and add the Madeira, if desired. Reheat the soup and correct the seasoning. Garnish each portion with a lemon slice, or serve with chopped onion, chopped tomato, and cooked rice.

◆

SOUP-ER MOMENTS IN THE HISTORY OF SOUP

Americans consume more than 10 billion bowls of soup each year and January has been declared National Soup Month.

6,000 B.C. . . . An anonymous caveman creates a hippopotamus soup. Archaeologists dig up the evidence approximately 7,980 years later.

300 B.C. . . . Esau sells his birthright for a bowl of red lentil pottage. The original recipe is lost, but variations of the dish are still cooked throughout the Middle East.

A.D. 500 . . . The word "sop" comes into use in medieval Europe as a predecessor to the word "soup."

1729 . . . The government of the state of Maine passes a law forbidding the use of tomatoes in clam chowders made within the state; since then all New England clam chowders have been made with cream.

1750 . . . King Louis XV of France creates French onion soup from onions, butter, and champagne.

1800 . . . Napoleon Bonaparte says, "An army travels on its stomach and soup makes the soldier."

◆

SENATE BEAN SOUP
HAY ADAMS HOTEL ◆ WASHINGTON, D.C.

MAKES 8 SERVINGS

1 pound (Michigan) navy
  beans
¼ cup vegetable oil
2 cups chopped onion
1 cup chopped celery
1½ teaspoons minced
  garlic
3 smoked ham hocks
  (about 2 pounds)
2 quarts water
2 teaspoons vinegar
½ cup ketchup
1 teaspoon dried thyme
2 cups peeled, diced
  potatoes
2 cups peeled, diced
  carrots
1 cup tomato juice

The U.S. Senate is a complex place and nobody is ever quite sure what is going on inside. But whatever conflict and confusion may exist inside, there is at least one thing we can count on—the Senate Restaurant will be serving bean soup at lunch every day. No one is quite sure how it happened, but during the early years of this century one of our senators slipped in a resolution requiring that bean soup be on the daily menu.

1. Cover the beans with cold water and soak overnight. Drain, discard water.

2. Heat the oil in a large pot. Over medium heat, sauté the onion, celery, and garlic, about 10 minutes.

3. Add the ham hocks, water, and drained beans to the onion mixture. Stir the mixture and add the vinegar, ketchup, and thyme. Bring to a boil, lower the heat, and simmer for 2 hours.

4. Add the potatoes, carrots, and tomato juice. Simmer until the vegetables are tender, about 30 minutes.

5. Remove the ham hocks from the soup and discard. (If desired, meat may be removed from the bones and added to the soup.)

GREEK LENTIL SOUP
GEORGE'S RESTAURANT ◆ ASTORIA, NEW YORK

1. In a 3-quart sauce pan, heat the olive oil over medium heat. Add the onion and sauté until translucent, about 3 minutes.

2. Add the garlic and salt and pepper; sauté for another 3 minutes, stirring occasionally.

3. Add the celery and carrot and sauté for another 3 minutes, stirring occasionally.

4. Add the remaining ingredients and bring to a boil. Reduce the heat and simmer for 35 minutes, or until the lentils are tender. Remove the bay leaf before serving.

MAKES 8 SERVINGS

1 tablespoon olive oil
1 medium onion, chopped
1 clove garlic, minced
Salt and freshly ground
  black pepper, to taste
1 stalk celery, diced
1 carrot, diced
4 cups chicken stock or
  broth
1 cup water
1 bay leaf
1 cup dried red lentils (or
  other lentils), rinsed
1½ cups canned plum
  tomatoes and their juices
½ teaspoon dried basil,
  crushed
½ teaspoon dried thyme,
  crushed

Mozart's Favorite Fish Soup
Goldener Hirsch Hotel ◆ Salzburg, Austria

MAKES 4 SERVINGS

DUMPLINGS

3 slices stale white bread
   (dried out overnight)
¼ cup finely chopped
   onion
1 tablespoon vegetable oil
1 cup ground catfish (about
   10 ounces), ground in
   processor—don't puree
1 egg white
1 egg
Pinch of dried thyme
¼ teaspoon salt
⅛ teaspoon freshly ground
   black pepper

VEGETABLE GARNISH

1 carrot, peeled and cut
   into thin matchsticks—
   1½ inches long × ⅛ inch
   thick
1 medium zucchini,
   unpeeled, seeded, cut
   into matchsticks as above
1 stalk celery, cut into
   matchsticks as above
Fresh chives or tender
   scallions, cut as thin as
   chives, in 1-inch-long
   pieces

For the past twenty-five years, chef Herbert Perkel-hopher has been cooking in the kitchens of Salzburg's Hotel Goldener Hirsch. He has also been researching and re-creating recipes from the period of Mozart's life in Austria during the late 1700s. One of Mozart's favorite recipes appears to have been fish soup. The following recipe shows its preparation.

TO MAKE THE DUMPLINGS:

1. In a bowl, cover the bread with water and soak until softened, about 2 minutes. Then squeeze out the water from the bread with your hands—you should have about 1 cup of damp, broken-up bread. Empty the bowl of water and return the bread to the bowl. Sauté the onion in oil over low heat until translucent, about 5 minutes. Add the bread to the onion and sauté for an additional 5 minutes, breaking up the bread in the pan. Put the mixture back into the bowl, add the fish, egg white, egg, thyme, salt, and pepper. Mix very well. Cover the bowl with plastic wrap and refrigerate for 1 hour.

FOR THE GARNISH:

2. Bring a small pan of water to a boil. Add salt and parboil (blanch) each garnish vegetable, except the chives or scallions, individually until almost tender (al dente) and brightly colored, about 1 to 1½ minutes. Retrieve quickly with a slotted spoon and immerse in a bowl of ice water to stop the cooking. When all are done, drain and place on a paper towel to absorb excess water. Set aside.

3. Bring a shallow pan of water to a boil and salt it moderately, then turn down the heat to a steady simmer. Remove the dumpling mixture from the refrigerator and with wet hands (dipped into cold water) form egg yolk–sized balls (about 12). Gently place them into the simmering water in one layer as you form them. Simmer the dumplings for about 8 minutes. Cut one open and taste to check for doneness. Remove them carefully with a slotted spoon or a skimmer. Keep warm.

FOR THE FISH:
4. Heat the oil in a skillet over medium heat. Sprinkle the catfish with salt and pepper on both sides and dredge in the flour. Shake off excess flour. Fry in the oil for 2 to 5 minutes per side, depending on the thickness. The thin crust should be golden and the fish tender (you can test it with the tip of a small knife). Place the fish on a paper towel to absorb excess oil. Keep warm.

FOR THE SOUP:
5. Bring the 3 cups of water to a boil. Add the bouillon cubes and dissolve. Turn down heat to low simmer and add the saffron, crushing it between your fingers as it is added. Allow to simmer for 5 minutes. Remove from the heat and add the buttermilk, salt, pepper, and lemon juice. Return to *low* simmer for 2 minutes. Do not bring to a boil.

6. Place about ¾ cup of hot soup in each of 4 shallow soup bowls. Place 2 to 3 dumplings in each bowl and 1 piece of the fried fish fillet in each. Place vegetable garnish on the fillet and sprinkle with the chives or scallions.

FISH
4 tablespoons vegetable oil
2 skinned catfish fillets (approximately 1 pound total), each halved
Salt and freshly ground black pepper
½ cup flour

SOUP
3 cups water
1½ fish bouillon cubes
Pinch of saffron
1 cup low-fat buttermilk
¾ teaspoon salt, or to taste
Freshly ground white pepper, to taste
1 teaspoon fresh lemon juice

SALZBURG'S OPEN MARKET

The open market in Salzburg is one of the cleanest, neatest, and best organized markets in Europe. It has all of the fruits and vegetables that you would expect, lots of nuts, fresh herbs, meats, great breads, cheeses, and flowers. It's set up every morning except Sunday in University Square in front of University Church. The townspeople come in by foot, buy what they need for the day's cooking, and walk home. It's been pretty much like this for about one thousand years. Throughout the changing seasons, different specialties show up in the market. Salzburg is well known for its decorative bouquets made from herbs and spices, as well as, Krampus: stick-figure dolls made from raisins, prunes, and dried pears. These are given to children around December 6, which is celebrated as St. Nicholas' Day. The doll is a reminder to behave properly during the holiday season, or else the dried fruits may be your only gift.

ABOUT MOZART

Wolfgang Amadeus Mozart was born on the twenty-seventh of January, 1756. He grew up in Salzburg and produced some of his finest music in that city. By the time he was five years old, he had learned how to play the harpsichord from his father. He could also play the violin, but he learned that from just watching. At the age of seven he went on tour with his father and his sister (she was eleven at the time). A woman in the audience was so impressed with Mozart that she decided if she ever had a son, she would make him a musical prodigy just like little Wolfgang—and she did. Her son's name was Ludwig van Beethoven.

So . . . not only did Mozart produce an enormous amount of magnificent music on his own, he inspired a second body of work in Beethoven. But Mozart's inspirational qualities were not just limited to music. Evidence, the Mirabelle Mozartkugel, the national candy of Austria. It was originally produced in 1891 to mark the one hundredth anniversary of Mozart's death.

PEA SOUP
OLD FORT WILLIAM ◆ THUNDER BAY, ONTARIO, CANADA

Old Fort William was constructed during the early 1800s near Thunder Bay, Ontario. For a time, it was a major fur trading post used by Canadian trappers. The hunters would often come in from the forest by boat and land their skins at the dock. Employees of the Northwest Company would keep track of their arrival, and the disposition of their goods. Most of the fur trading here was beaver, which was in great demand in Europe for men's beaver hats.

Today, the fort is a living museum with all the individual facilities that existed almost two hundred years ago. Members of the Old Fort William historical staff dress up in period costume and go about the same tasks that occupied the original residents of the area.

1. Pour hot water over split peas and soak for 1 hour.

2. In a 6-quart saucepan, cook the bacon and onion over medium heat, or until the onion is transparent. Add the carrots, turnip, and potato.

3. Drain and rinse the split peas, add to the saucepan along with the mustard, Tabasco, and water. Add salt and pepper to taste. Simmer for 1 hour.

4. Remove half of the liquid and vegetables, and place in a blender or processor. Puree until smooth. Mix with unblended soup and serve.

MAKES 6 SERVINGS

1 pound green split peas
¼ pound bacon, sliced thick
1 medium onion, diced
2 carrots, peeled and diced
1 turnip, peeled and diced
1 medium potato, peeled and diced
1 teaspoon dry mustard
1 teaspoon Tabasco sauce
6 cups water
Salt and freshly ground black pepper

YELLOW SPLIT PEA SOUP
HOTEL D'ANGLETERRE ◆ COPENHAGEN, DENMARK

MAKES 8 CUPS

1 pound dried yellow split
  peas
2 quarts water
2 teaspoons dried thyme
1 medium onion, chopped
2 carrots, peeled and
  chopped
2 leeks, trimmed and
  chopped
2 stalks celery, chopped

The Hotel D'Angleterre, in Copenhagen, opened in 1755. It's a national landmark, upholding the country's tradition, especially in the kitchen. Yellow split pea soup is Denmark's national soup.

1. Soak the split peas in water to cover overnight, then drain and rinse. Or simmer peas for 45 minutes in boiling water; drain.

2. Place the peas and the 2 quarts fresh water into a saucepan. Add the remaining ingredients and simmer until tender, approximately 1½ to 2 hours. Stir occasionally.

3. Puree the soup in a food processor until smooth.

ABOUT PEAS

Peas are high in fiber, iron, zinc, phosphorus, magnesium, thiamin, and vitamin B$_6$. Peas are also high in niacin, which is an important nutrient, and may become more important to us as we get older. Pea soup is packed with vitamin E, and some scientists are telling us that food rich in vitamin E, as well as foods rich in vitamin C, can help protect our eyesight as we get older.

When you're picking out peas in the market, look for ones with bright color. Also, you don't want any with pinholes or cracks; those are the first signs of decay. And if you can get them so they're pretty much uniform in size, that's even better, because they will cook more evenly.

VIENNESE POTATO SOUP
HOTEL IMPERIAL ◆ VIENNA, AUSTRIA

Potatoes originated in South America and were brought to Europe in the late 1500s. After a few years, they became a favorite food for the European peasant farmers because they grew underground and the invading armies that wandered over Europe could not see them.

Chef Karl Malafa is the executive chef at Vienna's famed Imperial Hotel. The following is his recipe for a hearty potato soup.

1. Put the 3 tablespoons vegetable oil in a large pot. Add the onions, leeks, and marjoram and sauté over medium heat, stirring occasionally, until the vegetables are softened, about 15 minutes.

2. Add the potatoes and beef broth, cover, and simmer for 25 minutes.

3. Add the buttermilk or yogurt, pepper, and cardamom, if using.

4. Puree the soup in a food processor or blender.

5. In a skillet, sauté the mushrooms in the oil for 1 minute, or until the liquid evaporates and the mushrooms are golden. Season with salt and pepper, to taste.

6. Divide the mushrooms and precooked carrots and potatoes among 8 bowls. Add the soup and serve immediately.

NOTE: If you use yogurt instead of buttermilk, do not *reheat* the soup. Yogurt can separate when reheated.

MAKES 8 SERVINGS

3 tablespoons vegetable oil
2 cups sliced onions (large Bermuda or Spanish)
2½ cups sliced leeks (about 3), cleaned thoroughly
1 tablespoon fresh marjoram, chopped, or 1½ teaspoons dried
8 cups peeled, sliced potatoes (approximately 4 pounds)
7 cups beef broth
¾ cup buttermilk or plain low-fat yogurt
½ teaspoon freshly ground black pepper, or to taste
Pinch of ground cardamom (optional)

GARNISHES
½ pound fresh mushrooms, sliced
1 tablespoon vegetable oil
Salt and freshly ground black pepper
½ cup peeled, diced carrots, precooked
1 cup peeled, diced potatoes, precooked

RICE AND POTATO SOUP
FELIDIA RESTAURANT ◆ NEW YORK, NEW YORK

MAKES 10 SERVINGS

2 tablespoons olive oil
2 potatoes, peeled and
  diced
2 carrots, peeled and
  shredded
2 stalks celery, diced
2 tablespoons tomato paste
10 cups chicken stock,
  simmering
2 bay leaves
Freshly ground black
  pepper
1 cup long-grain rice

GARNISHES
Grated Parmesan cheese
Chopped parsley

The restaurant Felidia is well-known for its fine Northern Italian cooking. The executive chef is Lydia Bostianich. Born on the Adriatic coast of Italy, she has devoted her life to good cooking. Besides the work in her restaurant, she teaches, writes cookbooks, and studies nutrition at Hunter College. She graciously shared her recipe for a delicious, nutritionally well-balanced rice and potato soup.

1. In a large saucepan or stockpot, heat the olive oil over medium heat. Add the potatoes and sauté for approximately 10 minutes. Add the carrots, celery, tomato paste, chicken stock, and bay leaves. Simmer for 40 minutes. Season with black pepper to taste. Stir in the long-grain rice and cook for 15 minutes more, until the rice is tender. Remove the bay leaves and skim off any foam.

2. Serve garnished with a few tablespoons of grated Parmesan and chopped parsley.

POTATO AND RED PEPPER SOUP
THE HEATHMAN HOTEL ◆ PORTLAND, OREGON

Portland's Heathman Hotel opened in 1927. The local newspapers called it the city's finest hotel and praised the amenities that were available to its guests. The Italian Renaissance design of the structure was a source of great pride for the neighborhood. The hotel was built next to the Portland Center for the Performing Arts ... and soon became the home away from home for the actors who performed at the Center.

1. Place the sliced potatoes in a large pot of boiling water to cover. Simmer for 20 minutes, or until tender. Drain and set aside.

2. Place the peppers on a baking sheet or metal pie pan. Grill or roast under a preheated broiler, about 4 inches from the heat source. Rotate about every 3 minutes until all sides of the peppers are black and the skin is blistered. Remove the peppers and place in a bowl to cool. When cool enough to handle, remove the cores. Cut the peppers into quarters and remove the ribs, seeds, and skins.

3. Heat the olive oil in a skillet over moderate heat. Sauté the peppers, onions, and garlic for 5 minutes, or until the onion is softened and slightly golden, stirring often. Crush the thyme and add to the skillet. Add the minced jalapeño or chili peppers. Cook for 2 minutes.

4. In the container of a food processor or blender, combine half the potatoes, half the red pepper/onion mixture, and half the chicken stock. Process until smooth. Remove, repeat with the remaining potatoes, red pepper/onion

MAKES 6 SERVINGS

6 russet or all-purpose potatoes (about 3 pounds), peeled, sliced into ½-inch discs
3 large red bell peppers
2 tablespoons olive oil
2 cups chopped onion
2 tablespoons minced garlic
2 teaspoons fresh thyme
1 jalapeño or 2 chili peppers, seeded and minced
4 cups chicken stock
Salt and freshly ground black pepper

◆

mixture, and stock. Combine both batches. Season with salt and pepper to taste.

5. Reheat the soup in a saucepan over moderate heat if serving hot, or chill if preferred cold. If the soup is too thick, adjust consistency by stirring in additional chicken stock or water.

◆

PORTLAND—THE CITY OF ROSES

Portland is officially known as the city of roses and it is home to the International Rose Test Garden, the country's oldest continuously operated site of its kind. Its three terraces have over 10,000 bushes and 400 varieties of roses. These flowers have had a mystical quality through most of their history. Scientists have found fossilized roses that date back over 40 million years. Roses are the symbol of the Virgin Mary. A rosary originally consisted of 165 dried rolled up rose petals. Ancient societies used roses to make medicine, perfume, and love potions. Rose petals made pillow stuffings, carpets, hats, and umbrellas.

The rose has been a cooking ingredient for centuries, usually as the basis for desserts and baked goods, especially in Middle Eastern recipes. Even American cooks used rose-scented water as an ingredient right into the twentieth century. You can still pick up a bottle of rose water in markets that have a selection of Middle Eastern ingredients. Substitute a few tablespoons of rosewater for some of the liquid that is already in the recipe. It works well with cakes, pastries, sherbets, ice creams, and rice dishes.

◆

TOMATO AND BASIL SOUP
TOP NOTCH INN ◆ STOWE, VERMONT

1. Heat the oil in a saucepan or stockpot. Add the onion and thyme; sauté until the onion is soft, but not brown. Add the tomatoes and stir briefly.

2. Add the flour, and stir for about 3 minutes, or until the flour is fully incorporated into the mixture.

3. Stir in the sugar, chicken stock, and tomato paste. Simmer, partially covered, for 30 minutes, stirring occasionally to prevent sticking.

4. Puree the soup mixture in a food processor and return to the pot. Season with salt and pepper, to taste.

5. Just before serving, add the basil. Serve with a dollop of yogurt, if desired.

MAKES 6 SERVINGS

4 tablespoons vegetable oil
1 large onion, chopped
1 teaspoon dried thyme
2 pounds ripe tomatoes, coarsely chopped
¼ cup all-purpose flour
2 tablespoons sugar
2 cups chicken stock
½ cup tomato paste
Salt and freshly ground black pepper
½ cup chopped fresh basil
Plain low-fat yogurt (optional)

BASIL

Basil is a deep green plant with 2-inch-long glossy leaves. Basil originated in ancient India where it was sacred to the gods Vishnu and Shiva. The ancient Greeks, Romans, and the Hebrews believed that basil had the power to give great strength.

SALMON SOUP

REGENT BEVERLY WILSHIRE HOTEL ◆
HOLLYWOOD, CALIFORNIA

MAKES 4 SERVINGS

4 cups chicken stock
1 pound boneless, skinless
  salmon, cut into bite-
  sized cubes
½ teaspoon cornstarch
  dissolved in ¼ cup water
¼ cup chopped chives
1 cup peeled, sliced
  carrots
1 teaspoon celery seed
Freshly ground black
  pepper

1. In a medium saucepan, bring the chicken stock to a simmer.

2. Add the salmon, cornstarch mixture, chives, carrots, and celery seed to the chicken stock. Bring to a low boil and cook for 7 minutes. Season with black pepper, to taste.

RESTORATIVE SOUPS

For hundreds of years, the cooks of Europe were organized into very specialized craft unions. Roasters did the roasting, sauciers did the sauces, pâtissiers did the pastry, bakers did the breads, ragout-makers did the stews, and each group controlled the production and distribution of their product.

Then one day in the 1700s, a Parisian named Boulanger noticed a loophole in the law which would allow him to sell food to the public without belonging to a guild. What he found he could legally sell was soup. The major claim that he made for his recipes was that they were healthful and would restore one's strength. As a matter of fact, the word "restaurant" comes from the sign on Boulanger's shop, describing his "restorative" soups.

BEEF STEW
CORNELIUS O'DONNELL ♦ CORNING, NEW YORK

I originally met Cornelius O'Donnell in 1970, when we were both cooking at a charity event. Cornie works for Corning Incorporated as Manager of Creative Services, and he's one of the world's leading authorities on cooking in glass. He writes a monthly magazine column, and has produced an award-winning cookbook called Cooking with Cornelius. The following is his recipe for basic beef stew.

1. Preheat the oven to 350° F.

2. Pat the beef dry with a paper towel. In a large nonstick skillet, heat 2 tablespoons of the vegetable oil over high heat. Add half the beef and cook for 5 to 6 minutes until browned. (Do not overcrowd.) Remove the meat to a large oven-proof casserole with a lid. Repeat with the remaining 2 tablespoons of vegetable oil and the rest of the meat.

3. To the casserole with the meat, add the flour and stir until combined. Stir in the garlic, carrots, onions, turnip, orange peel, and bay leaf. Toss to mix. Add enough beef broth to cover the meat. Cover with a lid and bring to a simmer over medium heat.

4. Place in the oven and simmer for 2 hours. You may have to lower the oven temperature to 300° F. to maintain the simmer, and you may have to add additional beef broth to keep the meat covered in liquid. Stir occasionally.

5. Remove the bay leaf and serve.

MAKES 12 SERVINGS

3 pounds lean stewing beef (chuck or round), trimmed and cut into 1½-inch cubes
4 tablespoons vegetable oil
3 tablespoons flour
2 cloves garlic, minced
4 carrots, peeled and chopped into small pieces
3 onions, peeled and chopped into small pieces
1 white turnip, peeled and chopped into small pieces
3 strips orange peel
1 bay leaf
4 cups canned beef broth

CASSOULET WITH CHICKEN AND WHITE BEANS
WINDSOR COURT HOTEL ◆ NEW ORLEANS, LOUISIANA

MAKES 4 SERVINGS

1 pound dried Great
  Northern or navy beans
3 bay leaves
3 cloves garlic
2 boned chicken breasts
2 teaspoons vegetable oil
Salt and freshly ground
  black pepper
¼ pound lean bacon, cut
  into 1-inch pieces, cooked
  but not crisp (fat
  reserved)
¼ pound dried sausage,
  cut into ¼-inch slices
1 tablespoon chopped
  garlic
1½ cups canned peeled
  tomatoes, chopped, with
  juices
1½ cups chicken broth
½ cup dry bread crumbs
1½ tablespoons butter or
  margarine

The Windsor Court Hotel in the heart of New Orleans is regularly selected by travel authorities as one of the very best hotels in the world. It houses an excellent collection of seventeenth, eighteenth, and nineteenth century art and furniture that you would normally expect to see in museums.

The executive chef, Kevin Graham, has put some of his favorite recipes into a book called Simply Elegant, *which is a perfect description of this dish. The preparation is simple; the result elegant.*

1. Soak the beans overnight in cold water. Drain the beans, put them into a pot with fresh water that covers the beans by 4 inches. Add the bay leaves and garlic cloves. Bring to a boil over high heat, lower the heat, and simmer until tender—about 45 minutes. Drain and place in an oven-proof casserole. Remove and discard the bay leaves. Set the beans aside.

2. Preheat the oven to 325° F.

3. Rub the chicken breasts with the oil and seasonings. Place in a shallow baking dish and bake for 30 minutes, turning after 15 minutes. Remove the chicken from the oven, remove the skin, and cut into bite-sized pieces. Add to the beans, along with the bacon and sausage.

4. Over low heat in the reserved bacon fat, sauté the chopped garlic for 1 minute. Add the tomatoes and their juices and simmer, turning the heat up to medium,

5 minutes more. Add the chicken broth, cook over high heat for about 10 minutes, stirring occasionally. Pour over the bean mixture in the casserole and blend well.

5. Place the bread crumbs in a bowl and rub the butter or margarine into them. Sprinkle over the beans, cover, and bake for 15 minutes. Uncover the casserole and bake an additional 15 minutes.

◆

ABOUT THE HISTORY OF FOOD IN NEW ORLEANS

The original inhabitants of New Orleans were the native American Choctaws. The first Europeans to arrive were the French; they came in around 1700. Then the Spanish came up from the Caribbean, Mexico, and Latin America. Africans were brought in, and later the French Canadian Cajuns arrived. In 1805, the French sold all of their Louisiana lands, including the city of New Orleans, to the United States government. We paid $15 million for it. It wasn't even a leveraged buy-out. In those days the United States had a balanced budget—we actually paid cash. People from the original colonies began to wander in to see what was going on in the newly purchased land, plus lots of immigrants from Italy, Ireland, Germany, and Greece. As each group arrived, they took their basic techniques and recipes and adapted them to the local ingredients.

The process of adapting recipes has been going on in New Orleans since the very beginning when the French arrived and took their classic soup, bouillabaisse, gave up the Mediterranean fishes, and put in the local shellfish. The Choctaw Indians taught them how to thicken that soup with ground sassafras leaves. The sassafras was called filé and the new soup gumbo.

Three hundred years of serious gastronomic adaptation and invention have turned New Orleans into a city of food lovers. In no other American town is there a greater interest in food. It's the subject of much conversation, the basis of the major social activities, and the occupation of the local heroes. One result is a series of New Orleans specialties that have become the gastronomic signature of the city. The dish most often associated with New Orleans is gumbo, a rich soup of vegetables, shellfish, meat and/or poultry. Next is jambalaya, a rice-based dish with pork or shellfish or sausage or all of the above. Jambalaya is the adaptation of paella.

◆

VEGETARIAN CHILI
LA COSTA RESORT AND SPA ♦ CARLSBAD, CALIFORNIA

MAKES 4 SERVINGS

1 cup chopped onion
¾ cup chopped celery
¾ cup chopped carrots
2 cups chopped red and
    green bell peppers
1 tablespoon chopped
    garlic
1½ cups low-sodium
    tomato juice
Pinch of white pepper
Cayenne pepper, to taste
1 tablespoon ground cumin
1 teaspoon dried oregano
1 tablespoon chili powder
1 cup chopped fresh
    tomato with skin on
1½ cups precooked kidney
    beans
1½ cups precooked chick-
    peas (garbanzo beans)
Cooked brown rice, for
    serving

GARNISHES
Firm tofu, cut into ½-inch
    strips
1 to 2 tablespoons chopped
    fresh cilantro (coriander)

1. Place a heavy saucepan over high heat. Let it get very hot, then add the onion, celery, carrots, and peppers. Stir to mix and dry-sauté for 5 minutes. Add the garlic and stir for 1 minute more.

2. Add the tomato juice and seasonings. Cook for 5 minutes.

3. Lower the heat to medium, add the tomato, and cook for 1 minute. If using canned beans, drain and rinse the beans with cold water, then add them to the mixture. Heat thoroughly.

4. Serve the chili over cooked brown rice and garnish with the tofu strips and cilantro.

ABOUT BROWN RICE

Brown rice is brown because the bran layer on the outside has not been polished off to expose the white underneath. The bran layer gives the rice a light tan color, a subtle nutlike flavor, and a nice chewy texture. Brown rice has about ninety calories in a half-cup serving. It's low in fat and low in sodium. Like all grains it's totally free of cholesterol. It's a good source of vitamin E, protein, phosphorus, and riboflavin, and it has more fiber than white rice. Recent research has also shown that rice bran can help lower your cholesterol level.

FIREHOUSE CHILI
ENGINE COMPANY 212 ◆ BROOKLYN, NEW YORK

A few years ago, I conducted a chili cook-off among the firehouses of New York City. The following was the winning recipe.

1. In a large heavy skillet, brown the ground meat and sausage in 2 tablespoons of the oil. Transfer to a 4-quart pot. In the same skillet, add the beef stock and bring to a boil.

2. Remove the stock from the heat, then crumble the saffron and add to the stock. Set this aside.

3. Add the remaining 3 tablespoons of oil to a second skillet and cook the shallots and garlic for 5 minutes, stirring frequently. Remove from the heat.

4. To the second skillet add the chilies and seasonings. Stir together.

5. Add the tomato paste and beef stock to the second skillet. Mix together thoroughly, then add this to the meat and bring to a boil. Stir. Reduce heat and simmer in a half-covered pot for 1½ hours.

6. Add the beans 10 minutes before completion.

MAKES 8 SERVINGS

2 pounds ground round beef
1 pound Italian sausage, skinned and crumbled
5 tablespoons vegetable oil
4 cups fresh or canned beef stock
1 teaspoon saffron threads
2 cups coarsely chopped shallots
2 tablespoons finely chopped garlic
One 10-ounce can green chilies, chopped to form a rough puree
1 teaspoon dried oregano, crushed
1 teaspoon ground cumin
½ teaspoon cayenne pepper
2 tablespoons chili powder
1 teaspoon salt
Freshly ground black pepper, to taste
One 6-ounce can tomato paste
One 30-ounce can red kidney beans, drained

◆

LEAN CHILI
THE CINCINNATIAN HOTEL ◆ CINCINNATI, OHIO

MAKES 6 SERVINGS

4 tablespoons vegetable oil
3 pounds very lean ground
  beef
1 medium onion, finely
  diced
1 tablespoon minced garlic
¼ teaspoon crushed red
  chili peppers
⅛ teaspoon cinnamon
1 tablespoon freshly
  ground black pepper
½ teaspoon allspice
1 tablespoon salt
1 tablespoon chili powder
1 bay leaf
6 cups V-8 juice or tomato
  juice
2 tablespoons
  Worcestershire sauce
½ teaspoon Tabasco sauce

FOR SERVING
Cooked spaghetti
Chopped raw onions
Cooked red beans
Shredded Cheddar cheese

The Cincinnatian Hotel in Cincinnati is well-known for its excellent food, which is prepared by Executive Chef Anita Cunningham. Her specialty is the development of recipes that keep in the flavor and leave out as much of the fat and calories as possible. An example is her recipe for Lean Chili. Anita reduces the fat content by putting the meat into a strainer to let some of the fat drain out. That's a good technique for most ground beef recipes: after the meat has been browned, put it into a colander for a few minutes and press out the excess fat. Fewer calories from fat, healthier recipes.

1. Heat 2 tablespoons of the oil in a large saucepan over low heat. Cook the ground beef until the meat is brown, about 15 minutes. Place the meat in a colander and let drain out. Set the meat aside.

2. In the same pan add the remaining 2 tablespoons of oil, and sauté the onion until it softens. Add the garlic and the dry seasonings, and sauté for 2 to 3 additional minutes.

3. Add the cooked meat to the pan and pour in the V-8 or tomato juice, along with the Worcestershire and Tabasco sauces. Continue to simmer for 1 hour.

4. Adjust seasoning to taste.

5. Traditionally, Cincinnati chili is served over spaghetti and topped with chopped onions, red beans, and Cheddar cheese.

ABOUT CINCINNATI CHILI

The Empress Burlesque House and Moving Picture Theater was a major cultural attraction in Cincinnati during the 1920s and '30s. Next to the theater was a chili restaurant, and that's where the Cincinnati chili craze got started. The old Empress is gone, but the city's affection for chili lives on. From the beginning the basic approach has been the same. A thick ground beef and tomato sauce is cooked and called "chili," but it's served in very unorthodox ways. A plain bowl of chili is called Cincinnati Chili 1 Way, but 2 Way is served over spaghetti; 3 Way, over spaghetti with a topping of cheese; 4 Way adds chopped onions; 5 Way is all of the above, plus beans; and Coneys are hot dogs smothered with chili, onions, cheese, and oyster crackers. Show-business folks traveling on the burlesque circuit passed along the word that when you got to Cincinnati, you had to try the chili.

Chili is so much a part of this town's food that when a local bank was robbed and a photo of the robber circulated, he was quickly spotted by a chili parlor waitress and identified as an out-of-towner. He had come into the restaurant to eat prior to the robbery and had to have the five different ways of chili explained. No local bandit—obviously.

◆

ABOUT SALT AND HIGH BLOOD PRESSURE

Some people are "salt sensitive": too much salt in their diet can lead to a rise in blood pressure and eventually to heart disease. Historically people have fought and died for salt, now it looks like some people die from it. When there is too much salt in the blood, the blood gets thirsty and draws in liquid from the tissues to balance things out. But with more liquid in the circulatory system, your heart has to pump harder to move that liquid around. And for many people, the result is high blood pressure. The Federal Food and Drug Administration estimates that as many as thirty-five million Americans have a problem with high blood pressure, and there are no apparent symptoms. The only way to find out if you have a problem is to have your blood pressure checked. So it's important to do that a couple of times a year to find out how serious you should be about your salt intake.

◆

CLAM CHOWDER
THE EMPRESS HOTEL ◆ VANCOUVER ISLAND, BRITISH COLUMBIA, CANADA

MAKES 6 SERVINGS

1 tablespoon vegetable oil
½ cup diced bacon
1 cup chopped onion
1 cup chopped celery
1 cup chopped carrot
1 cup chopped green bell
  pepper
1 tablespoon chopped
  fresh thyme, or
  ½ teaspoon dried
¼ cup flour
2 tablespoons tomato paste
6 cups hot clam broth or
  juice
2 potatoes, peeled and
  diced (about 2½ cups)
1 small tomato, chopped
Freshly ground black
  pepper
2 cups chopped canned
  clams

1. Combine the oil and bacon in a large pot. Over medium heat sauté for 1 minute.

2. Add the onion, celery, carrot, bell pepper, and thyme. Stir and sauté the vegetables until they begin to soften, about 15 minutes.

3. Add the flour, stir, and cook for 1 minute. Add the tomato paste, stir, and cook for 30 seconds. Add 1 cup of broth and stir, then add another cup of broth, stir.

4. Add the remaining 4 cups of broth, the potatoes, tomato, and pepper, to taste. Bring to a boil, lower the heat, and simmer for 15 minutes, or until the potatoes are tender.

5. Add the clams and their juice, heat through for about 5 minutes, and serve.

ABOUT CLAMS

Clams contain iron, which could help remind all of us of our youthful strength. Iron is an essential nutrient for aging eaters like me, and clams are a nice way to get it. The word "clam" comes from an Old English word that means "bond"—to be bonded together like a clam shell. There are about two thousand different kinds and they're found all over the world. People have been eating clams for tens of thousands of years. When cooking clams, check to make sure all the shells have opened. Any clam that has not opened during cooking may be bad, in which case you want to toss it out.

DUNGENESS CRAB CHOWDER
THE HEATHMAN HOTEL ◆ PORTLAND, OREGON

The city blocks of Portland were designed to be 200 feet long, which is thought to be the ideal length for travel by foot. The result is that you are never very far away from the Heathman Hotel.

1. Heat the oil in a 5-quart stockpot over medium heat. Add the peppers and corn and sauté for 2 minutes over high heat.

2. Add the garlic, thyme, and cumin; sauté for 2 minutes. Add the scallions and sauté for another minute.

3. Add the chicken stock and cornstarch mixture. Reduce the heat to medium and simmer for about 2 minutes.

4. Season the chowder with Tabasco to taste, then add the cooked crabmeat. Season to taste with salt and pepper.

5. Garnish the individual servings with the scallion.

MAKES 8 SERVINGS

2 tablespoons vegetable oil
1 cup diced red bell
  pepper
1 cup diced green bell
  pepper
4 cups fresh or frozen corn
  kernels
1 teaspoon finely chopped
  fresh garlic
1 teaspoon fresh thyme, or
  ½ teaspoon dried
1 tablespoon ground cumin
1 cup diced scallions
4 cups hot chicken stock
¼ cup cornstarch, mixed
  with 3 tablespoons cold
  water
Tabasco sauce, to taste
2 cups cooked Dungeness
  crabmeat
Salt and freshly ground
  black pepper
Chopped scallion, for
  garnish

◆

THE HISTORIC BEGINNINGS OF WEIGHT-LOSS PROGRAMS

These days about 150 million Americans are following some sort of weight-control program, including me. There is a theory that all these diet programs can be divided into two groups. The first is usually directed toward men—there's a romantic appeal to this type of diet. It calls for a rediscovery of your youth and an ability to find your original strength in terms of self-cotrol. The guy who first put this pitch forward was an Italian living in Venice during the 1500s. He wrote a book about what he ate and drank and claimed that it helped him rediscover the strength of his youth. It was a best-seller of the time, and he kept telling his story over and over until he died at the ripe old age of ninety-one. He was the Jack LaLanne of the 1500s, and his name was Luigi Coronaro of Venice.

The second approach to weight control was for many years directed primarily toward women—it was much more scientific. It was about weighing and measuring, detail and control. Many of today's successful weight-loss programs are based on this approach. It was also developed by an Italian during the 1500s. He lived in Padua and appears to have spent much of his life sitting on a scale, recording his weight and the weight of everything he ate and drank. His name was Santorio Santorio.

◆

FISH AND SEAFOOD

CLASSIC FRIED CATFISH
PEABODY HOTEL ◆ MEMPHIS, TENNESSEE

MAKES 2 SERVINGS

2 catfish fillets
1 egg
2 tablespoons milk
Vegetable oil
½ cup cornmeal
Lemon wedges, for serving

The Peabody Hotel in Memphis has been a hall-mark of Southern hospitality since 1869. It has become world famous for the Peabody Ducks who live in their own suite and spend the day in the lobby pool. The Peabody is equally famous for Chez Philippe, the hotel's elegant French restaurant. Jose Gutierrez is the head chef at Chez Philippe. The following is his recipe for Classic Fried Catfish.

1. Pat the fillets dry with paper towels.

2. In a shallow bowl, using a fork, combine the egg and milk.

3. Heat ¼ inch of vegetable oil in a large skillet.

4. Dip the fillets in the beaten egg-milk mixture, then into the cornmeal to coat the entire surface.

5. Sauté the fillets in the hot oil—about 3 minutes on each side, or until golden. Serve with lemon wedges.

STORING FISH

Fresh fish should be wiped with a damp cloth, wrapped in wax paper, and placed in a covered container. It can then be stored in the coldest part of your refrigerator for two days, maximum. Frozen fish should be kept frozen until just before cooking.

CORNMEAL COLORS

Cornmeal is available in two colors: yellow and white. The former is ground from yellow corn kernels, the latter from white corn. In cooking, they are interchangeable. If a recipe calls for yellow cornmeal, you can use white; the color is the only difference. Generally, yellow cornmeal is used in down-home-style foods and white cornmeal is used when a more refined presentation is desired.

◆

ABOUT CATFISH

In the 1970s, a new breed of catfish was developed that thrives in breeding beds made by flooding fields that used to be used for growing soybeans. These controlled ponds range from ten to twenty acres, and are supplied with fresh water from deep wells.

The catfish are fed a specially developed diet that gives them a delicate flavor and tender meat. When fully grown, in about eighteen months, the fish are taken in huge waterbed trucks to be processed.

◆

FISH TIPS

Do everything you can to keep the fish cold from the time you buy it until the time you cook it. When you're preparing to cook the fish, cut away any dark-colored areas of flesh. If the fish has absorbed any of the man-made contaminants from the sea, they will most likely be in the dark flesh. When you're cooking a fish, grill it or broil it; that will let much of the extra fat drip away.

◆

FISH FILLETS WITH TOASTED ALMONDS
ED McMAHON ◆ BEVERLY HILLS, CALIFORNIA

MAKES 4 SERVINGS

2 ounces slivered almonds
Vegetable oil spray
1 pound boneless, skinless
  flounder or other firm-
  fleshed fish fillets
Freshly ground black
  pepper
Steamed fresh carrots and
  asparagus, for serving

Ed McMahon is a man for all seasons. As one of America's most recognizable faces, he has taken the job of announcer and made it a starring role. He has become more familiar to most Americans than their own next-door neighbor.

Ed recently lost fifty pounds and took about fifty weeks to do it. The slow rate is very important. You don't want to try and lose more than a pound or two a week. Most of us spend a lot of time putting on our extra weight; we should give it a lot of time to come off. If you lose your weight fast, you usually put it right back on. The following recipe is one of Ed's basic low-cal dinners.

1. Preheat the oven to 350° F.

2. Toast the almonds on a baking sheet for 12 minutes until golden. Reserve.

3. Cover the baking sheet with foil and spray with vegetable oil spray. Place the fish fillets on the sheet and season to taste with pepper. Bake for 10 minutes per inch of thickness.

4. Top the fish with the toasted almonds and serve immediately with steamed carrots and asparagus.

THE HEALTH FOODS OF THE NATIVE MEXICANS

The native tribal cultures of Mexico have a great understanding of healthful foods. Their meals are high in fiber from an extraordinary amount of fruits and vegetables. Beans are a basic part of almost every meal, lots of nuts and seeds, too. Even their bread, the tortilla, when it's baked instead of fried, has a fabulous nutritional balance. Almost all of their recipes manage to combine small amounts of meat, fish, or poultry with lots of grains, peas, and beans. The result is a very high concentration of valuable nutrients in a low-fat, high-fiber system.

◆

ABOUT THE MAYANS AND THE AZTECS

Mexico's earliest settlers, which included the Mayans and Aztecs, created incredibly sophisticated civilizations, evidenced by the magnificent ruins that remain today. The Mayans believed that the gods had created them for the express purpose of producing great foods for the deities to dine on. The Mayans were convinced that they had been made from corn.

Mayan actually means "the men of corn." The Mayans' sacred texts also told them that if they did not produce the appropriate foods, the universe would come to an end. Talk about feeling pressure to cook . . . the recipe fails, and so does the planet!

This pressure to be great farmers led them to develop reliable calendars. In fact, it was the Mayans who first calculated the solar year to be 365 days. The Mayans became skilled astronomers, mathematicians, and builders. The ancient Aztec central market was so gigantic that it regularly held over sixty thousand people. And it stocked an astounding variety of foods—foods that were at the time unknown to the rest of the world: corn, beans, potatoes, tomatoes, eggplants, avocados, chilies, vanilla, and chocolate. All gifts from the ancient Mayan or Aztec cultures.

◆

FISH WITH MEXICAN VERACRUZ SAUCE
PATRICÍA QUINTANA ◆ VERACRUZ, MEXICO

MAKES 4 SERVINGS

¼ cup plus 2 tablespoons
   olive oil
3 cloves garlic, minced
1 large onion, pureed
One 28-ounce can Italian
   tomatoes and their juices,
   pureed
One 4-ounce can mild
   peeled green chilies,
   chopped and drained
2 bay leaves
1 teaspoon dried marjoram
1 teaspoon dried thyme
One 3¾-ounce jar green
   olives stuffed with
   pimientos, drained, finely
   chopped
¼ cup drained capers
1 pound boneless red
   snapper fillets, skin on

The Aztecs believed that at some point in time a great savior would arrive from across the sea. When a group of Spanish explorers led by Hernando Cortez showed up in the early 1500s, they looked like they had just stepped out of the legend. Within a short time and without much difficulty, Cortez took control of the land and the history of New Spain began. On August 13, 1521, the Empire of the Sun was eclipsed. The capital city of the Aztecs was captured by the conquistadores, and a new society was born, a society that contained the richness and complexity of both parents—not Indian, not Spanish, and yet clearly the child of the two.

You can see this mixture in the architecture of the period. The buildings were designed by Spanish missionary builders who remembered the architecture of their homeland. All the construction was done by Indian artisans with their ancient values and talents. The colonial period lasted almost four centuries. It was a time of European rule, with Spanish, French, and Austrian influences.

Along with the architecture, religion, and language, the conquistadores brought rice, wheat, cinnamon, cloves, beef, butter, cheese, and European cooking techniques. The marriage of the Old and the New World is apparent in the cooking of Patricía Quintana.

An accomplished chef for twenty-five years, Patricía Quintana is also a best-selling cookbook author who believes that the essence of Mexican cooking is

*as rich and provocative as the Mexican culture it-
self. The following is her recipe for Fish with Mexican Veracruz Sauce.*

1. In a large sauté pan, heat ¼ cup of the olive oil over high
heat. Add the garlic and sauté until golden, approximately
1 minute. Add the onion, tomatoes, chilies, bay leaves,
marjoram, and thyme. Reduce heat and simmer for
40 minutes. Remove the bay leaves. Add the olives and
capers to the sauce.

2. In a second sauté pan, heat the remaining 2 tablespoons
of olive oil. Sauté the fish for 4 to 5 minutes per side, skin
side down first.

3. Place some of the sauce on each plate and top with the
fish. Cover with more sauce and serve immediately.

COLORED OILS

*You can create a final decoration with some colored
oils. Green oil is created by letting oil sit in spinach
for a couple of weeks, but you can make any color
by letting the oil sit with an intensely colored fruit
or vegetable.*

FISH WITH TOMATOES AND GRAPES
GUAYMAS RESTAURANT ◆ TIBURON, CALIFORNIA

MAKES 4 SERVINGS

2 tablespoons unsalted
  butter
1 tablespoon chopped
  fresh cilantro leaves (also
  known as coriander or
  Chinese parsley)
1 teaspoon tomato paste
1 tablespoon chopped
  onion
Salt and freshly ground
  black pepper
¾ cup tomato juice
1 cup chopped tomato
4 white firm-fleshed fish
  fillets or steaks,
  preferably striped bass or
  halibut
2 cups seedless grapes
1 lemon, cut into slices, for
  garnish

The Spanish were the first Europeans to come into the area that we now call San Francisco. For 200 years their missionaries and explorers colonized the land. For all intent and purposes it was part of Spain's adventure in Mexico, and even today, people of Spanish and Mexican heritage make a major contribution to the culture of the city financially, intellectually, artistically, and gastronomically.

San Francisco's Guaymas restaurant is one of the finest Mexican restaurants in the country. It has a fantastic location at the edge of the Tiburon Ferry Pier facing Angel Island and San Francisco across the bay. For years it has worked hard to serve authentic regional Mexican dishes to its guests.

1. In a large sauté pan over medium heat, melt the butter. Add the cilantro, tomato paste, onion, black pepper to taste, tomato juice, and chopped tomato. Bring the mixture to a simmer and continue to cook for 5 minutes.

2. Season the fish with salt and pepper to taste and place on the simmering sauce. Cook the fish fillets for 8 minutes, then turn the fillets over and cook for 8 minutes more. Add the grapes and cook until the second side of the fish is cooked through.

3. Remove the fillets and sauce to 4 plates. Garnish with the lemon slices.

CREOLE RED SNAPPER
CLUB MED 1

Club Med I is the world's largest sailboat, over 600 feet of luxury, designed to take guests to the islands of their fantasies. At lunchtime the kitchen offers specialties from the local cuisine. The following red snapper recipe was presented near the Caribbean Island of Barbados.

1. Put the vegetable oil in a sauté pan. Over medium heat sauté the onion, pepper, and scallions until the pepper loses its raw green color, about 5 minutes.

2. Add the garlic and sauté for 1 minute.

3. Add the tomatoes and cook for another minute.

4. Add the lemon, olives, and saffron, crushing the saffron between your fingers before you add it, in order to bring out the flavor. Stir and cook for 5 minutes.

5. Put the fish fillets, flesh side down, into the pan. Cook for 3 minutes.

6. Turn fish over carefully, using a spatula or two, and sprinkle with lemon juice, salt and pepper, to taste.

7. Cover and continue to cook until desired doneness, approximately 3 more minutes.

8. Carefully remove from the pan, and garnish with fresh dill if desired.

MAKES 4 SERVINGS

4 tablespoons vegetable oil
½ cup finely chopped onion
½ cup finely chopped green bell pepper
½ cup chopped scallions
2½ teaspoons finely chopped garlic
1 cup chopped tomatoes, fresh or canned with juice
1 lemon, peeled, seeded, and chopped
16 small pitted whole olives
Pinch of saffron
4 red snapper fillets, skin on
Juice of ½ lemon
Salt and freshly ground black pepper
Fresh dill, for garnish (optional)

FISH AND PEPPERS
LA COSTA RESORT AND SPA ◆ CARLSBAD, CALIFORNIA

MAKES 4 SERVINGS

2 tablespoons vegetable oil
Approximately 2 pounds
  sea bass, halibut, or other
  white, firm-fleshed fish,
  bones and skin removed,
  divided into 4 pieces
Freshly ground black
  pepper
½ cup flour, for dredging,
  placed in a shallow bowl
1 cup dry bread crumbs,
  for coating
Salt
1 teaspoon dried thyme

SAUCE
1 tablespoon vegetable oil
1 cup thinly sliced red
  onion
2 cups thin strips of
  seeded red, yellow, and
  green bell peppers
2 teaspoons finely chopped
  garlic
2 tablespoons chopped
  pitted black olives
2 teaspoons capers
½ cup chopped fresh
  tomato
2 tablespoons chopped
  fresh parsley

1. Preheat the oven to 350° F.

2. Heat the oil in a sauté pan over medium-high heat.

3. Season the fish with pepper to taste, dredge in the flour, tapping off the excess. Carefully place the fish in the pan and cook for 2 minutes, turn, and cook for 2 minutes more. Remove the fish, discard the remaining oil in the pan, and wipe out with a paper towel.

4. Season the bread crumbs with salt and pepper to taste and the thyme. Coat one side of the fish with the seasoned crumbs. Press the fish into the crumbs to help them stick. Place the fish in an oven-proof pan, breaded side up, and bake for 8 to 10 minutes, depending on thickness.

5. While the fish is baking, prepare the sauce by heating the oil in the original sauté pan. Cook the onion and peppers over medium heat for 4 minutes. Add the garlic and cook for 30 seconds. Add the olives and capers. Stir and sauté for another 30 seconds. Add the tomato and parsley, lower the heat, cover, and cook for 5 minutes, or until the vegetables are tender.

6. Place some of the vegetable sauce on each plate, top with the fish.

CAPERS

Capers are actually the flower bud of a plant that grows in the countries around the Mediterranean Sea. The best flavor comes from the tiny variety.

DANISH FISH WITH CUCUMBERS
HOTEL D'ANGELTERRE ◆ COPENHAGEN, DENMARK

TO MAKE THE FISH:

1. In a deep sauté pan, combine the water, vinegar, peppercorns, bay leaves, dillseed, and mustard seeds. Bring to a boil. Reduce the heat and add the fish. Simmer for 8 minutes. Remove the fish and keep warm.

TO MAKE THE SALAD:

2. In a medium saucepan, combine the vinegar, mustard seeds, peppercorns, bay leaves, brown sugar, and water. Bring to a boil and boil for 3 minutes. Strain over the cucumbers.

3. Serve the fish with boiled new potatoes, lemon wedges, and the cucumber salad.

MAKES 4 SERVINGS

FISH

4 cups water
½ cup white vinegar
½ tablespoon white
  peppercorns
3 bay leaves
½ tablespoon dried
  dillseed
1 tablespoon dried mustard
  seeds
1 pound firm-fleshed
  boneless, skinless white
  fish fillets

CUCUMBER SALAD

1½ cups white vinegar
½ tablespoon dried
  mustard seeds
½ tablespoon white
  peppercorns
2 bay leaves
½ cup brown sugar
½ cup water
2 cucumbers, peeled and
  thinly sliced

Boiled new potatoes and
  lemon wedges, for serving

A B O U T   D I L L

Dill is best known for the pungent seed that gives dill pickles their flavor, but its feathery green leaves are highly aromatic. Finely chopped, they are used to season soups, salads, and fish.

Though a native of Asia, dill is grown throughout Europe and America. Its name is derived from the Norse word dillâ, *meaning "to cure." Roman gladiators ate dill as a tonic. It once had a sinister reputation as a potent magical herb; anyone growing it was condemned as a witch.*

◆

FISH WITH BANANAS AND ALMONDS
COMMANDER'S PALACE ◆ NEW ORLEANS, LOUISIANA

MAKES 4 SERVINGS

SAUCE
Juice of 2 large lemons, to
   equal ⅓ cup
Juice of 3 limes, to equal
   ⅓ cup
1 clove garlic, crushed
1 teaspoon peppercorns

BANANA GARNISH
Vegetable oil
3 medium bananas, peeled
   and sliced ¼ inch thick
Salt and freshly ground
   black pepper

FISH
1 egg, beaten with
   2 teaspoons water
¼ teaspoon dried basil
¼ teaspoon dried thyme
⅛ teaspoon powdered
   garlic
¼ teaspoon powdered
   onion
⅛ teaspoon cayenne
   pepper
¼ teaspoon paprika
½ teaspoon salt
1 cup flour

Commander's Palace restaurant occupies a beautiful Victorian mansion in the garden district of New Orleans. It's one of the truly great restaurants in the United States, and the original home of the jazz brunch.

FOR THE SAUCE:
1. Place the lemon and lime juice, garlic, and peppercorns in a small saucepan over high heat. Boil until the mixture is slightly syrupy, about 10 to 15 minutes, stirring occasionally. Strain the liquid into a clean saucepan and set aside.

FOR THE BANANA GARNISH:
2. Oil a small baking sheet and place the bananas on it; sprinkle with salt and pepper. Place them under the broiler for 1 minute, then remove and set them aside.

FOR THE FISH:
3. Place the egg mixture in a shallow bowl. Combine the seasonings in another bowl. Place the flour on a plate and season with salt and pepper.

4. Heat the oil in a skillet over medium heat. Sprinkle each fillet with the seasonings, dip into the beaten egg, allowing any excess egg to drain, then dredge in the flour. Shake off excess flour and place the fillet in the hot oil. Sauté until golden brown on each side; cook until desired degree of doneness. Repeat for all the fillets. Place the fish on a paper towel to drain.

TO FINISH:

5. Reheat the lemon and lime mixture until warm. Over the lowest possible heat, whisk in the butter or margarine 1 tablespoon at a time. The sauce should look creamy; if it begins to look like melted butter remove the pan from the heat and continue whisking until the sauce looks emulsified.

6. Place a quarter of the warmed sauce on a plate. Place a fillet on top. Place a quarter of the banana slices on top of the fillet. Sprinkle one quarter of the almonds over the bananas and sprinkle with parsley.

7. Garnish each plate with optional capers, tomatoes, and sautéed onions.

3 tablespoons vegetable oil
4 red snapper, trout, or
   flounder fillets

1 stick (4 ounces) butter or
   margarine, at room
   temperature
¾ cup toasted almond
   slices
2 tablespoons chopped
   parsley

OPTIONAL GARNISHES

2 teaspoons capers, rinsed
   and drained
2 tablespoons chopped
   seeded tomatoes
12 small red onions, sliced
   thin and lightly sautéed
   in oil

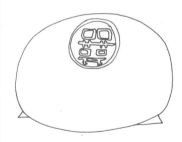

A FEW WORDS
ABOUT THE BANANA

In October of 1987 my doctor informed me that my blood pressure was too high and that my diet needed to be modified in accordance with the most recent information on food and hypertension. One of the results has been that I now eat a banana each day. First of all, bananas are high in potassium, which can help lower blood pressure. In addition, bananas are very low in sodium, high in natural fiber, and, like all other plants, totally free of cholesterol. Bananas contain vitamins C, B_1, B_2, B_6, 1 gram of protein, almost no fat, and only about 95 calories.

There is evidence that bananas have been cultivated for almost 5,000 years. Its Latin name means "food of the wise." The banana is actually a giant herb rather than a fruit.

I try to get my daily banana in the following shake:

1 banana
4 ounces skim milk
¼ cup fresh or frozen strawberries
4 ice cubes

In a blender container, combine all the ingredients. Blend for 60 seconds, or until smooth.

◆

THE LIBRARY OF CONGRESS AND THE AMERICAN COOKBOOK

The Library of Congress was originally established in 1800 to purchase books that members of the legislature might need to consult. It started out as a small reference collection but like most things that originate in Washington, D.C., it just kept getting bigger and bigger and bigger. Today it has almost one hundred million items, including a tremendous collection of American cookbooks, cookbooks that tell the story of how the American family has been transformed from food producers to food consumers. Gone are the instructions to readers to pick your vegetables early in the day because they'll taste better.

The library also has an extensive variety of what are called "charitable" cookbooks. They were developed by Ladies' Aid Societies during the Civil War in order to raise funds for charitable organizations. These charitable cookbooks are a particularly American invention.

The Complete Cook was the first cookbook printed in America, in 1742. Next came The Frugal Housewife and The New Art of Cookery, but these were basically English cookbooks reprinted in America. The first really American cookbook was published in 1796 and was called American Cookery. It's the first cookbook to call for ingredients that were only available in the American colonies. It was the first book to use words like squash, cookie, coleslaw, and shortening. It had the first recipes for Indian pudding, hasty pudding, johnnycake, and pumpkin pie. It was the first to recommend the combination of turkey and cranberries. Where would we be on Thanksgiving without this book? In 1828, Robert Roberts, a servant in the home of a Massachusetts senator, published The House Servant's Directory. It was the first commercially printed cookbook by an African American.

During the late 1800s most of our cookbooks came out of cooking schools, where half the students were the daughters of immigrant families who hoped to earn a living as cooks and half were the daughters of upper-class families who wanted to learn how to give orders to the cooks. The most important book to come out of the schools was Fannie Farmer's The Boston Cooking School Cook Book. It set the basic style for recipe presentation that we use today and it was the first to use precise measurements—it called for an 8-ounce cup instead of two handfuls.

◆

HEART-HEALTHY FISH
THE CINCINNATIAN HOTEL ◆ CINCINNATI, OHIO

MAKES 4 SERVINGS

Four 6- to 7-ounce firm,
  white-fleshed fish fillets,
  such as Red Snapper
Salt and freshly ground
  black pepper, to taste
1 egg, beaten with
  2 teaspoons water
1 cup flour
3 tablespoons vegetable oil
2 heads minced shallots, or
  ½ of a small onion,
  minced
One 10-ounce bunch fresh
  spinach, washed
  thoroughly, trimmed of
  stems, and chopped, or
  one 10-ounce package
  frozen spinach, thawed
  and chopped
1½ cups sliced mushrooms
1 large tomato, roughly
  diced
½ pound diced cooked
  lobster or crabmeat
Juice of 2 lemons
½ cup chicken stock or
  broth

The Cincinnatian Hotel was constructed in 1882. The structure is of such architectural importance that it has been placed on the National Registry of Historic Buildings. For its 105th birthday, the place was given a complete renovation. Twenty-three million dollars turned it into an elegant European-style establishment. An atrium rises through the building's eight floors. Many of the guest rooms have balconies that look down into the area. I wouldn't mind being refurbished for my 105th birthday. The only problem is I don't think $23 million is going to get the job done.

Today The Cincinnatian is considered by critical guide books to be the hotel in Cincinnati with the best rooms, the best service, and the best food.

1. Season the fish fillets with salt and pepper. Place the egg mixture in a shallow bowl. Place the flour in a second shallow bowl or plate.

2. Heat the oil in a skillet over medium heat. Dip each fillet into the egg mixture and allow the excess egg to drain, then dredge in the flour. Place the fillets into the hot oil. Sauté until golden brown on each side. Repeat for all fillets. Place fish on a paper towel to drain. Set aside.

3. Add the shallots or the onion to the pan and sauté for 2 minutes. Add the spinach, mushrooms, and tomato and sauté for 2 minutes. Add the lobster or crabmeat, lemon juice, chicken stock, and herbs and cook until most of the liquid evaporates and the spinach is wilted. Season with salt and freshly ground black pepper, to taste.

4. Ladle the sautéed vegetables and lobster or crab mixture over the warm fish and serve with rice or couscous.

¼ cup chopped fresh
  herbs, such as basil,
  parsley, or chives
3 cups cooked rice or
  couscous, for serving

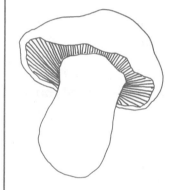

OMEGA 3

Eating more fish may be one of the best things you can do to help reduce your risk of heart disease. Research continues to indicate that a special type of fat found in fish can lower the level of the "bad" cholesterol in your blood, while at the same time, raising the level of "good" cholesterol. That fat is called Omega 3. It's found in all types of fish, but it is in greatest supply in sardines, bluefish, tuna, mackerel, and salmon. Remember to get your Omega oil from fish, not fish-oil capsules. It looks like the capsules are just about useless.

◆

THREE GRILLED FISH
HOTEL LE BRISTOL ◆ PARIS, FRANCE

MAKES 4 SERVINGS

½ pound each of three
  kinds of boneless,
  skinless fish fillets, cut
  into 4 pieces (Choose fish
  for a variety of colors and
  flavors.)
2 tablespoons vegetable
  oil, or as needed
4 cups water
1 cup peeled, diced turnips
1 cup peeled, diced carrots
1½ tablespoons red wine
  vinegar
½ tablespoon prepared
  mustard
3 tablespoons olive oil
Salt and freshly ground
  black pepper

1. Preheat the oven to 350° F.

2. Brush the fish with a light coating of vegetable oil. Grill under the broiler or sauté in a nonstick skillet for 1 minute on each side. Place on an oiled baking sheet in the oven for 5 minutes.

3. In a medium saucepan, bring the water to a boil. Cook the turnips and carrots for 10 to 12 minutes. Drain.

4. In a small bowl, whisk together the vinegar, mustard, and olive oil. Season with salt and pepper, to taste.

5. Serve 1 fillet of each fish with the warm vegetables, vinaigrette on the side.

FISH IN A PACKAGE WITH GINGER AND LIME
RAINBOW ROOM ◆ NEW YORK, NEW YORK

New York's Rockefeller Center has been a national landmark since the 1930s. On the sixty-fourth and sixty-fifth floors of the Center building is the Rainbow Room. When it opened, it was the meeting place for elegant café society. Today, after a full reconstruction, it's a major attraction for both New Yorkers and visitors. One of its specialties is this fillet of sea bass cooked in a bag. The bag helps hold in the food's nutrients and natural juices.

1. Preheat the oven to 375° F.

2. Place a bed of watercress or spinach slightly off the center of each circle of parchment or foil.

3. Pepper the fillets and place them on top of the greens. Arrange 3 slices of tomato and a layer of mushrooms on top of each fillet. Sprinkle both fillets with the ginger, lime juice, and wine. Dot them with butter and top each fillet with a slice of lime.

4. Fold the paper over the fillets so that the edges of the paper are even. Starting from one corner, fold the edges, about 1 inch at a time, until the paper is sealed airtight.

5. Place the packages on a baking sheet. Bake in the middle rack of the oven for 12 minutes.

6. Remove the packages from the oven. Slit the package along the top and the sides. Carefully slide the contents onto a serving plate. Serve the fillets with their own juices.

MAKES 4 SERVINGS

4 ounces fresh watercress or spinach
2 16-inch circles of parchment paper or aluminum foil
Freshly ground black pepper, to taste
Two 8-ounce bass fillets or similar white-fleshed fish
6 slices tomato
½ cup sautéed thinly sliced mushrooms (about 1 cup uncooked sliced mushrooms)
1 teaspoon finely chopped fresh ginger
1 teaspoon fresh lime juice
1 tablespoon white wine
1 tablespoon butter
2 thin slices of lime

◆

GRILLED HALIBUT WITH SAUTÉED VEGETABLES
HOTEL NORGE ◆ BERGEN, NORWAY

MAKES 4 SERVINGS

3 tablespoons vegetable oil
1 small onion, chopped
1 small red bell pepper,
  chopped
½ cup chopped celery
½ small eggplant, peeled
  and chopped (about
  1 cup)
1 small zucchini, chopped
3 cloves garlic, minced
One 10-ounce package
  frozen spinach, thawed,
  chopped, and drained
⅛ cup white wine
Salt and freshly ground
  black pepper
1 pound halibut fillets or
  other firm-fleshed white
  fish

1. In a large skillet, heat the oil, add the onion, and cook for 3 minutes.

2. Add the bell pepper, celery, and eggplant and cook for 4 minutes, stirring constantly to keep the vegetables from sticking to the bottom of the pan.

3. Add the zucchini, garlic, and spinach and continue cooking for 3 minutes.

4. Add the white wine and cook for 3 minutes.

5. Season with salt and pepper to taste. Set aside and keep warm while you cook the fish.

6. Grill the halibut over high heat, or place under a broiler for 4 to 5 minutes on each side, depending on the thickness of the fish.

7. Place the vegetables in a serving dish and top with the fillets.

NOTE: This is a very pretty dish for home entertaining and is very easy to prepare, since the vegetable mixture can be made early in the day and then reheated before serving. Simply bring the vegetables to room temperature before warming.

NORWEGIAN FISH FARMS

The ancient city of Bergen has been around for over a thousand years. It's ideally situated at the end of a giant fjord. A fjord is a riverlike body of water that comes inland from the sea, sometimes for hundreds of miles. I traveled by boat through the fjord that leads from Bergen to the sea. It cuts through some of the most dramatic and beautiful landscapes in Europe and comes to an end at the ocean community of Fitjar, a small bustling fishing village that clings to an outcropping of rocks. Fitjar is not just any little fishing village. Each day, the hardy individuals who live there leave the small island community and boat out to giant floating platforms that are anchored off the coast. The platforms contain nets inside of which salmon are raised. The fish start out in hatcheries on the shore, and are shifted into the netted areas as they grow older. They are fed a specially designed diet, one prepared by scientists with the objective of producing the ideal fish. It is really a traditional farm operation, only it is floating in the sea. When these guys go off to the north forty, it's not acres, it's fathoms. The entire system is made possible by the warm water current that comes up to Norway from the Gulf of Mexico.

◆

ABOUT THE VIKINGS

The ancient Vikings who lived in Norway perfected the technique for preserving fish so that most of the nutrients in the fish lasted for months at a time. Once the Vikings were able to do that, they put the fish on board their Viking boats and made longer voyages than anybody had ever made before. As a matter of fact it was the ancient Viking Leif Eriksson who traveled across the North Atlantic to North America, and he did it hundreds of years before Christopher Columbus. He could not have done it without his preserved fish.

◆

SALMON WITH CABBAGE LEAVES
HOTEL NORGE ◆ BERGEN, NORWAY

MAKES 4 SERVINGS

1 tablespoon vegetable oil
1 small onion, chopped
4 pieces parchment or wax
  paper, approximately
  12 inches long
1 tablespoon margarine
8 large cabbage leaves,
  ribs removed and
  blanched in boiling water
  for 3 to 4 minutes, rinsed
  in cold water, and
  drained
2 tomatoes, seeded and
  chopped
Freshly ground black
  pepper
1½ pounds salmon, cut
  into 8 thin slices
1 bunch chives, chopped
¼ cup chopped fresh
  parsley
1 lemon, peeled and thinly
  sliced into 8 slices
¾ cup clam juice

1. Preheat the oven to 450° F.

2. In a medium skillet, heat the oil. Add the onion and sauté until translucent, approximately 3 minutes. Set aside.

3. Fold each of the parchment or wax papers in two and rub the insides with the margarine. On the lower inside part of each paper, place two leaves of the cabbage and top with the chopped tomatoes and cooked onion. Season with the pepper, to taste. Place 2 slices of salmon on each of these beds, sprinkle with chives and parsley, and top with 2 slices of lemon. Divide the clam juice evenly among the 4 packages.

4. Close the packages, folding the edges over, all around the envelopes. Place on a baking sheet. Bake for 6 to 7 minutes. The packets can be prepared 3 or 4 hours in advance, and placed in the refrigerator. If chilled, add 5 minutes to the cooking time.

GRILLED SALMON WITH BEAN SALSA
MICKEY MANTLE'S RESTAURANT ◆ NEW YORK, NEW YORK

Mickey Mantle is the quintessential baseball player. A farm boy from Oklahoma who was an extraordinary natural athlete. He was signed to the New York Yankees in 1951, and remained there for his entire seventeen-year career—the shining superstar of the greatest winning team in baseball history. These days he is continuing his winning stretch with Mickey Mantle's restaurant in New York City. The walls are covered with one of the most extensive private collections of sports memorabilia, including the uniforms worn by Babe Ruth and Joe DiMaggio. It's a place where Mickey can sign autographs, talk sports, and hang out with old fans like me.

1. Place the salsa ingredients in a bowl and toss gently to combine without breaking up the beans. Set aside.

2. Brush the salmon very lightly with the oil, only enough to prevent sticking. Preheat a ridged cast-iron stove top grill or fry pan, or outdoor grill. When the grill or pan is very hot, place fish on it and cook for approximately 5 to 7 minutes on each side, depending on thickness. Turn carefully with a spatula.

3. Place a serving of salmon on each of 4 plates and divide the salsa equally among the plates. Garnish with a slice of lime.

MAKES 4 SERVINGS

SALSA
2 cups precooked white beans or drained and rinsed canned
2 cups precooked black beans or drained and rinsed canned
⅔ cup finely chopped red onion
1 cup medium seeded, diced tomato
⅓ cup chopped cilantro (coriander)
Juice of ½ lime, or more, to taste
Salt and freshly ground black pepper, to taste
2 tablespoons olive oil

FISH
2 boneless, skinless salmon fillets, each cut into 2 pieces (approximately 1½ pounds total)
Vegetable oil
Lime slices, for garnish

SALMON WITH CARROT JUICE

MAKES 2 SERVINGS

1½ cups fresh, canned, or
  bottled carrot juice or
  low-sodium V-8 juice
1 teaspoon ground
  cinnamon
1 tablespoon curry powder
Juice of 1 lemon, strained
½ teaspoon dried tarragon
12 ounces boneless,
  skinless salmon fillet
2 carrots, peeled and cut
  into thick slices
1 zucchini, cut lengthwise,
  ends trimmed, seeded,
  and cut into strips with a
  vegetable peeler

1. In a large sauté pan, bring the carrot or V-8 juice, cinnamon, and curry powder to a boil. Reduce the heat and simmer until thickened and syrupy, approximately 18 to 20 minutes. Stir in the lemon juice and tarragon and remove from the heat.

2. Steam the salmon for 6 minutes until cooked through.

3. In a medium saucepan with salted boiling water, cook the carrots until tender, approximately 5 to 7 minutes. Add the zucchini strips and blanch for 30 seconds. Drain.

4. Place the salmon in the center of the plate with the vegetables on both sides. Spoon the sauce around the salmon.

STEAMED FILLET OF SOLE
SHUN LEE DYNASTY ◆ NEW YORK, NEW YORK

The Shun Lee Dynasty was the first restaurant in New York City to introduce a refined Chinese cuisine to affluent uptown communities. Prior to its establishment, Chinese cooking of this quality had been primarily available only within Chinatown. The following recipe illustrates the Shun Lee approach to elegant and healthful cooking.

MAKES 2 SERVINGS

2 sole fillets (about ¾ pound total)
12 snow peas
12 black mushrooms; if dried, soak in hot water for 40 minutes or until soft, remove stems and discard
2 tablespoons finely julienned fresh ginger
2 scallions, cut into 2-inch pieces
2 tablespoons dry sherry or rice wine
1 tablespoon soy sauce
½ tablespoon vegetable oil

1. Rinse the sole fillets and pat them dry with paper towels. Cut each fillet in half lengthwise, then in half crosswise.

2. In a large heat-proof plate with a raised rim, place the fillet pieces in one layer. Distribute the snow peas and the mushrooms over the fillets. Sprinkle with the ginger and scallions.

3. In a small bowl, mix the sherry or rice wine, soy sauce, and the oil. Pour this mixture over the fillets.

4. In a shallow saucepan or skillet large enough to hold the plate, place a steamer rack that stands about 2 inches above the bottom. Add 1 inch of water to the saucepan and bring to a boil. Place the plate of fish on the steamer rack. Cover the saucepan and steam the fish for 6 minutes over high heat.

5. Carefully remove the plate from the saucepan. There will be about ¼ cup of liquid on the plate. Spoon the liquid over the fish and serve.

NOTE: If you do not have a steamer rack, try a plate on top of three empty cans with both tops and bottoms removed. Low tuna cans work extremely well.

TILAPIA FISH WITH LEMON SAUCE
THE SHERMAN HOUSE ◆ SAN FRANCISCO, CALIFORNIA

LEMON SAUCE
¼ cup lemon juice

1 teaspoon chopped
  shallots or onions

Salt and freshly ground
  black pepper

1 tablespoon chopped
  capers

¼ cup sliced pitted black
  olives

½ teaspoon chopped
  lemon zest

¾ cup vegetable oil

3 tablespoons chopped
  Italian parsley

FISH
4 boneless, skinless Tilapia
  fillets or other firm,
  white-fleshed fillets

Salt and freshly ground
  black pepper

1 teaspoon vegetable oil

GARNISHES
Cooked asparagus

Baby cherry tomatoes

Chopped parsley

The Sherman House was originally built in 1876 as the home of Leander Sherman. Sherman was an influential patron of the arts and his elegant home became a center for San Francisco's writers, musicians, and artists. In 1980, the structure was purchased by a Persian economist named Manou Mobedshahi. Manou and his wife Vesta, a trained art historian, restored the structure and turned it into what many people describe as the world's finest small hotel. There are only fourteen rooms and suites. No two are alike, but all of them are elegant. They have bathrooms with sunken bathtubs and television sets. They also have wood-burning fireplaces, four-poster feather beds, antique period furniture, private butlers, private flower gardens attached to the rooms, and a Victorian hothouse imported from England so you can have fresh flowers every day. The garden pathways are built of cobblestones that were once used in the roadways of the city's cable cars. There is a team of five chefs who do all of the cooking for the fourteen rooms. That's roughly one chef for every three rooms. With a ratio like that, you can get some fabulous cooking. And that is precisely what's happening under the direction of executive chef Donia Bijan. Donia says that expressing yourself through your cooking is like expressing yourself through a well-spoken language: you should try to be clear, direct, honest, and interesting. I can definitely hear what she's saying with her recipe for farm-raised Tilapia fish.

1. In a bowl, combine the lemon juice, shallots, salt and pepper to taste, capers, olives, and lemon zest. Slowly whisk in the oil until the sauce is emulsified. Stir in the parsley. Set aside.

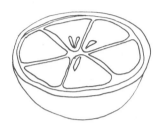

2. Season the fish with salt and pepper, to taste. Pour the teaspoon of oil into a nonstick skillet, and heat over medium-high heat. When hot, add the fillets and cook for about 2 minutes on each side, depending on thickness of fish.

3. Put the fillets on a serving plate, garnish with the asparagus and tomatoes, some lemon sauce, and a sprinkle of parsley.

PACIFIC WHITING AND SHRIMP
THE HEATHMAN HOTEL ◆ PORTLAND, OREGON

MAKES 4 SERVINGS

3 tablespoons vegetable oil
4 large or 8 small whiting
  fillets, skinned
Salt and freshly ground
  black pepper
Flour, for dredging
1 egg, beaten with
  1 tablespoon milk
Bread crumbs
Dash of ground cayenne
  pepper
1 tablespoon fresh
  chopped basil, or
  ½ teaspoon dried
1 teaspoon fresh chopped
  oregano, or ½ teaspoon
  dried
1 teaspoon fresh chopped
  thyme, or ½ teaspoon
  dried
1 teaspoon fresh chopped
  rosemary, or ½ teaspoon
  dried
1 pound small or medium
  shrimp, peeled and
  cleaned

1. Heat 2 tablespoons of the vegetable oil in a large sauté pan over medium heat. Season the whiting with the salt and pepper, to taste. Dredge the fillets in the flour, and shake off the excess. Dip in the egg wash and allow the excess to drip back into the bowl. Dip into the bread crumbs until coated on both sides. Then place the fish into the hot oil. Sauté for 2 to 3 minutes on each side, until golden. Remove from the pan to serving plates.

2. Wipe out the pan and add another tablespoon of oil to heat up over medium heat. Add the cayenne pepper and herbs and sauté for 30 seconds before adding the shrimp. Sauté, stirring, until the shrimp turn pink and are cooked through, about 2 minutes. Do not overcook.

3. Place equal portions of shrimp over each fillet and serve.

BASIL

Basil is a deep green plant with 2-inch-long glossy leaves. Basil originated in ancient India where it was sacred to the gods Vishnu and Shiva. The ancient Greeks, Romans, and the Hebrews believed that basil had the power to give great strength.

◆

FOUNTAINS OF GOOD HEALTH

Portland, Oregon, is a city of fountains. The Ira Keller Fountain was designed to echo the natural waters that surround the city, the Columbia River and the watershed that comes from the melting snow of Mount Hood. The Skidmore Fountain was put up in 1888 by a man who was impressed with the fountains of Europe and wanted something similar in his own town. The Benson Fountains are twenty identical drinking stations each with four spigots. They were donated to the city in 1912 by lumber baron Simon Benson. Legend has it that Benson put up the water fountains all over town to discourage his loggers from drinking stronger stuff.

You don't see it on essential nutrient lists, but water is our most important nutrient, we can only live for a few days without it. Unfortunately, thirst is not a reliable guide to your need for water. You can desperately need water and not be thirsty, and that's why scientists recommend that we drink six to eight cups of water every day, thirsty or not. It's important to your good health.

ABOUT WHITING

Pacific whiting is a fish that is found off our coast from northern California to Washington State. In fact, more than half the fish swimming off the West Coast are whiting. It is mild tasting, with a flaky white meat that has a soft texture. Years ago it was all taken by the Soviet Union and other Eastern bloc countries —previously known as the Communists. But these days U.S. fishermen make the catch. Last year we brought in over 200,000 tons. Because whiting is so delicate, it should be handled with care and cooked the same day you get it home. The best whiting is actually the perfect fish for the microwave. When you microwave a fish like whiting and add a low-fat sauce, you end up with a dish that is almost perfect from a nutritional point of view: lots of taste, easily prepared, high-quality protein, low in calories, and low in fat.

PACIFIC WHITING WITH GARLIC AND LEMON SAUCE

THE B. MOLOCH/HEATHMAN BAKERY & PUB ◆
PORTLAND, OREGON

MAKES 4 SERVINGS

4 large or 8 small whiting
  fillets, skinned
Flour, for dredging
2 tablespoons vegetable oil
2 tablespoons chopped
  garlic
¼ cup lemon juice
¼ cup sherry or chicken
  stock
¼ cup grated Parmesan
  cheese
Cooked asparagus spears,
  for garnish

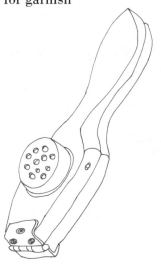

The name at the door reads, "B Moloch-Heathman Bakery & Pub." B. Moloch was the name of a French caricaturist whose paintings decorate the walls of the restaurant. The kitchen has a ten-ton custom-designed brick wood-burning oven which produces over 20,000 loaves of whole-grained bread each month . . . and hundreds of pizzas each day. The sous chef was born in West Africa but is perfectly at home in western Oregon. His recipe for Pacific whiting reflects his love of satisfying foods that are painless to prepare.

1. Preheat the oven to 350° F.

2. Lightly coat the whiting fillets with flour.

3. Heat the oil in an oven-proof skillet. Brown the fish for 2 minutes on each side. While the fish is cooking, add the chopped garlic, lemon juice, and sherry or chicken stock. Let that cook down for a moment. Sprinkle the Parmesan cheese over the fish and put the entire pan into the oven for 5 minutes.

4. Remove the pan from the oven, add the cooked asparagus spears, and return the pan to the oven to heat through for a moment more.

5. Place the asparagus on a serving plate next to the fish and cover with the garlic and lemon juice pan drippings.

CRABCAKES IN CREOLE SAUCE
REGENT BEVERLY WILSHIRE HOTEL ◆
BEVERLY HILLS, CALIFORNIA

The elegant and stately Regent Beverly Wilshire Hotel has been in the Hollywood spotlight since it first opened its doors in 1928. It is an architectural gem, designed in the Italian Renaissance style. The builders imported rare marble from Italy to embellish the detail. The hotel's popularity with the Hollywood set has been legendary. The following crabcake recipe is a great favorite with the hotel's regular guests.

1. In a mixing bowl, combine the crabmeat, bell pepper, garlic, corn, and egg whites. Sprinkle a cutting board with half the bread crumbs. Divide the crab into 12 portions and working on the crumbed surface press into patties, about 1 inch in diameter. Sprinkle with the remaining bread crumbs and press until they hold their shape.

2. In a large sauté pan, heat 2 tablespoons of the vegetable oil over medium-high heat. Sauté 4 of the crabcakes until golden and crispy, approximately 2 minutes per side. Drain on paper towels. Add 2 more tablespoons of the oil to the pan and sauté 4 more patties. Repeat a third time.

3. Make the Creole sauce in a food processor. Puree all the ingredients until smooth.

4. Divide the sauce into 4 bowls and place 3 crabcakes on top.

MAKES 4 SERVINGS

1 pound fresh lump crabmeat, well drained and broken into small pieces
1 red bell pepper, seeded, ribs removed and finely chopped
2 cloves garlic, minced
1 cup canned or frozen corn kernels, drained
2 egg whites
1½ cups dry bread crumbs
6 tablespoons vegetable oil

CREOLE SAUCE
1 small onion, roughly chopped
½ jalapeño pepper, or more to taste, seeded, ribs removed, and roughly chopped
One 14½-ounce can tomatoes and their juices
2 tablespoons tomato paste
¼ teaspoon cayenne pepper

CRABCAKES
1789 RESTAURANT ◆ WASHINGTON, D.C.

MAKES 10 CAKES

1 cup low-calorie or low-cholesterol mayonnaise, or 1 cup egg whites
2 tablespoons lemon juice
1 teaspoon ground ginger
4 teaspoons Old Bay seasoning or a mixture of your favorite herbs
¼ cup chopped parsley
2 tablespoons chopped chives
4 cups fresh lump crabmeat
¼ cup crushed oyster crackers
Vegetable oil, for sautéing
Dry bread crumbs, for dredging

SAUCE
¼ cup mustard
½ cup low-calorie mayonnaise
4 teaspoons lemon juice

In the heart of Georgetown, in a cozy three-story town house that feels like a private home is the 1789 Restaurant. Seventeen eighty-nine was a big-deal year in the history of Washington. It was the year the Constitution of the United States was finally adopted, which marks it as the first year of our federal government. It was the year that Georgetown was incorporated as a village, and it was the year that George Washington was inaugurated as the first president of the United States. Good year. Good restaurant, too: a warm, romantic atmosphere decorated with period prints, antiques, and fine reproductions. There's an old English Parliament clock that dates back to the time when the English Parliament passed a tax on watches, a tax that was so unpopular, the pubs installed clocks to help patrons avoid the tax.

One thing that is definitely not taxing is the food at 1789. Chef Rick Steffan chooses simple ingredients of outstanding quality and presents them in a straightforward way. Classic American food at its best.

1. Combine the mayonnaise or egg whites, lemon juice, ginger, seasonings, parsley, chives, crabmeat, and oyster crackers, and blend thoroughly. Cover with plastic wrap and refrigerate for 15 to 30 minutes.

2. Pour enough of the oil into a large frying pan to cover the bottom by about ⅛ inch. Heat the oil over medium-high heat.

3. Quickly form the crab mixture into patties, using about ½ cup for each crabcake. Dredge the patties in the bread crumbs and carefully place in the hot oil. Cook for 2 to 3 minutes on each side, until a golden crust forms. Turn the crabcakes carefully. Add more oil if needed. Drain the crabcakes on a paper towel.

4. For the sauce, combine the mustard, mayonnaise, and lemon juice and serve on the side of the crabcakes.

A B O U T   W A S H I N G T O N ,   D . C .

Washington was the first modern city designed from scratch to be the capital of a nation. In 1790 Congress authorized the newly elected President, George Washington, to select a site on the Potomac River for a federal city. Washington had done an enormous amount of traveling during his life and was fed up with the idea of commuting to work, so he chose the nearest town to his own home, Alexandria, Virginia, as a starting point for the capital. The President's official home —the White House—was placed on top of a small hill, looking down a wide avenue with the Houses of Congress at the other end. That way they could keep an eye on each other. Today most of the sights to see are concentrated in this one area of town, which makes it a great place to get in your walking. Three miles in forty-five minutes four times each week could help reduce your need for federal medical assistance.

DUNGENESS CRAB WITH PASTA
SALISHAN LODGE ◆ *LINCOLN CITY, OREGON*

MAKES 6 SERVINGS

¾ pound angel hair pasta
2 tablespoons vegetable oil
½ teaspoon hot pepper
  sauce
2 tablespoons minced
  garlic
2 tablespoons finely
  chopped fresh ginger
1½ cups thinly sliced
  vegetables, such as
  zucchini, celery, broccoli,
  whole snow peas, and/or
  green beans
1 teaspoon cornstarch
3 tablespoons regular or
  low-sodium soy sauce
2 tablespoons rice wine
  vinegar
2 cups cooked Dungeness
  or lump crabmeat,
  cleaned

The Salishan Lodge is a beautiful resort complex on the Pacific Coast near the town of Lincoln City in Oregon. In addition to its fine kitchen, it has a truly magnificent wine cellar.

1. Cook the pasta according to the package directions.

2. In a large skillet, heat the vegetable oil and hot pepper sauce over moderate heat for 1 minute. Add the garlic and ginger. Cook about 30 seconds, stirring often.

3. Add the vegetables and cook, stirring often, for about 4 minutes, until they are tender-crisp, not quite cooked through.

4. In a small bowl, dissolve the cornstarch in the soy sauce. Add the mixture to the skillet and stir. Add the rice wine vinegar and crabmeat to the skillet and stir to combine.

5. Add the cooked and drained pasta to the sauce in pan and toss to combine. Serve immediately.

◆

DUNGENESS CRABS

There are over 4,000 different types of crabs, but when it comes to taste, the Dungeness is unsurpassed. We have been landing Dungeness crab on the Pacific Coast since the 1880s. The clean, cold waters of the area offer up their harvest nearly all year round and the fishermen have learned to cook and freeze their catch so it can be shipped throughout the world. In fact, they have recently developed a system for shipping live crabs. Dungeness make an ideal source of high-quality protein, they are low in saturated fat, low in calories, and contain something called Omega 3 oil which appears to help protect us against heart disease. When you've got something that tastes as naturally good as a Dungeness crab and is good for you, too, it's important to choose a cooking method that keeps the dish healthful. Broiling, poaching, steaming, and boiling are your best techniques and keep the other ingredients low in fat.

◆

ABOUT CELERY

Celery is available all over the country, all year long. It is inexpensive and it adds a crunchy texture to whatever you're cooking. It is used in first courses, main courses, soups, salads, stuffings, and all by itself.

Don't wash celery before you store it in your refrigerator. The moisture that stays on it will shorten the storage life. Cut off the top leaves and take off any limp outer stalks, then place it in a plastic bag and into the refrigerator. It will hold for about a week. Just before you use your celery, give it a quick rinse in cold water to refresh the ribs.

A cup of celery has about twenty calories, a significant amount of vitamin A and vitamin C, and some calcium, phosphorus, iron, and fiber.

Before the seventeenth century, celery was used as a seasoning or a garnish, the way we use parsley today. In the 1600s in Italy, it became a salad ingredient. They served it with a little vegetable oil and a pepper dressing. In the early 1800s in the United States of America, it became a very fashionable food like caviar is today. It was served in its own specially designed vase, which was placed in the center of the table as a centerpiece. At the time, those pressed-glass vases became the most popular wedding gift that anybody could give.

◆

PAELLA
CHITA RIVERA ◆ NEW YORK, NEW YORK

MAKES 8 SERVINGS

½ cup flour
4 chicken breasts, split,
  skinned, and halved
  (8 pieces)
6 tablespoons vegetable oil
24 clams, well scrubbed
24 mussels, well scrubbed
4 cups boiling chicken
  broth or water
2 cloves garlic, unpeeled,
  plus 3 cloves, minced
1 large onion, finely
  chopped
3 cups long-grain rice
Generous pinch of saffron,
  soaked in 2 tablespoons
  water
Salt and freshly ground
  pepper
1 pound chorizo,
  pepperoni, or poached
  hot Italian sausages,
  sliced ½ inch thick
1½ cups peeled, seeded,
  and chopped fresh
  tomatoes, or one
  14½-ounce can chopped
  Italian plum tomatoes,
  drained

Tony Award–winning actress Chita Rivera has been delighting audiences with her amazing performances and dynamic dancing since she was sixteen years old. Over the years, her tremendous talent has brightened the lights of Broadway and made theatrical history. The following recipe is for her favorite dish . . . paella.

1. Preheat the oven to 325° F.

2. Lightly flour the chicken breasts and set aside.

3. In a large, heavy skillet or stockpot, heat the oil. Add the chicken and brown on all sides, then reduce the heat and continue to cook until the chicken is tender, about 20 minutes.

4. In 2 separate pans, steam the clams and mussels each in 1 cup chicken broth or water with an unpeeled garlic clove just until the shells open, being sure to discard any that do not open. Drain the clams and mussels and set aside, reserving the broth.

5. Add the onion and minced garlic to the pan in which the chicken was cooked, and sauté, stirring until soft and golden, approximately 3 minutes. Scrape up the brown bits. Add the rice and cook, stirring, until it turns translucent, approximately 3 minutes. Add the saffron and the reserved clam and mussel broths and remaining 2 cups of broth or water to the rice and season with salt and pepper, to taste. Bring to a boil, then reduce the heat, and simmer the rice until the liquid has been absorbed and the rice is almost done, approximately 15 minutes, adding chicken stock or water if the liquid cooks away too fast.

6. Add the sausages and tomatoes and mix into the rice. Cook for 5 minutes. Add the shrimp to the rice and cook for 4 to 5 minutes, or until they turn pink. Add the peas; stir.

7. Arrange the chicken pieces and the opened clams and mussels on top of the rice. Garnish with warmed pimiento strips and serve immediately.

12 raw shrimp, unpeeled
5 ounces frozen peas,
   thawed in boiling water
   and drained
One 4-ounce jar pimientos,
   drained, sliced, and
   warmed, for garnish

N O   S A L E

When supermarkets first came to Puerto Rico, they used standard cash registers from the States. But things would go nuts and long lines would form when someone would ring up the No Sale sign; in Spanish, No Sale means "don't leave."

♦

Stir-Fried Shrimp, Scallops, and Snow Peas

THE EMPRESS HOTEL ◆ VANCOUVER ISLAND, BRITISH COLUMBIA, CANADA

MAKES 4 SERVINGS

2 tablespoons vegetable oil
2 teaspoons finely chopped
  garlic
1 teaspoon finely chopped
  fresh ginger
½ cup thinly sliced carrots
½ cup sliced onion
½ cup baby corn (optional)
16 medium shrimp, peeled
  and deveined
16 sea scallops
¼ pound snow peas, stem
  ends removed
1 tablespoon sesame oil
1½ tablespoons oyster
  sauce
1 pound vermicelli or thin
  spaghetti, cooked in
  chicken broth
Sliced scallions, for
  garnish

1. Heat a wok or large sauté pan over high heat. Add the oil, garlic, ginger, and carrots. Stir-fry for 1 minute. Add the onion and corn, if desired, and stir for another minute.

2. Add the shrimp and scallops and stir for 2 minutes. Add the snow peas, sesame oil, and oyster sauce. Stir-fry until the shrimp and scallops are cooked, about 5 minutes total.

3. Serve over cooked vermicelli or thin spaghetti and garnish with scallions.

VANCOUVER'S CHINATOWN

The first European settlers to arrive in Vancouver were mostly from Great Britain. But in the late nineteenth century, a large number of Chinese laborers came into the area to help with the construction of the Cross-Canada Canadian Pacific Railway. The railway was completed in 1885, but the Chinese laborers stayed on. Today, Vancouver's Chinatown may be the largest Chinese community in North America.

The port of Vancouver reminds many people of the harbor area of Hong Kong. As a result, many of the folks leaving Hong Kong for North America settled in this region. These days, the town has some of the world's finest Chinese restaurants.

Sautéed Shrimp and Vegetables
The Sea Grill ◆ New York, New York

The Sea Grill restaurant is in a handsome space facing the ice-skating rink and outdoor garden at New York's Rockefeller Center. The following dish was taught to me by The Sea Grill chef, Seppi Renggli, who has been a superstar on our national food scene for the past twenty-five years.

1. In a large skillet or wok, heat the olive oil over high heat. Add the garlic, shallot or onion, and ginger and sauté for 1 minute. Add the shrimp and sauté for 1 minute on each side, until pink.

2. Add the peppers, scallions, and mushrooms and cook for 2 minutes more. Add the basil, pepper, Tabasco, and soy sauce. Cook for 1 minute. Mix well.

3. Remove from heat and serve over cooked rice.

ABOUT SHRIMP

Shrimp is the most popular shellfish in the United States. We eat over 500 million pounds of them each year. We know we have eaten shrimp in this country as far back as we have recorded information. Wherever we have had access to an ocean, shrimp have popped onto the local menu. And "local" is the key word, because fresh shrimp doesn't last very long. In 1917 we began putting refrigeration on the fishing boats and in the 1950s we began freezing shrimp for shipment.

MAKES 4 SERVINGS

2 tablespoons olive oil
1 clove garlic, slivered
1 shallot, minced, or
   2 tablespoons chopped
   onion
One 1-inch piece fresh
   ginger, peeled and cut
   into matchsticks
1 pound large shrimp,
   peeled and deveined
½ red bell pepper, seeded,
   ribs removed, and cut
   into thin strips
½ yellow bell pepper,
   seeded, ribs removed,
   and cut into thin strips
½ green bell pepper,
   seeded, ribs removed,
   and cut into thin strips
1 bunch scallions, cut into
   1-inch pieces
1 cup trimmed, sliced
   mushrooms
½ cup basil leaves,
   coarsely chopped
½ teaspoon freshly ground
   black pepper
2 to 5 drops Tabasco sauce
2 tablespoons reduced-
   sodium soy sauce
Cooked rice, for serving

A B O U T   T U N A

Tuna is a firm-fleshed, oily member of the mackerel family. Six different varieties of tuna come to the market fresh, frozen, and canned. Canned is by far the most popular. Light tuna comes from yellowfin, skipjack, and small bluefin tuna. White tuna comes only from albacore. Generally speaking, darker fleshed tuna tends to be less delicately flavored than lighter fleshed tuna.

Seamen in the Mediterranean hunted tuna for thousands of years before the birth of Jesus. Tuna travel in schools and swim close to the surface when migrating, so fishermen in ancient times would post scouts on steep cliffs or in cedar trees along the coastal waters. The lookouts would signal the fishermen, who would capture the tuna. Today, in fishing tournaments off the coast of Long Island, a tuna scout is posted in a crow's nest high above the powerboat's deck.

To people in the eastern United States, bluefin tuna has always been a sporting fish and not an eating fish, but the Japanese love bluefin for sushi and sashimi and are now buying all the bluefin tuna caught in New York fishing tournaments. They pack the freshly caught tuna in ice and ship them straight out of Kennedy Airport to Japan. Tuna is a low-fat source of protein. It also contains high amounts of Omega 3 fish oil, which has been found to fight heart disease.

*P*OULTRY

CHICKEN WITH LENTILS
GRAND HYATT HOTEL ◆ NEW YORK, NEW YORK

MAKES 4 SERVINGS

1½ tablespoons olive oil
1 clove garlic, minced
1 carrot, peeled and
   minced
1 stalk celery, minced
2 cups cooked lentils, if
   canned, rinsed and
   drained
1 teaspoon dried thyme
1 teaspoon cayenne pepper
1 teaspoon ground cumin
Salt and freshly ground
   black pepper, to taste
1 pound boneless, skinless
   chicken breast
One 6½-ounce jar
   pimientos, drained
2 cucumbers, peeled and
   sliced into thin strips, for
   garnish

One of New York's brightest stars, Anne Jackson has been delighting audiences for decades. Her superb acting has earned her three Tony Award nominations. In addition, she received the Obie Award for her work in The Typists *and* The Tiger, *two one-act plays in which she starred opposite her actor/husband, Eli Wallach. Their marriage has blossomed for over forty years, and has been a colorful match both on and off stage. Anne ordered this dish when we were videotaping together at New York City's Grand Hyatt Hotel. It was designed as a heart-healthy recipe, and meets the standards of the American Heart Association.*

1. Heat ½ tablespoon of the olive oil in a large sauté pan. Add the garlic and sauté for 1 minute. Add the carrot and sauté for 2 minutes more. Add the celery and sauté for 1 minute. Add the lentils and seasonings; stir to combine and heat through.

2. Brush the chicken on both sides with the remaining tablespoon of olive oil and season with salt and pepper. Broil or grill for 8 to 10 minutes per side, or until cooked through. Add the pimientos to the pan or grill for the final 8 to 10 minutes.

3. Divide the cucumbers on the outside of 4 dinner plates. Place ½ cup of the lentils in the center, a piece of chicken on top, and garnish with some pimiento.

CHICKEN WITH PEAS AND CAULIFLOWER

1. Heat the oil in a sauté pan. Add the garlic and cook for 1 minute. Add the chicken, salt and pepper, to taste, and cook, uncovered, for 15 minutes, or until the chicken is browned and fully cooked. Turn the pieces occasionally.

2. Cook the cauliflower in boiling water for 4 minutes. Drain and set aside.

3. When the chicken is cooked add the vinegar, rosemary, and parsley. Cover, reduce the heat, and cook for 3 minutes more. Remove the cover, turn up the heat, and let the vinegar evaporate, which will take about 2 minutes.

4. Add the tomato, black olives, cauliflower, and peas. Cover and simmer for 10 minutes. Remove the garlic before serving.

MAKES 6 SERVINGS

2 tablespoons vegetable oil
3 cloves garlic, unpeeled
One 3-pound chicken, cut into 6 pieces
Salt and freshly ground black pepper
1 head of cauliflower, broken into flowerets
¼ cup wine vinegar
1 tablespoon chopped rosemary
1 tablespoon chopped parsley
1 cup chopped tomato
½ cup pitted black olives, drained
One 10-ounce package frozen peas, thawed

CHICKEN SHOULD BE FULLY COOKED

We are still having a salmonella bacteria problem with our poultry. Make sure that all of your chicken is fully cooked. The best way to do that is to use a thermometer. You want an internal temperature of 170° F. on white meat, 180° F. on dark meat.

CHICKEN AND ARTICHOKES
LA COSTA ◆ CALIFORNIA

MAKES 4 SERVINGS

½ cup flour, for dredging
1½ tablespoons vegetable
  oil
2 whole chicken breasts,
  split in half to equal
  4 pieces, all skin, fat,
  and bones removed
1½ teaspoons finely
  chopped garlic
2 tablespoons chopped
  fresh parsley
Salt, to taste
1 cup fresh, frozen, or
  canned cooked artichoke
  hearts or bottoms
¼ cup thinly sliced sun-
  dried tomatoes
½ cup chicken broth
Parsley, for garnish

1. Place the flour in a shallow bowl. Heat the oil in a nonstick pan. When the oil is hot, dredge the chicken in the flour, tap off the excess, and sauté until golden brown, about 2 to 3 minutes on each side. Pour off the oil and add the garlic to the pan with the chicken, stir to combine. Add the parsley and salt, artichokes, and sun-dried tomatoes. Stir to combine.

2. Add the broth and bring to a boil. Cover, lower the heat, and simmer for 5 to 8 minutes, turning the chicken 2 to 3 times until cooked through.

3. Place the chicken on plates, arrange the artichokes and tomatoes around the chicken, and pour the sauce over all. Garnish with parsley.

ABOUT THE SPA

The idea of the spa—a place to relax, get your body and mind into shape, and cleanse yourself of the pollutants of society—has been around for thousands of years. The ancient Romans had places with hot mineral springs that they loved. They were fascinated with the idea of water that came up hot from deep inside the earth. And because the water contained so much salt, you were more buoyant when you sat in it; you felt lighter, and that contributed to the idea of being rejuvenated by the water of a hot spring. The ancient Roman soldiers loved the spas. They thought that after a good battle there was nothing like coming home and sitting in the bathtub for a couple of days. The word "spa" itself goes back almost two thousand years. At one point in time, the Roman Legion was marching home from northern Europe, stopped for a night in a Belgian village, and discovered that the place had the same hot mineral springs that they had in Rome. The word was passed along, and the town became a common resting place for Roman troops who needed to recover their strength after a battle. The name of the Belgian town was Spa.

Eventually, the world's mineral springs became valuable commercial properties with magnificent resorts built around them, but the basic objective has not changed. People still come to a spa to be restored between battles.

THE ORIGIN OF SPORTS

The anthropologists who study the history of our early societies suggest that the men in primitive tribes had only a few major responsibilities. They had to develop a perimeter wherein women could give birth to the members of the next generation and raise them, and they had to do the big hunting. Important tasks, but not always very time consuming. If no other tribe was challenging the territory and the local animals were generally available, there wasn't very much for the men to do. In those days men's bodies were built for real activity. Imagine all these men built like Schwarzenegger standing around without anything serious to do. Unacceptable. So they began developing a series of activities in which they would practice their defensive and hunting skills. They formed groups that would compete with each other. They wanted things to be realistic so they could see who was the fastest, smartest, and strongest. And it was out of these groups of people practicing their defensive and hunting skills that our first sports teams evolved.

◆

CHICKEN WITH RICE
MIGUEL DOMENECH ◆ SAN JUAN, PUERTO RICO

MAKES 6 SERVINGS

4 tablespoons olive oil
One 3-pound frying
 chicken, cut into
 8 pieces, skin removed
1 large onion, chopped
1 green bell pepper, ribs
 and seeds removed,
 chopped
2 tablespoons capers
¼ cup small pimiento-
 stuffed olives
1 cup prepared tomato
 sauce
1 tablespoon dried oregano
1 teaspoon red pepper
 flakes
3 cloves garlic, minced
3 cups long-grain rice
4½ cups chicken broth
½ cup chopped parsley

GARNISHES
½ cup cooked peas
3 tablespoons chopped
 pimiento

When tourists come to Puerto Rico, they see the elegant hotels, the beautiful beaches, the sixteenth- and seventeenth-century architecture of Old San Juan, the Fortress El Moro, and the rain forest of El Yunque. What they don't see is the man who spends his life making these things available to the tourist . . . Miguel Domenech, the executive director of Puerto Rico Tourism. Let me be quite blunt about the following recipe. Miguel negotiated a deal with me. If I showed pictures of the great attractions of Puerto Rico in my television report, all of which are really good to look at, then Miguel would show me his recipe for chicken with rice, which is really good to eat. It's an excellent one-pot meal.

1. In a stockpot or Dutch oven large enough to hold all of the ingredients, heat the oil and brown the chicken on all sides. Cover, lower the heat, and simmer for about 15 minutes.

2. Add the onion and green pepper and cook for 4 minutes. Add the capers, olives, tomato sauce, oregano, pepper flakes, and garlic, and cook for another 4 to 5 minutes.

3. Add the 3 cups of rice and stir the mixture well. Add the chicken broth and parsley and stir. Cover the pot, reduce the heat, and simmer for approximately 20 minutes, or until the liquid is absorbed and the rice is tender.

4. Garnish with the peas and pimiento and serve.

CHICKEN WITH MUSTARD
HOTEL LE BRISTOL ◆ PARIS, FRANCE

In the 1700s the ultimate tourist was Britain's fourth Earl of Bristol. He spent his entire life and a considerable part of his vast fortune traveling around Europe looking for the best of everything. He actually had his chef travel a half day ahead of him so when he got someplace to eat, the food would be perfect. The Bristol Hotel in Paris is named after his lordship as a constant reminder to everybody who works there to keep things up to the standard that the Earl demanded.

MAKES 4 SERVINGS

Vegetable oil spray
1 tablespoon plus
  1 teaspoon vegetable oil
1 pound boneless, skinless
  chicken breast
Freshly ground black
  pepper
3 tablespoons prepared
  mustard
2 tablespoons dried bread
  crumbs
1½ tablespoons butter
1 pound three-color
  linguini, cooked

1. Preheat the oven to 350° F. Spray a baking sheet with vegetable oil.

2. In a large sauté pan, heat the 1 tablespoon of vegetable oil over high heat. Season the chicken with pepper, to taste. Sauté the chicken over high heat for 3 minutes per side, or until golden. Remove the chicken and drain on paper towels.

3. In a small bowl, combine the mustard, the remaining teaspoon of vegetable oil, and the bread crumbs. Spread on both sides of the chicken and place on the baking sheet. Bake for 15 minutes, or until the chicken is cooked through.

4. In a large sauté pan over medium heat, melt the butter. Sauté the pasta for 3 minutes, tossing in the butter.

5. Arrange the pasta in 3 stacks on each plate and place the chicken in the center.

CHICKEN BREASTS WITH BUTTERMILK STUFFING

HOTEL VANCOUVER ◆ VANCOUVER, BRITISH COLUMBIA, CANADA

MAKES 4 SERVINGS

1 tablespoon chopped
  shallots, or ¼ of a small
  onion, chopped
3 tablespoons vegetable oil
1 teaspoon chopped fresh
  rosemary, or ½ teaspoon
  dried, crushed
⅛ pound prosciutto ham,
  minced or chopped
1 tablespoon chopped
  fresh parsley
1½ cups small bread cubes
¼ cup buttermilk
Salt and freshly ground
  black pepper
4 skinless, boneless
  chicken breasts, cut
  almost in half
  horizontally, to create
  more surface for stuffing

The steeple-pitched copper roof of the Hotel Vancouver is a feature of the Vancouver skyline. The main restaurant in the hotel is the Timber Club, which is decorated with memorabilia from the world of logging. The executive chef is Elio Guarnori, and the following recipe comes from his mother's kitchen in Italy.

1. Preheat the oven to 400° F.

2. In a skillet, sauté the shallots or onion in 1 tablespoon of the oil over medium heat for 1 minute. Add the rosemary and sauté for another minute. Add the prosciutto and stir for 1 minute more. Stir in the parsley and add the bread cubes. Stir and sauté for about 4 minutes, until the bread absorbs the oil and the ingredients are well blended. Remove from the heat and add the buttermilk. Allow to cool slightly; season with the salt and pepper, to taste.

3. Place some stuffing along the middle of each breast, press it slightly to condense it, then fold the chicken over it in thirds to enclose the stuffing. Tie with kitchen string or use toothpicks to secure.

4. Heat about 2 tablespoons of the oil in a sauté pan over medium heat. When hot, brown the chicken on each side for a total of 4 minutes.

5. Place the chicken in an oven-proof pan and bake for 20 minutes. Remove the string or toothpicks and slice each chicken roll diagonally. Arrange the slices on 4 plates.

TO PREPARE THE FRUIT CHUTNEY:

6. In a small pan combine all the ingredients except the blueberries and cook over medium-high heat for about 5 minutes, stirring constantly.

7. Add the blueberries and continue to cook and stir until the berries break down slightly and the chutney thickens, about 10 minutes. Let cool slightly and serve as a garnish for the chicken.

FRUIT CHUTNEY (OPTIONAL)

3 tablespoons brown sugar

1 tablespoon sherry or apple cider vinegar

1½ cups peeled, chopped pears

2 teaspoons peeled, grated or minced fresh ginger

1 cup fresh or frozen blueberries

N A T I V E
V A N C O U V E R

The earliest native legend about the area which is now called Vancouver describes the local river basin as filled with so many fish that it could feed all of mankind. The first inhabitants of this land were settled populations with well-developed cultures and histories that went back for thousands of years. They lived on the shores of the rivers and the Pacific Ocean. The water was the highway on which they traveled and the source of much of their food. They had salmon, halibut, herring, mussels, and clams. The necessities of life came easily; the climate was relatively mild. They had time to develop their artistic skills and an extraordinary level of craftsmanship that went into everything, even the most common objects. And especially those that dealt with food.

GRILLED MESQUITE CHICKEN
JOE THEISMAN'S RESTAURANT ◆ FALLS CHURCH, VIRGINIA

MAKES 4 SERVINGS

MARINADE
1 medium onion, coarsely
  chopped
1 tablespoon mesquite
  flavoring (optional)
1 stalk lemongrass,
  chopped (optional)
Juice of 2 limes
Freshly ground black
  pepper, to taste, use at
  least ½ teaspoon
2 to 3 cloves garlic,
  crushed, or ½ teaspoon
  garlic powder

4 skinless, boneless
  chicken breasts, about
  1½ pounds total

RED PEPPER SAUCE
2 red bell peppers
2 tablespoons olive oil
½ teaspoon finely chopped
  garlic
Salt

OPTIONAL GARNISHES
Parsley
Lime slices

From the first time he ran out on the Notre Dame field, Joe Theisman was working toward his dream of quarterbacking an NFL team to a world championship. While at the University of Notre Dame, Joe set a series of important Fighting Irish records, many of which still stand. He holds the single-season records with 268 attempts, 155 completions, 2,429 yards gained, and 16 touchdown passes. In 1970, after earning All-American honors and leading his team to a victory in their second consecutive Cotton Bowl, Joe was runner-up in the Heisman Trophy balloting. That same year he was named Academic All-American for combining his football success with an outstanding performance in the classroom. Following his 1971 graduation with a degree in sociology, Joe was drafted by the Miami Dolphins as well as a major league baseball team, the Minnesota Twins. But he elected to play professional football with the Canadian Football League.

In 1974 he returned to the States and began his twelve-year NFL career with the Washington Redskins. He played in 163 consecutive games, leading them to back-to-back Super Bowl appearances, including the victory over the Dolphins in Super Bowl XVII. These days, Joe owns and runs a group of restaurants near Washington, D.C.

1. Combine the marinade ingredients in a container large enough to accommodate the chicken.

2. Place the chicken in the marinade, cover with plastic wrap, and marinate for several hours, or several days, in the refrigerator.

3. Make the red pepper sauce. Peel the peppers with a potato peeler, cut in half, and discard the seeds. Slice the pepper thinly. Heat the oil in a sauté pan over medium heat and add the peppers, garlic, and salt, to taste. Sauté over medium heat for 15 minutes, then cover the pan and cook until the peppers are soft. When cool, put the mixture into a food processor and pulse until coarsely chopped. If the sauce is too thick, thin it with a little chicken stock or water. Set aside.

4. Allow the chicken to remain at room temperature for 30 minutes before grilling. You can grill over mesquite wood or charcoal or use a stovetop grill. Make sure the grill is very hot. If using a stovetop grill, oil it lightly before grilling the chicken to prevent sticking.

5. Dry the chicken with paper towels and place on the grill until cooked on one side. Turn the chicken over and continue grilling until done. Alternatively, you can broil the chicken under the broiler.

6. Serve with the red pepper sauce and a garnish of parsley and lime slices.

GRILLED CHICKEN WITH YOGURT
HALCYON HOTEL ◆ LONDON, ENGLAND

MAKES 6 SERVINGS

MARINADE
1 tablespoon grated fresh
  ginger
1 teaspoon ground
  cardamom
1 teaspoon coriander
Juice of 1 lemon
1 tablespoon minced fresh
  mint
1 cup plain low-fat yogurt

SAUCE
½ cucumber, peeled,
  seeded, and coarsely
  grated (about ⅓ cup)
1 tablespoon chopped
  fresh mint
1 clove garlic, minced
Juice of ½ lemon
1 cup plain low-fat yogurt
Salt and freshly ground
  black pepper, to taste

3 boneless, skinless
  chicken breasts, halved
Fresh mint, for garnish

The Halcyon Hotel is a small and very elegant establishment in a quiet part of London called Holland Park. The hotel was recently constructed inside two handsome private homes. Each of the hotel's forty-four suites has a unique style of decoration. The rooms give you the feeling that some very rich friends have invited you to spend a few days in their London home. (I wish I had friends like that.) Its restaurant has become well-known for a series of healthful dishes that are as good for you as they are good tasting.

1. In a baking dish mix all of the marinade ingredients. Place the chicken breasts in the marinade, turning once to coat both sides of the chicken. Cover and refrigerate for 24 hours.

2. In a small bowl combine all of the sauce ingredients. Cover and chill until ready to use.

3. Remove the chicken from the marinade and grill until done, about 4 minutes per side.

4. Place a generous serving of the sauce on each dinner plate, top with a chicken breast, and garnish with a fresh sprig of mint. Serve at once, with a dollop of homemade yogurt (recipe follows).

HOMEMADE YOGURT

1. In a very clean saucepan, heat milk to 180° F. Then allow it to cool to 110° F. Meanwhile, wash a heat-proof glass jar with a tight-fitting lid in very hot soapy water. Rinse well with boiling water.

2. Stir the store-bought yogurt into the milk. Pour the mixture into the glass jar and seal tight.

3. Put the jar into a preheated 100° F. oven or insulated picnic cooler for 7 hours. The longer the incubation, the more tangy the yogurt. Once you refrigerate, the process stops.

4. Refrigerate the yogurt for 2 hours before using. It will hold in the refrigerator for about 1 week. Save some of the yogurt from this batch to use as a starter for your next batch of yogurt.

MAKES 2 CUPS

2 cups milk
2 tablespoons plain low-fat
  yogurt

ABOUT YOGURT AND GOOD HEALTH

Louis Pasteur was a Parisian chemist who developed the technique of vaccination. He also invented the process of pasteurization, which extends the shelf life of milk products. In the 1880s the Pasteur Institute was founded to continue his work.

In 1908, Dr. Ilya Metchnikoff won the Nobel Prize for the research that he was doing at the institute. Metchnikoff's books on prolonging life and avoiding the problems of premature aging led him to investigate various populations around the world. One of his conclusions was that the people of Bulgaria lived longer and healthier lives because they ate yogurt. He was able to isolate the organism that turns milk into yogurt, and that made the large-scale production of yogurt possible.

Metchnikoff pointed out that yogurt helped purify the large intestines and introduced substantial amounts of vitamin B. It was Ilya Metchnikoff who first described yogurt as a "health food." One of his friends, a Spaniard named Isaac Cartasso, purchased some yogurt cultures from the institute and began manufacturing yogurt for the European market. When World War II started, Cartasso's son came to the United States and started to make yogurt from his father's cultures. The son's name: Dan; his company name: Dannon.

◆

CHICKEN BAKED IN YOGURT SAUCE
LOEWS LE CONCORDE ◆ QUEBEC CITY, CANADA

French culture is clearly the strongest influence in the Canadian province of Quebec, with British traditions a close second. But Quebec has hosted some massive migrations. People have come from Scotland, Ireland, Poland, Hungary, Italy, China, Germany, Greece, Portugal, the countries of Africa, the islands of the Caribbean, and India. Over eighty different nationalities have come to Quebec. In proportion to its population, more people have been taken in here and protected from political and economic hardship than in any other singular-size area of the world. The point was clearly made in the kitchens of Loews Le Concorde Hotel. The pastry chef is from Tangier, the sous chefs are from France, Switzerland, and Martinique, and the executive chef is from India. The result is an exchange of ideas and techniques that produce some outstanding dishes. A perfect example is Nanak Chand Vig's Chicken Baked in Yogurt Sauce.

1. In a cup or small bowl, combine the seasonings, shallots, lemon juice, and yogurt.

2. Pour the mixture into a baking dish and add the chicken breasts, turning them over to coat well with the yogurt mixture. Cover and refrigerate overnight or for several hours.

3. Preheat the oven to 350° F. Uncover the chicken and bake for 1 hour.

MAKES 4 SERVINGS

1 tablespoon minced garlic
1 tablespoon minced fresh peeled ginger
⅛ teaspoon red pepper flakes, to taste (optional)
1½ teaspoons ground cumin
1½ teaspoons ground paprika
1½ teaspoons turmeric
2 teaspoons chopped fresh rosemary, or 1 teaspoon dried
Salt, to taste
1 tablespoon chopped shallots
2 teaspoons fresh squeezed lemon juice
2 cups (1 pint) plain low-fat yogurt
2 whole chicken breasts, skinned, fat removed, and split in half to equal 4 pieces

◆

CARIBBEAN LEMON CHICKEN
CLUB MED 1

MAKES 4 SERVINGS

MARINADE
1 cup fresh squeezed
  lemon juice
1½ cups sliced onions
½ cup chopped fresh
  parsley, with stems

1 medium whole chicken
  (about 3 pounds), cut into
  8 pieces, with the skin
  removed
3 tablespoons vegetable oil
1½ cups thinly sliced
  onions
1½ teaspoons minced
  garlic
Salt and freshly ground
  black pepper
½ cup fresh squeezed
  lemon juice
1 cup lime sections, with
  peel and white pith
  removed (about 4 limes)
¼ cup low-fat buttermilk
  or heavy cream

OPTIONAL GARNISHES
Chopped parsley
Lime slices

1. In a small bowl, combine the marinade ingredients.

2. Put the chicken pieces into a bowl with the marinade. Cover and refrigerate for at least 3 hours, turning the chicken pieces occasionally. Drain and discard the onions and parsley.

3. Heat the oil in a sauté pan over medium heat. Add the onions and garlic, and sauté for about 2 minutes, or until the onions begin to soften.

4. Add the chicken pieces, salt and pepper, to taste, and cook for about 5 minutes, turning occasionally. Add the lemon juice and lime sections, then turn up the heat to bring the liquid to a boil. Cover and lower the heat to a simmer. Simmer for 20 minutes.

5. Remove the chicken pieces and keep warm. Add the buttermilk or cream *over low heat* and heat through.

6. Put the chicken pieces back into the sauce and turn to coat. Place 2 pieces of chicken on each plate. Garnish with the parsley and lime slices, if desired.

CHICKEN CURRY
THE EMPRESS HOTEL ◆ VANCOUVER ISLAND, BRITISH COLUMBIA, CANADA

1. Preheat the oven to 375° F.

2. Put the oil in a heavy oven-proof sauté pan over medium heat; add the garlic and ginger. Add the chicken to the pan and sauté, turning to color the chicken evenly.

3. After a few minutes, add the seasonings. Sauté and stir for 1 minute. Add the remaining ingredients (except the rice), and bring the mixture to a boil. Cover and place in the preheated oven.

4. Bake for 30 minutes, turning the chicken pieces occasionally. Remove the cover 5 minutes before done. Serve with the cooked rice.

MAKES 4 SERVINGS

3 tablespoons vegetable oil
2 teaspoons chopped garlic
2 teaspoons chopped fresh peeled ginger
One 4- to 5-pound chicken, using legs, thighs, and breasts, all skin removed
2 tablespoons curry powder
2 bay leaves
1 tablespoon ground cumin
1 teaspoon ground coriander
2 teaspoons turmeric
½ cup chopped onion
½ cup chopped celery
½ cup chopped carrot
2 tablespoons tomato paste
1 small tomato, chopped (about ½ cup)
1 green apple, peeled, cored, and chopped (about 1½ cups)
2 tablespoons fresh lemon juice
1 cup chicken stock
Salt and freshly ground black pepper, to taste
Cooked rice, for serving

◆

MEXICAN CHICKEN IN A BAG
ROSA MEXICANO ◆ NEW YORK, NEW YORK

MAKES 4 SERVINGS

One 4-ounce can chopped
  chilies, drained
One 15-ounce can tomato
  sauce
1 tablespoon
  Worcestershire sauce
1 tablespoon cider vinegar
½ tablespoon dried ground
  mustard
1 teaspoon cayenne pepper
3 cloves garlic, minced
1 tablespoon ground cumin
½ teaspoon ground cloves
4 pieces chicken, skin on
  and bone in (about 2½ to
  3 pounds)

Josephina Howard is the owner of a great Mexican restaurant in New York City called Rosa Mexicano. Following is her delicious recipe for Chicken in a Bag. Originally, this recipe was made with leaves . . . but these days, for ecological reasons, it's made with parchment paper.

1. In a mixing bowl, combine all the ingredients except the chicken. Mix well.

2. Lay out 4 pieces of parchment paper approximately double the size of each piece of chicken. Lay the chicken on half of each foil piece, skin side down. Paint the chicken with the sauce. Turn the chicken, skin side up, and paint with the remaining sauce. Fold the foil piece over the chicken and fold the edges to seal tightly. Place in a steamer basket over simmering water and steam for 45 minutes. This can also be baked in a preheated 350° F. oven on a cookie sheet for 45 minutes. Make sure the chicken is fully cooked.

3. Serve each pouch on a plate, and let your guests open them at the table.

CHICKEN NIKOLA
IL NIDO ◆ NEW YORK, NEW YORK

*Il Nido is a classic and classy Northern Italian res-
taurant on New York's East Side. It is regularly selected by restaurant authorities as one of the very
best Italian restaurants in a city packed with Italian eateries. Nikola Jovic is the chef.*

1. Preheat the oven to 350° F.

2. Lightly dredge the chicken in the flour.

3. In a large sauté pan, heat the vegetable oil over medium
heat. Sauté the chicken pieces until lightly browned on all
sides, about 8 to 10 minutes. Remove the chicken to an
oven-proof pan and bake for 10 minutes, until the chicken is
fully cooked.

4. Pour off the excess grease remaining in the sauté pan
(brown bits are fine), pour in the olive oil, and heat. Add the
garlic and jalapeños and cook until the garlic is golden,
approximately 2 minutes. Add the wine or broth and simmer
for 3 minutes, scraping up the brown bits.

5. Return the chicken to the sauté pan and add the broth.
Bring to a boil over high heat. Let the sauce boil until
thickened, approximately 5 minutes.

6. Place the chicken with the sauce on a serving plate and
garnish with the slivers of Pecorino Romano cheese.

MAKES 6 SERVINGS

3 whole skinless, boneless
  chicken breasts, cut into
  1- × 2-inch strips
¼ cup flour
¼ cup vegetable oil
2 tablespoons olive oil
3 cloves garlic, thinly
  sliced
2 jalapeño peppers,
  seeded, ribs removed,
  and thinly sliced
¼ cup white wine or
  chicken broth
1 cup chicken broth
½ cup slivers Pecorino
  Romano cheese, for
  garnish

CHICKEN WITH PEACH SAUCE
JACKSONVILLE INN ◆ JACKSONVILLE, OREGON

MAKES 4 SERVINGS

One 20-ounce bag frozen
   peaches, or 4 large fresh
   ones
1 cup white wine or
   chicken stock
1 teaspoon ground
   cinnamon
⅛ cup sugar
½ cup flour
1 egg, beaten with
   1 tablespoon water
¾ cup finely chopped
   hazelnuts or pecans
2 tablespoons vegetable oil
2 boned, skinned chicken
   breasts, split in half and
   slightly flattened

During the 1850s, gold was discovered near the town of Jacksonville, Oregon, and the joint began to jump. Prospectors arrived from all over the world searching for wealth beyond their wildest dreams. The miners went up into the hills and used their pans to separate the gold from the earth. Then the cooks in Jacksonville used their pans to separate the gold from the miners. The gold prospectors did not spend much effort cooking while they were searching for gold. They were therefore quite willing to spend big bucks for good food when they came into town.

These days the good cooking takes place at the Jacksonville Inn and chef Diane Menzie is in charge of the mother lode.

1. In a large skillet, place the peaches, white wine or chicken stock, cinnamon, and sugar and stir gently over medium heat until the peaches are tender and heated through. The sauce will reduce slightly and thicken. Set aside and keep warm.

2. Set up an assembly line: place the flour on a flat plate, the egg mixture in a large bowl, and the chopped nuts on a flat plate.

3. In a large skillet, heat the oil until it is hot.

4. Dip the chicken into the flour and shake off any excess, then dip into the egg mixture and then into the chopped nuts. Place the coated chicken into the skillet and sauté over moderate heat for approximately 3 minutes on each side, until completely cooked.

5. To serve, place half a chicken breast on each dinner plate and top with a portion of the peach sauce.

THE RESTAURANT MENU AS A LIST OF INGREDIENTS

There is a technique you can use in most restaurants to make sure you have a low-fat meal when you want one. Think of the menu not as a list of finished dishes, but as a list of ingredients that you can reassemble. For example, if you are ordering French onion soup . . . tell the waiter to leave off the cheese. Look to fresh fruit as a dessert. I can often get a waitress to give me the melon for dessert that was on the menu as an appetizer.

SALBUTES *(MEXICAN CHICKEN APPETIZERS)*
THE PLAZA HOTEL ◆ *NEW YORK, NEW YORK*

MAKES 30 APPETIZERS

6 skinless, boneless split
  chicken breasts

MARINADE
3 cloves garlic, crushed
½ teaspoon freshly ground
  black pepper
½ teaspoon ground allspice
1 tablespoon chopped
  fresh oregano, or
  1 teaspoon dried
½ cup red wine vinegar
½ cup orange juice
½ cup grapefruit juice
½ cup olive oil
Salt, to taste

ONION GARNISH
2 medium red onions,
  julienned
½ cup red wine vinegar
¼ cup orange juice
¼ cup grapefruit juice
⅓ cup olive oil
3 cloves garlic, crushed
1 teaspoon freshly ground
  black pepper
Salt, to taste

Tortillas, crackers, pitas,
  or bread

1. Place the chicken breasts in a baking dish. Combine all of the ingredients for the marinade and pour over the chicken. Marinate for 2 hours in the refrigerator.

2. Place the onions in a mixing bowl. Add the remaining garnish ingredients. Allow the onion mixture to marinate for 2 hours.

3. Preheat the oven to 350° F.

4. Remove the chicken from the marinade and place into a roasting pan. Bake the chicken for 45 minutes, brushing with the marinade as needed. Let cool. Cut into bite-sized pieces.

5. Top the tortillas with the chicken mixture, and garnish with the marinated onions.

STIR-FRY CHICKEN
MARLA'S MEMORY LANE SUPPER CLUB ◆ HOLLYWOOD, CALIFORNIA

As Florence Johnson, the hot-stuff housekeeper on the television hit series "The Jeffersons," Marla Gibbs portrayed a woman who was full of the spice of life. These days those spices also go into the cooking at her restaurant. The following is an example.

1. In a large skillet or wok, heat the olive oil and margarine over high heat. Add the onion and garlic and sauté for 1 minute.

2. Add the chicken strips and sauté for 5 minutes. Stir constantly. Stir in the soy sauce and vinegar.

3. Add the carrots, broccoli, and cauliflower and sauté for 2 minutes more. Add the cabbage, red bell pepper, celery, snow peas, and bean sprouts and sauté for 3 minutes. Add the sesame seeds.

4. Serve immediately with brown rice.

MAKES 4 SERVINGS

2 tablespoons olive oil
2 tablespoons margarine
½ red onion, sliced
2 cloves garlic, chopped
1 pound boneless, skinless chicken breast, cut into strips, and seasoned with salt and freshly ground black pepper, to taste
2 tablespoons reduced-sodium soy sauce
½ cup rice wine vinegar
2 carrots, peeled and sliced very thin
2 cups broccoli flowerets
2 cups cauliflower flowerets
1½ cups chopped red cabbage
½ red bell pepper, seeded, ribs removed, and sliced very thin
1 stalk celery, chopped very thin
1 cup snow peas
½ cup bean sprouts
½ tablespoon sesame seeds
Cooked brown rice, for serving

NIKE CHICKEN
NIKE HEADQUARTERS ◆ BEAVERTON, OREGON

MAKES 4 SERVINGS

¾ cup Canola oil
2 teaspoons paprika
Salt and freshly ground
  black pepper, to taste
1 teaspoon finely chopped
  garlic
4 skinless, boneless
  chicken breast halves
1½ cups plain nonfat
  yogurt
¼ cup honey
2 teaspoons ground
  cinnamon (optional)
1 cup pureed fresh or
  frozen blueberries
1 pound cooked pasta, at
  room temperature

GARNISHES
Lettuce
Cubes of cantaloupe or
  honeydew melon
Strawberries
Grated Swiss cheese
Chopped pecans

1. Combine the oil, paprika, salt and pepper, and garlic in a shallow bowl. Add the chicken breasts, toss carefully to mix, and marinate for at least 30 minutes at room temperature.

2. Combine the yogurt, honey, cinnamon, if used, and blueberries in a bowl. Mix thoroughly. Combine ½ cup with the pasta and set the remaining yogurt mixture aside.

3. Preheat an indoor or outdoor grill, or broiler to high heat. Remove the chicken from the marinade, allowing any excess marinade to drip off. Grill the chicken breasts for 4 to 6 minutes on each side, depending on thickness. Remove the chicken when cooked throughout. Cool slightly.

4. On each plate, arrange lettuce, top with pasta, garnish with melon, strawberries, and Swiss cheese. Slice the chicken lengthwise and arrange over the top. Spoon the remaining yogurt mixture over all and top with pecans.

ABOUT CANOLA OIL

Scientists have come to the conclusion that saturated fat raises your blood cholesterol level more than any other food. So if somebody came up with a cooking oil that was almost free of saturated fat . . . that would be a giant and healthful step in the right direction. And that's exactly what a group of Canadian scientists did. They based it on a relative of the mustard plant, pressed out the oil, and named it Canola—after Canada. Canola oil is processed from the seeds of a beautiful yellow-flowered plant. The oil is lower in saturated fat than any other type of cooking or salad oil; 50 percent lower than corn oil or olive oil, and 60 percent lower than soybean oil. Members of the American Dietetic Association recommend that we keep our saturated fat down to 10 percent of our total caloric intake. Canola oil can help.

◆

THE WAFFLE OF FITNESS

Bill Bowerman was a track coach at the University of Oregon. Phil Knight was a miler that Bowerman was training. Bowerman was pleased with Knight's showings but not with his shoes. As a matter of fact, Bowerman wasn't pleased with the shoes of any of his athletes. Bowerman had been experimenting with different sole patterns in the hope of getting better traction and better cushioning, but nothing seemed to work very well.

Then one day in 1971, Bowerman was looking at the breakfast waffle that his wife had just made for him and suddenly realized the surface of the waffle could be the perfect surface for the sole of his new running shoe. He took his wife's waffle iron, filled it with rubber, and there it was—the new running shoe. Bowerman and Knight formed a company to market that shoe and many other sports shoes. Today that company is called Nike after the ancient Greek goddess of victory. So next time you see Bo Jackson or Michael Jordan or John McEnroe wearing their Nikes to victory, they owe it all to Mrs. Bowerman's waffles.

◆

CHICKEN SAUTÉED IN APPLE CIDER
LA CITÉ ◆ NEW YORK, NEW YORK

MAKES 4 SERVINGS

SAUTÉED CHICKEN
3 tablespoons vegetable oil
1 small onion, chopped
2 whole skinless, boneless
  chicken breasts, halved,
  fat removed
¼ cup all-purpose flour
¼ teaspoon freshly ground
  black pepper, to taste
3 cups apple cider

CARAMELIZED APPLES
3 Granny Smith apples
2 tablespoons margarine
1 tablespoon brown sugar

VEGETABLE GARNISH
2 tablespoons vegetable oil
2 cups small mushroom
  caps, brushed clean and
  stems removed
Pinch of freshly ground
  white pepper
½ tablespoon fresh thyme,
  or ½ teaspoon dried
1 tablespoon margarine
¾ cup pearl onions, peeled
  and trimmed on the ends

La Cité is a restaurant in New York City. But its style is based on the classic bistros and brasseries of Paris. Following is one of my favorite dishes from La Cité, Chicken Sautéed in Apple Cider.

1. In a large sauté pan, heat 1½ tablespoons of the vegetable oil over high heat. Add the onion and sauté until transparent, about 3 minutes. Scrape the onion into a bowl and set aside.

2. In the same sauté pan, heat the remaining 1½ tablespoons of vegetable oil. Lightly dredge the chicken in flour and season with pepper. Place the chicken in the sauté pan and sauté until golden, turning once, approximately 4 minutes per side. Add the apple cider and reserved sautéed onion to the pan. Reduce the heat and bring to a simmer, scraping up the brown bits. Continue simmering over low heat for 20 to 25 minutes, until cooked through, turning 2 or 3 times.

3. Core and peel the apples and cut into ¼-inch slices. Set the apple pieces aside. Place the peels on top of the pieces of chicken for additional flavor and to keep the juices in while simmering.

4. In a second smaller sauté pan, heat the vegetable oil over high heat. Place the mushroom caps in the oil, cap side down. Cook until the caps are very dark in color, about 6 minutes. Do not stir. Pour off the oil, if any, and add the white pepper and thyme. Stir to evaporate any remaining liquid. Remove the mushrooms and set aside. Add the margarine and the pearl onions to the pan. Cook over medium-high heat until the onions are browned, about 8 minutes. Return the mushroom caps to the pan and cook for 2 minutes more. Remove from the heat and cover to keep warm.

5. For the apples, in another medium sauté pan, melt the 2 tablespoons margarine over high heat. Add the brown sugar and stir until well blended. When it starts to bubble, add the apples and sauté for 4 to 5 minutes, until well wilted, tossing carefully to cook evenly.

6. When the chicken is cooked, remove it to a serving plate and cover loosely with foil. Increase heat and reduce the liquid, boiling for approximately 15 minutes. Strain the poaching liquid and skim off fat.

7. Make a nest of the caramelized apple slices on each plate, top with a chicken breast half, and arrange the mushroom caps and pearl onions over the chicken. Pour a little of the strained juice on top to finish.

IDEAL APPETITE SUPPRESSION

Research indicates that, contrary to popular belief, exercise does not increase your appetite. As a matter of fact, exercise tends to reduce your appetite.

◆

TURKEY LOAF

MAKES 6 SERVINGS

½ cup white wine or
  chicken broth
1 green bell pepper,
  chopped
1 medium onion, chopped
1 clove garlic, minced
1 medium yellow squash,
  grated
1 pound lean ground
  turkey meat
2 egg whites
3 large carrots, grated
½ cup cornmeal
1 teaspoon dried oregano
1 teaspoon dried basil
Salt and freshly ground
  black pepper
Tomato sauce

Yolanda Bergman is the Hollywood food cop, a refrigerator reformer and a diet guru. She's cleaned up the acts and cleaned out the refrigerators of many of Hollywood's Who's Who. Following is her low-fat, low-calorie recipe for Turkey Loaf.

1. Preheat the oven to 450° F.

2. In a medium sauté pan, heat the white wine or broth over medium heat. Add the green pepper, onion, and garlic. Simmer for 2 minutes.

3. In a medium mixing bowl, combine the yellow squash, ground turkey, egg whites, carrots, cornmeal, oregano, and basil. Add the sautéed vegetables and mix well. Season with salt and pepper, to taste.

4. Form the mixture into a loaf and place on a sheet pan sprayed with vegetable oil. Top with your favorite tomato sauce. Bake for 25 minutes. Slice and serve.

MEAT

STEAK WITH THREE PEPPERS
HOTEL LE BRISTOL ◆ PARIS, FRANCE

MAKES 2 SERVINGS

Two 6-ounce beef filets
1½ tablespoons vegetable
  oil
Cracked black
  peppercorns
½ cup beef stock
1 tablespoon green
  peppercorns, packed in
  brine and drained
½ tablespoon pink
  peppercorns
1 tablespoon margarine
1 teaspoon sugar
1 cup julienned vegetables
  (a combination of carrots,
  potatoes, zucchini)

1. Rub the filets with ½ tablespoon vegetable oil. Season both sides with freshly cracked black peppercorns.

2. In a large sauté pan over medium heat, heat the remaining tablespoon of vegetable oil. Sauté the filets on both sides until cooked to desired doneness, approximately 4 minutes per side for medium. Remove the filets from the pan and deglaze the sauté pan with the beef stock, scraping up the brown bits, and simmering until reduced by half. Add the green and pink peppercorns and simmer for 2 minutes more.

3. In a medium sauté pan, heat the margarine over medium heat. Stir in the sugar and dissolve completely. Sauté the vegetables until softened, but still slightly crunchy. Cooking time will vary depending on the vegetables chosen.

4. Place the vegetables in a circle on each plate. Place the beef in the middle and top with the peppercorn sauce.

A B O U T   S T E A K

Steak usually refers to beef cut against the grain. The most tender cuts can be broiled or pan fried. Chuck and round steaks need to be marinated or cooked in liquid to be tender. The flank, just under the tenderloin, contains one of the versatile cuts, the flank steak. The most common flank steak dish is London broil.

USDA prime, choice, and select are the main gradings for steak. They are based on the quality of fat or "marbling" in the meat. Ninety percent of the steak we eat is choice. Prime is very expensive and hard to come by except in restaurants. Select is the leanest grade and is now being upgraded by the beef industry. All beef is a good source of protein, iron, and B vitamins.

SESAME STEAK

SHUN LEE WEST ◆ NEW YORK, NEW YORK

The Lincoln Center complex of New York City's West Side is one of the town's cultural centers. The New York State Theater, Metropolitan Opera, and Avery Fisher Hall have made it a focal point for the arts, which of course, include the culinary crafts. The area has become a magnet for restaurants. One such restaurant, Shun Lee West, boasts the virtuoso Michael Tong. The following is his rendition of an old oriental favorite.

MAKES 4 SERVINGS

1 pound beef filet mignon
1 teaspoon Szechuan chili paste or hot sauce
2 teaspoons cornstarch
1½ tablespoons sugar
2 tablespoons dry sherry or rice wine
3 tablespoons soy sauce
2 tablespoons red wine vinegar
½ cup vegetable oil
1 tablespoon chopped garlic
2 tablespoons chopped scallions
½ cup thinly sliced bamboo shoots
¼ pound snow peas
1 teaspoon sesame seeds

1. Cut the beef filet into bite-sized pieces.

2. In a small bowl, thoroughly combine the chili paste or hot sauce, cornstarch, sugar, sherry or rice wine, soy sauce, and vinegar. Set aside.

3. In a wok or a skillet, over high heat, heat the oil. Add the filet pieces and cook for about 30 seconds, turning almost constantly. Remove the meat from the skillet and set aside. Discard all but 3 tablespoons of the oil.

4. Reheat the 3 tablespoons of oil over high heat. Add the garlic and scallions and stir-fry for 20 seconds. Add the bamboo shoots, snow peas, sesame seeds, and the steak and stir-fry for 1 minute. Stir in the soy sauce mixture and cook for 30 seconds.

SAUERBRATEN
GRAMMER'S RESTAURANT ◆ CINCINNATI, OHIO

MAKES 10 SERVINGS

MARINADE
2 cups chopped onion
1 cup chopped carrot
1 cup chopped celery
½ cup chopped red or
  yellow bell pepper
2 teaspoons chopped fresh
  thyme
1 lemon, cut and squeezed
  and dropped into
  marinade
3 cloves garlic, crushed
2 to 3 parsley stems
Pinch of allspice
4 cloves
½ teaspoon crushed black
  peppercorns
6 juniper berries, crushed
3 bay leaves
1 tablespoon sugar
Equal parts red or white
  wine vinegar and water to
  cover meat and
  vegetables

3 to 3½ pounds top round,
  brisket, or rump roast,
  tied up
2 tablespoons vegetable oil

In the heart of the Over-the-Rhine district of Cincinnati sits Grammer's Restaurant, established in 1872 and in continued operation ever since. It was originally opened up by a German baker. It soon established a reputation for great food and became the home of the German Baker's Singing Society. Don't laugh—the German Baker's Singing Society was very important, and if they sang in your restaurant, you had it made. Grammer's was also a center for important political meetings, and a favorite night spot for famous athletes and musicians. Under the direction of the present owner, Jim Tarbel, Grammer's is better than ever, and still has a culinary core of great German dishes. Example: Sauerbraten with Spaetzle: marinated sweet and sour beef slowly cooked with gingersnaps and served with homemade dumplings.

1. Place all the marinade ingredients into a glass bowl, add the meat, and cover and refrigerate for 3 to 5 days, turning the meat once each day.

2. Preheat the oven to 350° F.

3. Remove the meat from the marinade. Dry with paper towels. Strain the marinade and reserve the liquid. Discard the solids.

4. Heat the oil in a large oven-proof casserole. Add the meat and brown over medium heat until all surfaces are browned. Remove the meat to a plate.

5. Add the carrot, onions, celery, and a pinch of salt to the casserole pot. Sauté over medium heat until the onions are softened and beginning to brown. Add the bay leaves, cloves, and juniper berries and stir. Add the tomato paste and stir for 1 minute.

6. Put the meat back into the pot and add enough marinade to half cover the meat. Bring to a boil, cover, and place in the oven. Cook for 3 to 3½ hours, turning the meat over 3 times, adding stock or water if needed to maintain liquid level. Remove the meat when it is fork tender. Set aside.

7. Strain the cooking juices. Remove the bay leaves and cloves. Puree the remaining solids in a food processor. Pour everything back into the casserole, heat over medium heat, and add the gingersnaps. Season with salt and pepper, to taste. Cook slowly, until the gingersnaps are completely incorporated into the sauce, about 5 minutes. Slice the meat and serve with the sauce.

1 cup chopped carrot
4 cups sliced onions
1 cup chopped celery
Salt and freshly ground
  black pepper
2 bay leaves
4 cloves
4 juniper berries, crushed
2 tablespoons tomato paste
Beef stock or water, if
  needed
1 cup finely ground
  gingersnaps

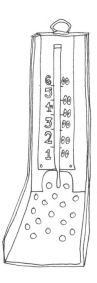

THE HISTORY OF
THE HOT DOG

The term "hot dog" was first used in 1901 at the Polo Grounds, which was the original home of the Giants baseball team. It was a cold day in April, and the food vendors were not doing well with their ice cream. They came up with the idea of selling a hot German sausage called a "dachshund sausage." It got that name because the shape of the sausage reminded people of a dachshund dog. A sports cartoonist at the game thought it was a great idea and he put a drawing of a barking sausage in the next day's paper. The cartoonist wasn't sure how to spell dachshund so he labeled the drawing "hot dog."

What makes hot dogs so good at sporting events is that they are easy to eat. It's the combination of the sausage and the roll that makes the play, and that team got put together at a World's Fair in St. Louis. A man named Anton Feuchtwanger was selling sausages, but they were so hot that people couldn't hold them; sales were slow. His brother-in-law was a baker who saw what the problem was and helped him out by producing a roll that would hold the meat. Talk about a great assist. It has been said that the most loyal and most noble dog of all is the hot dog—it feeds the hand that bites it.

◆

ASIAN-STYLE BEEF FILLETS
THE WINCHESTER INN ◆ ASHLAND, OREGON

When American settlers moved west in the 1800s, the unspoiled land of Oregon was a prime objective. It was and still is an ideal place for raising some of the world's finest beef cattle—a fact that is not lost on the man who gave me this recipe, chef Tad Platner at Oregon's Winchester Inn, located in Ashland.

1. Make a few incisions into both sides of the fillets and press in the lemon zest and peppercorns.

2. Combine the marinade ingredients in a container large enough to hold the liquid and the meat. Place the fillets in the marinade for several hours—ideally overnight in the refrigerator.

3. Grill the fillets until you reach the point of doneness you desire.

4. Serve sliced across the grain with heated marinade spooned on top.

MAKES 4 SERVINGS

BEEF FILLETS
Four 10-ounce portions of
  beef fillets
2 tablespoons lemon zest
2 tablespoons crushed
  black peppercorns

MARINADE
1⅓ cups water
1⅓ cups regular or low-
  sodium soy sauce
1 cup fresh lemon juice
½ cup sugar
1 tablespoon wasabi paste,
  Japanese horseradish, or
  2 tablespoons prepared
  white horseradish
½ teaspoon ground
  cinnamon
⅛ teaspoon grated nutmeg

AUSTRIAN BEEF BROTH AND BOILED BEEF
GOLDENER HIRSCH HOTEL ◆SALZBURG, AUSTRIA

MAKES 6 SERVINGS

3 pounds beef bones, cut up
5 quarts cold water
3 pounds brisket of beef, trimmed of excess fat
1 large Spanish or Bermuda onion
2 cups peeled, coarsely chopped white turnips
1 cup peeled, coarsely chopped carrots
4 cups carefully cleaned, coarsely chopped leeks, green tops removed
1 tablespoon salt
20 black peppercorns
3 bay leaves
White horseradish or horseradish sauce, for garnish

Mozart is probably Austria's most famous musician, but Tafelspitz is its most famous dish. It got that way because of Austria's most famous Emperor, Franz Josef I. Whatever Franz did, everyone else wanted to do too. So when the word got out that his Imperial Majesty preferred a boiled beef dish called Tafelspitz for lunch to everything else, it was Tafelspitz mania, and it still is.

1. Rinse the bones with cold, running water. Put into a stockpot large enough to accommodate all the ingredients. Cover with the cold water. Bring to a boil, turn down to simmer, and skim the surface.

2. When the surface is clean, add the brisket and continue to skim.

3. Cut the onion in half horizontally and place cut side up under a hot broiler. Broil until dark brown then add to the pot.

4. Add the turnips, carrots, and leeks. Simmer for 1 hour.

5. Add the salt, peppercorns, and bay leaves and simmer for 3 hours longer.

6. Remove the brisket from the broth.

7. Strain the broth into another container and discard the vegetables and bones.

8. To serve the brisket, thinly slice against the grain. Serve with white prepared horseradish or a simple horseradish sauce.

ABOUT THE HOTEL GOLDENER HIRSCH

In the heart of the antique city of Salzburg, on one of its oldest and most picturesque streets, sits the world famous Hotel Goldener Hirsch—the Golden Stag—with a history that dates back to 1407.

Amazing, almost a hundred years before Columbus set sail for the New World people were trying to get a reservation here. I understand that if Chris could have booked a room with a weekend rate, he would have come here rather than to America. Such are the small twists and turns in the course of history.

The present character of the hotel is a result of the work of Countess Harriet Walderdorff. She wanted the building to feel like a private manor house, and so she filled it with authentic period furniture: local works of art, traditional Austrian handicraft, and locks that date from the Renaissance. Today the hotel is managed by the Countess's son, Count Johannes Walderdorff, who is determined to maintain the atmosphere of a home away from home. His office has a small tunnel window that looks down on the entrance area. It gives him an opportunity to constantly note the arrival of his guests, and welcome them. And for the Count, nothing counts more than the hotel's cooking.

CURRIED BEEF AND RICE
WALDORF-ASTORIA HOTEL ◆ NEW YORK, NEW YORK

MAKES 8 SERVINGS

4 tablespoons vegetable oil
2 pounds lean boneless
  beef, cut into 1-inch
  cubes (Good cuts would
  be rump, chuck, or
  sirloin tip.)
1 cup finely chopped onion
½ cup finely chopped
  celery
1 teaspoon minced garlic
1 apple, peeled, cored, and
  cut into ¼-inch cubes
1 tablespoon curry powder
2 tablespoons tomato paste
2 cups long-grain rice,
  uncooked
4 cups beef broth
¼ cup raisins
¼ cup toasted pine nuts
  (optional)

The first rice to come to North America probably arrived on the coast of South Carolina in 1688. A sea captain named John Thurber ran into trouble and brought his ship in for repairs. He paid for the work with rice. Little did Captain Thurber realize that his rice was the starch of something grand.

1. Preheat the oven to 350° F.

2. In a 12-inch sauté pan or 5-quart heat-proof saucepan or casserole, heat 2 tablespoons of the vegetable oil over medium heat for 1 minute. In batches, add in the beef, and sauté for a few moments, stirring, until the sides of each piece are browned. Remove the beef to a dish and hold aside.

3. Add the remaining 2 tablespoons of oil and heat over medium heat for 30 seconds. Add the onion, celery, garlic, and apple and sauté for a minute. In batches, add in the beef, and sauté for a minute. Add the curry powder and tomato paste, mix well, and cook for a minute. Cooking the curry powder before the liquid is added to the dish will help bring out the curry flavor.

4. Mix all the cooked beef back into the pan. Add the rice, beef broth, raisins, and nuts. Mix well and cook, uncovered, in the oven for 30 minutes, until the rice is fully cooked.

NOTE: The better the quality of meat, the better the taste of the final dish. A recipe like this can be cooked either on top of the range or in the oven. Most professionals prefer the oven because the pot is fully surrounded by heat, which results in a cooking process that is more uniform.

PORK MEDALLIONS
JACKSONVILLE INN ♦ JACKSONVILLE, OREGON

When homesteaders first arrived in Oregon Territory they were astonished by the abundant supply of wild nuts that were in the forest. There was also a vast variety of wild berries. When you have a forest filled with wild food you have the perfect spot for raising pigs, and within a few years Oregon farmers were producing some of the finest pork. They still do. The following sautéed pork loin recipe was prepared by Chef Diane Menzie from the Jacksonville Inn. It's part of her low-fat menu and one of the inn's most popular dishes.

1. Lightly dredge the pork medallions in the flour.

2. In a large sauté pan, heat the oil. Place the medallions in the pan and cook 4 minutes on each side.

3. Add the mushrooms, rosemary, shallot or onion, and pepper to the sauté pan. Cook for 3 minutes. Add the ½ cup beef broth and the Marsala or additional beef broth and cook 8 to 10 minutes more.

4. Serve the meat with the sauce poured over it and garnish with chopped parsley.

MAKES 4 SERVINGS

1½ pounds pork tenderloin, trimmed and cut into ½-inch-thick medallions
4 tablespoons flour
2 tablespoons vegetable oil
2 cups sliced fresh mushrooms
1 tablespoon chopped fresh rosemary, or ½ tablespoon dried
1 shallot, minced, or 2 tablespoons minced onion
Freshly ground black pepper, to taste
½ cup beef broth
⅓ cup dry Marsala wine, or additional beef broth
Chopped parsley, for garnish

PORK LOIN WITH RICE
JAN D'ESPOSO ◆ OLD SAN JUAN, PUERTO RICO

MAKES 10 TO 12 SERVINGS

1 cup wild rice
1 teaspoon salt
1 teaspoon black
  peppercorns
3 cloves garlic, chopped
¼ cup chopped green
  olives
¼ cup dark rum
One 3- to 4-pound pork
  loin, trimmed but with a
  layer of fat on top
2 tablespoons butter or
  vegetable oil
3 jalapeño peppers,
  seeded, ribs removed,
  and minced
½ cup chopped onion
½ cup chopped red bell
  pepper
3 tablespoons chopped
  cilantro (coriander) or
  Chinese parsley
2 cups basmati or whole-
  grain rice
2 cubes chicken bouillon
3 drops Tabasco, or more
  to taste
Chopped cilantro, for
  garnish (optional)

Jan D'Esposo studied art at Bennington College in Vermont and Yale University. Today she lives in Puerto Rico's Old San Juan. She paints, runs an art gallery and a wonderful little inn with ten rooms and a serious kitchen. When she sets a table it's decorated with sculpture and plated with dishes that are produced in the gallery. She demonstrated her culinary art skills with this recipe for roast pork with rice.

1. Preheat the oven to 350° F. In a small bowl, soak the wild rice in water for 30 minutes.

2. Using a mortar and pestle, or the bottom of a heavy pot, grind the salt and peppercorns together. Place the mixture into a bowl and add the garlic, green olives, and dark rum to make a moist paste.

3. Place the loin, fat side down in an oven-proof roasting pan. With a sharp knife make a 1-inch-wide "X," about ¾ inch deep, every 2 inches along the roast. Stuff the paste in the holes. Turn the roast over, with the fat side up. Make diagonal slits in the meat about ¾ inch deep, 2 inches wide, and 2 inches apart. Insert the paste in the slits and smother the roast with the remaining paste. Place the pork in the oven and cook to an internal temperature of 160° F., for a medium-done roast, approximately 1½ hours or 20 to 25 minutes per pound. Let stand for 10 minutes before carving. Pour the pan drippings over the roast to serve.

4. In a large stockpot or saucepan with a tight-fitting lid, melt the butter or oil. Add the jalapeños, onion, and red pepper and sauté for 10 minutes. Add the cilantro or Chinese parsley and the basmati or whole-grain rice. Stir until the rice is thoroughly coated with butter. Drain and rinse the wild rice and add it to the pot. Cover with water, approximately 5 to 6 cups. Add the bouillon and stir to dissolve. Add the Tabasco and simmer for 50 to 55 minutes. Remove from the heat and let stand, covered, 10 minutes longer. Garnish with chopped cilantro, if desired.

ABOUT OLD SAN JUAN

Old San Juan is one of the two walled cities in our hemisphere. This town takes you back through five hundred years of living history. It sits between two fortresses. El Moro is the leading castle of the wall, dating back to 1540. The back door to the city was protected by the fort of San Cristobal.

Today, the city of Old San Juan is laced with cobblestone streets and boasts some of the finest examples of sixteenth- and seventeenth-century Spanish colonial architecture. It is a city steeped in history and culture. La Fortaleza, the home of the governor of Puerto Rico, was ordered into construction by Spain's King Carlos I in 1540. It must feel great to live in a building where the mortgage was paid off four hundred years ago.

CARIBBEAN SWEET AND SOUR PORK
CLUB MED 1

MAKES 6 SERVINGS

3 tablespoons vegetable oil
2 tablespoons finely
 chopped, peeled fresh
 ginger
1 tablespoon finely
 chopped garlic
1 cup coarsely chopped
 carrots
1 cup coarsely chopped
 onion
1 cup coarsely chopped
 green bell peppers
1 cup crushed pineapple in
 its own juice
¼ cup white wine vinegar
1 tablespoon sugar
½ tablespoon white or
 freshly ground black
 pepper
1½ cups ketchup
½ cup pineapple juice or
 water
2¼ pounds pork filets, cut
 into bite-sized cubes, at
 room temperature
Cooked rice, for serving

The following recipe calls for boiling the pork, which removes even more fat from the already lean pork filet. The sauce is practically fat free. You can also prepare this dish substituting cooked chicken, beef, fish, or shellfish for the pork.

1. In a large saucepan, heat the oil. Add ginger and garlic and sauté over a low flame for 5 minutes until fragrant. Do not brown the garlic or it will taste bitter. Add the carrots, sauté another 5 minutes. Add the onion and peppers and sauté about 3 minutes—until the green peppers lose their rawness, but aren't cooked thoroughly.

2. Add the cup of pineapple and its juice and the vinegar. Bring to a boil over high heat. Reduce the heat to medium and cook for 5 minutes.

3. Add the sugar, pepper, ketchup, and ½ cup of pineapple juice or water. Stir very well and continue to cook an additional 5 minutes.

4. Cook the pork in boiling water for 10 minutes, testing the meat for doneness after 5 minutes. Cut a piece open—if it's not pink inside, it's done. When done, drain and add the pork to the sauce. Cook together for 2 minutes.

5. Adjust seasoning, tasting for salt, pepper, and vinegar. Add more if desired. Serve with cooked rice.

NOTE: This dish should be served immediately. It toughens if held in the refrigerator.

ABOUT THE CARIBBEAN

The islands of the Caribbean start out just below Florida and form an arc that curves east and south for some twenty-six hundred miles until it comes to the last landfall in the chain just off the coast of South America. There are about seven thousand islands in the group. Sometimes they are called the West Indies, because when Christopher Columbus originally discovered them he was looking for India, and these islands are somewhat to the west of his original destination. Actually they are about half a planet to the west of his original destination. To say that Columbus had lucked out would be one of the great understatements of the past five hundred years. These islands are also called the Antilles, which was a name used by thirteenth-century map makers to designate a group of imaginary islands that they placed in the Atlantic. But there is nothing imaginary about the beauty and charm of the Caribbean. The islands were formed during the last ice age and were part of an unbroken land mass that connected Florida to Venezuela. Earthquakes and volcanic eruptions changed the geology, and today only the mountaintops of this land bridge remain above water, forming these magnificent enclaves.

For hundreds of years after Columbus arrived, the area was in constant conflict. The Spanish, the French, the Dutch, and the English were perpetually battling each other and the local natives. Piracy was big, slavery, rebellion . . . not the ideal environment to develop a great cuisine. And yet all of the natural ingredients were here. The sea supplied an endless variety of fish and seafood. The area's rich tropical soil produced excellent fruits and vegetables. Many of the foods we take for granted were first brought to Europe from the Caribbean by Columbus and other early explorers: grapefruit, pineapple, hot peppers, tomatoes—all from the Caribbean. Think about that: Columbus was the first European to taste a tomato. Talk about landmarks in culinary history—without Columbus, no tomato sauce on pizza. Just on the basis of that he deserves to be a major figure in Italian history.

Within the last hundred years the islands have become politically and culturally independent. Colonial ideas no longer suppress local flavors and techniques, and that has led to the birth of the rich and fascinating Caribbean cuisine. Today Caribbean cooking is hot stuff.

◆

GRILLED PORK LOIN WITH SWEET MUSTARD GINGER GLAZE
THE CINCINNATIAN HOTEL ◆ CINCINNATI, OHIO

MAKES 4 SERVINGS

MARINADE
¼ cup Dijon-style mustard
2 tablespoons light soy
  sauce
2 tablespoons peanut oil
1 tablespoon sesame oil
3 tablespoons sweet chili
  sauce. If not available,
  use 3 tablespoons plum
  sauce with ⅛ teaspoon
  cayenne pepper
¼ teaspoon minced garlic
¼ teaspoon minced ginger

1¼ pounds pork loin cut
  into 8 medallions

DRESSING
½ cup rice wine vinegar
1½ tablespoons light soy
  sauce
2 tablespoons Dijon-style
  mustard
¼ teaspoon each of
  chopped garlic, ginger,
  and shallots or onion
¼ cup sesame oil
¼ cup peanut oil

For many centuries in both Europe and the United States, the word "chef" brought to mind a picture of a man who was as wide as he was tall. If he didn't look like his own biggest customer, his talent was in question. Fortunately things are changing. Today many of the most talented American chefs are young women who are as interested in good health as in good taste. Anita Cunningham has been the executive chef at the Cincinnatian Hotel since 1988, and she's a perfect example of what I mean. She takes pork—the Cincinnati classic—and prepares a low-fat, high-taste recipe for grilled pork loin.

TO MAKE THE MARINADE:
1. Mix all the ingredients together.

2. Place the pork medallions in a glass dish or plastic container. Pour the marinade over the pork.

3. Cover and let marinate for 6–12 hours in the refrigerator.

4. Cook the pork on the grill or under the broiler for 2½ minutes on each side, or until cooked through.

FOR THE DRESSING:
1. In the container of a food processor or the bowl of an electric mixer, blend all ingredients except the oils.

2. Keeping the processor or mixer running, slowly pour in both oils, one at a time. Set aside.

TO PREPARE THE SALAD:

1. Pour the sesame oil into a hot pan or wok.

2. Add the onion, pepper, and mushrooms.

3. Add the spinach and pour the dressing all over the mixture as if you were stir-frying. When the spinach is slightly wilted, remove from the pan and place some on each plate. Serve the cooked pork on top.

WARM SPINACH GREENS SALAD

1 tablespoon sesame oil
½ large red onion, julienned
1 large red bell pepper, julienned
1 cup sliced mushrooms
1 pound spinach, thoroughly cleaned

PORKOPOLIS

The years between 1830 and 1840 were years of great industrial growth for the city of Cincinnati. The industry most responsible for this period of development was pork packing. From its earliest days, Cincinnati was surrounded with rich agricultural land that was put to good use. Almost every farmer raised a few hogs. Hogs were easy, they could be left free to roam the nearby forests, and they required very little care. In the 1820s, farmers around Cincinnati began to grow a lot more corn, which they fed to the hogs. They noticed the corn produced fatter animals with a better quality meat and a higher lever of profit. So the farmers raised more hogs, and by 1835, Cincinnati had become the nation's largest pork-packing center and was actually referred to as **Porkopolis.**

APPLE-CURRANT PORK CHOPS
BLOMIDON INN ◆ NOVA SCOTIA, CANADA

MAKES 6 SERVINGS

6 pork chops, 1¼ to
  1½ inches thick
1½ cups garlic croutons
½ cup chopped apple
½ cup shredded Cheddar
  cheese
2 tablespoons dried
  currants or raisins
2 tablespoons unsalted
  butter, melted
2 tablespoons orange juice
¼ teaspoon salt
⅛ teaspoon cinnamon

The Blomidon Inn in Wolfville, Nova Scotia, was built by a sea captain named Rufus Burgess in the late 1800s and it is quite a piece of work. Burgess brought home great planks of mahogany from the tropics, which he used for paneling throughout the house. He decorated the public and private rooms with period antique furniture. He also constructed the first bathroom in the district, which made him an object of great curiosity.

The captain was well known for his distrust of banks, and at the time of his death it was rumored that a considerable fortune had been left behind. Today there is a constant (though quiet) search for his treasure, which is believed to be hidden somewhere in the house or on the grounds. I can't tell you much about the old captain's treasure, but there's certainly a collection of treasured recipes in the kitchen.

1. Preheat oven to 350° F.

2. Cut a pocket in each of the pork chops.

3. In a bowl, lightly toss together the croutons, apple, cheese, and currants or raisins. In a second bowl, combine the remaining ingredients. Pour them over the crouton-fruit mixture and toss gently.

4. Lightly stuff the pork chops with the crouton-fruit mixture. Place them in a shallow baking pan. Bake uncovered for 1 hour, cover with foil, and bake 20 minutes longer. Serve.

ABOUT PORK

Pork is the flesh of the pig, one of our oldest sources of meat. The first pork recipes, dated about 500 B.C., stem from China and call for a suckling pig roasted in a pit. The Chinese and the Romans were adept at smoking and curing pork for use in the winter months. The tradition of slaughtering hogs for roasts, chops, sausages, ham, and lard continues to this day. Among the Cajuns of southwest Louisiana, slaughtering is a community event called La Boucherie. The Spanish conquistador Hernando de Soto brought the first pigs to Florida in 1525. The majority of pigs in the United States are raised in Iowa, Illinois, and Missouri.

Part of the art of pork cookery is to avoid overcooking. During the past few years, the pork producers have been working to produce a leaner cut of meat and reduce the older recommended cooking times. These days they recommend that pork be cooked to an internal temperature of 160° F. for medium doneness. That will keep the meat tender and juicy while still reaching an adequate temperature for healthfully cooked pork.

◆

ABOUT TAKE-OUT FOOD IN PARIS

The word charcuterie means, literally, "pork butcher's shop," and when the first one opened in Paris in the year 1475, that's exactly what it was. The most common meat at the time was pork; it was also a time when most of the people living in Paris did not have kitchens in which they could really cook. And so the charcuterie became "the place where you can buy cooked food," a community kitchen where you could stop in and buy something that was already cooked to take home to eat. In the past five hundred years, the Paris charcuterie has evolved into the world's ultimate take-out food shop. One of the most famous charcuteries is called Fauchon. They offer over twenty-two thousand different products. The prepared dishes sit in the window and are responsible for causing thousands of hunger attacks in passersby each day. They make fresh pasta, and, of course, a wide assortment of sauces to go on top. The selection of preserved meats from pâtés to sausages is beyond description. You could probably buy your food at Fauchon each day of your entire life and never repeat a dish.

◆

CHICKEN FRIED STEAKS

MARCH OF DIMES GALA COOK-OFF ◆ NEW YORK, NEW YORK

MAKES 4 SERVINGS

1 pound round steak,
  about ¼ inch thick, cut
  into 4 pieces
Freshly ground black
  pepper
2 eggs, lightly beaten
¾ cup flour
⅓ cup vegetable oil
¾ cup milk

The March of Dimes was originally organized by President Franklin D. Roosevelt to raise money for the fight against polio. When a protective vaccine was developed, the March of Dimes shifted its work toward improving the health of America's newborn babies. Funds are often raised as part of celebrity cooking contests. The following recipe was presented at a March of Dimes event by the columnist Liz Smith.

1. Using a mallet, pound the steaks until they are about ⅛ inch thick. Cut each steak in half. Sprinkle them with pepper, to taste.

2. Dip each steak in the beaten eggs and then in the flour. Set aside.

3. In a 10-inch skillet, heat the oil over medium heat. Add the steaks to the pan and fry for 1 minute on each side. Remove the steaks to a plate lined with paper towels.

4. Pour the milk into the skillet and simmer, stirring, until the gravy thickens, about 1 to 2 minutes.

5. Place the steaks on a serving platter. Serve with the gravy on the side.

MAPLE-GLAZED COUNTRY BAKED HAM
SHELBURNE FARMS ◆ BURLINGTON, VERMONT

Shelburne Farms is a 1,000-acre property on Lake Champlain, near Burlington, Vermont. It was donated to a nonprofit, educational group in 1976. Since then it has become a dynamic community of people working together to preserve the natural and agricultural resources of the farm . . . to offer consumers locally produced foods and provide regional jobs. The following is their recipe for Maple-Glazed Country Baked Ham.

1. In a deep covered pot, simmer the ham in the cider for 2 hours. If the cider does not cover the ham, add enough water to cover.

2. Preheat the oven to 325° F.

3. Drain the pot, reserving the cider. Remove any skin from the ham. Place the ham in a shallow baking pan and set aside.

4. In a large bowl, combine the remaining ingredients. Take ½ cup of the reserved cider and whisk into the mixture. Pour the mixture over the ham.

5. Bake the ham for about 45 minutes. Baste occasionally. Remove the ham from the oven, slice, and serve with caramelized cider gravy from the roasting pan.

NOTE: If the gravy is not caramelized, reduce the liquid by stirring over high heat.

MAKES 8 SERVINGS

4 pounds boneless smoked
  round ham
2 quarts apple cider
1 cup raisins
1 cup maple syrup
1 teaspoon dry mustard
½ teaspoon ground cloves
½ cup water

LAMB KEBABS
THE RUSSIAN TEA ROOM ◆ NEW YORK, NEW YORK

MAKES 4 SERVINGS

½ cup vegetable oil

Juice of one lemon, strained

3 cloves garlic, crushed

1 small onion, chopped

Freshly ground black pepper, to taste

1 pound boneless chunks of trimmed leg of lamb

½ medium onion, cut in ¾-inch squares

1 green bell pepper, seeded, ribs removed, and cut into ¾-inch squares

16 cherry tomatoes

Rice Pilaf, for serving (see following recipe)

The Russian Tea Room is one of the landmark restaurants of New York. It began life in 1926 when members of the Russian Imperial Ballet, who had fled to America after the Russian Revolution, needed a place where the members of the troupe could socialize and meet with other Russian émigrés. Today the interior of the restaurant is like a Christmas tree, decorated in green, red, and gold, with a collection of fascinating Russian art and objects. The Russian Tea Room is still a favorite meeting place for people of the theater. Kebabs are one of the specialties of the restaurant.

1. In a medium mixing bowl, combine the oil, lemon juice, garlic, onion, black pepper, and lamb. Stir to combine. Cover and marinate for 3 days in the refrigerator.

2. On 8-inch metal skewers, alternate pieces of lamb, onion, green pepper, and cherry tomatoes. Brush the vegetables with the remaining marinade.

3. Broil kebabs for 12 minutes, 4 inches below the heat, turning several times.

4. Serve with Rice Pilaf.

RICE PILAF

MAKES 4 SERVINGS

6 tablespoons butter
1 cup long-grain rice
1¾ cups chicken stock
½ teaspoon salt
¼ teaspoon freshly ground
   black pepper

1. In a heavy 2- to 3-quart saucepan with a tight-fitting lid, heat 2 tablespoons of the butter. Cut the remaining butter into small pieces and set aside. Add the rice to the pan and cook over medium heat, stirring constantly with a wooden spoon, for 2 to 3 minutes, or until the rice begins to turn opaque. Do not brown the rice.

2. Add the chicken stock, salt, and pepper to the rice. Bring the mixture to the boiling point, stirring constantly. Cover the pan tightly and turn the heat down as low as possible. Cook without stirring, for 12 to 15 minutes, or until all the liquid has been absorbed. The rice should be tender, but not mushy. Stir the reserved butter into the rice. Remove from the heat and let stand, covered, for 5 minutes. Serve immediately.

HOW CHEFS' HATS CAME TO BE

On May 29, 1453, the Turkish armies of the Ottoman Empire invaded Greece and overthrew the Byzantine Empire and the Greek government. Right after the Ottoman invasion, the local church leaders took over their neighborhoods and worked to preserve the Greek language, Greek culture, and the sense of family and family traditions.

Many of the rich and famous Greeks went into the monasteries to hide themselves from the Turks. The monks didn't know what to do with these nobles and at one point it was suggested that the nobles do the cooking. They dressed just like the rest of the monks, in black robes and tall black hats, so the Turks couldn't tell who they were. But then neither could the monks, and that became annoying. So the monks decided that the people who were the cooks should change their uniforms. Not a big change—they just insisted that the black uniforms become white, including the tall hats.

CONCORDE VEAL WITH TOMATOES
AIR FRANCE KITCHENS ◆ NEW YORK, NEW YORK

MAKES 4 SERVINGS

4 medallions of veal,
  ½ inch thick, cut from
  the veal steak or eye of
  round
Salt and freshly ground
  black pepper
Flour, for dredging
2 to 3 tablespoons butter or
  margarine
¾ cup finely chopped,
  peeled and seeded tomato
2 tablespoons finely
  chopped shallots or onion
1 tablespoon chopped
  fresh tarragon, or
  ½ teaspoon dried
Swiss cheese, cut into
  16 matchsticks, 2 inches
  long

Michel Martin is a master French chef. His job is to take the classics of French cuisine, prepare them perfectly, and serve them to you with the elegance and skill for which French chefs have become famous. But Michel has a special challenge. Though his kitchen is down to earth in all details, his one hundred dinner guests are up in the air—about 6,000 feet up in the air, jetting across the Atlantic between New York and Paris on Air France's supersonic Concorde.

1. Preheat the oven to 400° F.

2. Season the veal with salt and pepper, to taste. Dredge in flour and shake off the excess.

3. Heat the butter in a skillet over medium heat and sauté the veal for 2 to 4 minutes on each side, depending on the thickness, until golden brown on all sides. Remove the veal to a baking pan.

4. In the same pan used to sauté the veal, over medium heat, add the tomato, shallots or onions and tarragon and cook for two minutes. Spoon the mixture in equal amounts over the veal.

5. Place 4 matchstick slices of swiss cheese in a crisscross pattern on top of the veal and bake in the preheated oven for 5 minutes in order to melt the cheese and heat the veal.

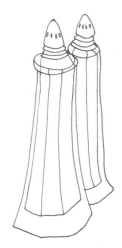

A B O U T   V E A L

Veal is young beef. It is more common in Europe than in America, but in cities with large Italian populations veal is readily available. European farmers do not have as much pasture and cropland as American farmers do, so they often slaughter young beef animals when they are two to five months old. They have been milk fed their entire lives and have not had a chance to exercise their muscles, so the meat is creamy white and very tender. Some American veal animals are allowed to become a few months older and feed on grass. This veal is called "calf."

Veal cutlets are thin, boneless pieces of meat cut from the rump or round portion of the animal. The best cutlets, called scaloppine, are cut across the grain from the single muscle of the top round. You may also come across cutlets cut from the whole hind leg that contain a small round bone in the center. This is a less desirable cut.

RINGNES BURGERS
FRAM MUSEUM ◆ OSLO, NORWAY

MAKES 6 SERVINGS

2 tablespoons vegetable oil
1 medium onion, chopped
¼ cup chopped pickled
  beets
¼ cup chopped sweet
  gherkins
1 tablespoon capers,
  chopped
2 pounds ground beef
2 eggs
½ teaspoon salt
¼ teaspoon freshly ground
  black pepper
¾ teaspoon chili powder
12 ounces Ringnes or your
  favorite beer

Just outside the city of Oslo, Norway, is a museum containing the ship that was used for a number of explorations to both the North and South poles. The name of the vessel is Fram, which means "forward."

Explorations are very expensive and are always funded by a sponsor. Columbus had Queen Isabella; Lewis and Clark, who mapped most of the American Northwest, were funded by a company that made fur hats; and the Norwegians were supported by the brewers of Ringnes beer. Of course, there were a few cases of Ringnes on board the Fram, and the cook often put the beer to good use in his recipes. My favorite is for Ringnes Burgers.

1. In a medium sauté pan, heat 1 tablespoon of the vegetable oil. Add the onion and sauté until it begins to turn golden, approximately 8 minutes. Add the beets, pickles, and capers and sauté for 3 minutes.

2. In a medium bowl, combine the vegetable mixture with the beef, eggs, salt, pepper, chili powder, and ¼ cup of the beer. Mix well. Shape the mixture into 6 patties, compressing firmly.

3. In a large sauté pan, heat the remaining tablespoon of vegetable oil. Pan fry the patties until done to taste, approximately 6 to 7 minutes on each side for a medium burger. Remove the patties from the pan and set aside.

4. Pour off the grease from the sauté pan. Add the remaining beer to the pan and cook for approximately 10 minutes, scraping up the brown bits with a spoon.

5. Pour the beer sauce over the burgers and serve.

A B O U T
H A M B U R G E R S

Along with hot dogs, hamburgers are the most American of all foods. The name "hamburger" is derived from the German port city of Hamburg. Through the latter half of the nineteenth century, some form of hammered beefsteak was served in restaurants there. But the first time the name "hamburger" was used was at the Louisiana Purchase Exposition and World's Fair in St. Louis in 1904.

The advent of the White Castle hamburger chain in the 1920s and the McDonald's chain in the 1950s spread hamburger culture far and wide in America.

Hamburgers should be called beef burgers because it is rare that hamburgers are made of veal, lamb, or pork. A hamburger should contain 20 to 25 percent fat, although it is possible to buy meat that is as lean as 10 percent fat. Ground chuck has the proper fat content and the beefiest flavor.

◆

VIENNESE WIENER SCHNITZEL
HOTEL IMPERIAL ◆ VIENNA, AUSTRIA

MAKES 4 SERVINGS

Flour, approximately
 ¾ cup
1 egg, beaten
¾ cup bread crumbs
2 tablespoons finely
 chopped parsley
Salt and freshly ground
 black pepper, to taste
½ to ¾ cup vegetable oil
4 veal cutlets (about
 1¼ pounds), cut from the
 loin, pounded between
 plastic wrap
1 lemon, cut into 4 wedges

1. Put the flour, egg, and bread crumbs into 3 separate shallow bowls. Add the parsley to the egg and mix. Season contents of each bowl with salt and pepper.

2. Heat ½ cup of vegetable oil in a skillet or frying pan until very hot—just *under* smoking, 375° F. The high heat helps reduce the absorption of fat.

3. Quickly dredge one cutlet in the flour, shaking off excess, then dip into the egg, and finally the bread crumbs. Place the breaded veal in the hot oil.

4. Repeat process with remaining cutlets, cooking each side until golden brown—anywhere from 45 seconds to 2 minutes, depending on thickness. Shake the pan as the cutlets cook so they don't stick. Add more oil to skillet if necessary.

5. Remove the cutlets as they finish cooking and place on paper towels to absorb any residual oil.

6. Serve each cutlet with a lemon wedge.

◆

BAKED HAM SLICE
AMERICAN FESTIVAL CAFÉ ◆ NEW YORK, NEW YORK

In 1608 three sows and a boar were brought from Great Britain to Jamestown, Virginia. Within two years, the pork population had increased to over sixty pigs. By 1625, Virginia, Maryland, and the Carolinas had become famous for their hams. Together they made pork the most popular meat in the colonies. Chef François Keller at the American Festival Café in New York has a collection of great American ham recipes; the following is an example.

1. Preheat the oven to 350° F.

2. Combine the mustard and nutmeg and rub onto both sides of the ham slice. Place ham in a baking dish. Pour the cider and maple syrup over the ham. Bake for 1 hour, basting occasionally. Slice and serve.

MAKES 2 SERVINGS

1 teaspoon dry mustard
¼ teaspoon nutmeg
One 2-inch-thick slice
  of ham steak (about
  1½ pounds)
½ cup apple cider
¼ cup maple syrup

SWEDISH MEATBALLS
OPERAKALLAREN RESTAURANT ◆ STOCKHOLM, SWEDEN

MAKES 4 SERVINGS

3 tablespoons dried bread
  crumbs
¼ cup heavy cream
½ teaspoon salt
½ teaspoon freshly ground
  black pepper
1 pound ground chuck
½ cup chopped onion
4 tablespoons vegetable oil

During the sixteenth century, the cooks of Sweden began developing a serving style that put all the food for the meal on one table at the same time. Eventually there were five distinct courses, but they were all laid out together.

When the custom first got started, the offerings were very simple, consisting primarily of a little bread, butter, cheese, and some herring. It was really a small appetizer buffet that guests could stand around before the actual dinner party began. In those days the roads in Sweden were rather rough, and not all the dinner guests could arrive at the same time, no matter how hard they tried. The smorgasbord, which actually means "bread and butter table," would be to one side, and there the guests could find enough food to hold body and soul together until everyone arrived and dinner was served.

Little by little, however, more and more dishes were added to the table. The invention of canning allowed people to increase the selection with foods that were out of season, which was a great luxury at the time. Today the traditional smorgasbord is still served at the Operakallaren restaurant in Stockholm, Sweden. Meatballs are a standard part of the Operakallaren smorgasbord.

1. In a bowl, combine the breadcrumbs, cream, salt, and pepper.

2. Add the ground chuck and onion to the bread crumb mixture and combine.

3. With wet hands, form the mixture into meatballs about the size of small walnuts.

4. In a 12-inch skillet, heat the vegetable oil over medium heat. Carefully add the meatballs and sauté until well browned on all sides, about 5 minutes. Shake the pan back and forth during cooking to prevent the meatballs from sticking.

A B O U T   S A L T

Salt has played such an important role in human history that the very word has become symbolic of value. The word "salary" comes from the word "salt"; it's a reference to the fact that in ancient times Roman soldiers received part of their payment in salt. To call someone the salt of the earth is to describe them as trustworthy and responsible. Salt was so valuable that if you spilled any of it at the table, you were thought to be in the presence of evil spirits, but you didn't have to worry, you just took a little and threw it over your left shoulder, and the spirits would run away. Evil spirits were thought to congregate behind you and slightly to the left.

Salt was also wonderful for finding out who was a witch. You put a little salt under a seat cushion, invited someone to sit down, and if they refused—that was it, you were stuck with a witch.

Salt had a negative image too: salt is a rock, and most people thought that eating a rock was kind of strange. This, perhaps, gave rise to a negative salt phrase. If you had a gold mine that was totally worthless, but you wanted to sell it to somebody, you'd take a little gold and stick it around to convince the buyer that the mine was filled with gold, and that was called "salting the mine."

CLYDE'S MEATLOAF
CLYDE'S OF RESTON ✦ RESTON, VIRGINIA

MAKES 6 TO 8 SERVINGS*

½ cup old-fashioned
  oatmeal (not the quick-
  cooking type)
½ cup plus 2 tablespoons
  honey
½ cup milk
2 tablespoons vegetable oil
1½ cups chopped onion
1½ teaspoons minced
  garlic
Salt and freshly ground
  black pepper
2½ pounds ground chuck
¾ cup grated carrots
⅓ cup ketchup
1 teaspoon dry mustard

The places where people come together can be divided into three categories: The first place is the home, the second is the workplace, and the third is where people in a neighborhood "hang out"—a café, a coffee house, a soda fountain, a place where folks from the area come together to talk, to get a sense of belonging to a group, to reduce the stress of daily life. Neighborhood gathering places are very common in European cities and they were a regular part of the American scene until the middle of this century. In recent years, however, very few real estate developers have included this type of gathering place in their plans. An exception is Clyde's of Reston, just outside of Washington, D.C. From the beginning, it was designed to be one of those "third places," with a cast of regular neighborhood customers. One of the ways Chef Tom Meyer keeps those customers is by serving dishes that are associated with the warmth of Ma's home cooking. An example is his Clyde's Meatloaf.

1. Combine the oatmeal, honey, and milk in a large mixing bowl. Allow to sit at room temperature for 30 minutes. Preheat the oven to 375° F.

2. Heat the oil in a sauté pan over medium heat and add the onion and garlic. Add salt and pepper, to taste, and sauté until the onion is translucent and softened slightly.

✦

3. Add the onion to the oatmeal mixture, along with the meat, add salt to taste, and plenty of black pepper. Add the grated carrots, mix thoroughly, and place in a nonstick 9-×-5-×-3-inch loaf pan. (If using a regular loaf pan, oil it lightly.) Place the loaf pan on a cookie sheet to catch any spills and put in oven.

4. Bake the meatloaf for 50 minutes. Remove from oven and carefully tip the pan to drain off the excess fat and liquid, then turn the meatloaf out onto the cookie sheet. Turn right side up. Combine the ketchup and mustard and spread the mixture over the top and sides of the meatloaf. Return meatloaf to the oven and bake for an additional 20 minutes.

*NOTE: Ingredients may be doubled and baked in a large bundt pan or tube pan to make 12 to 16 servings.

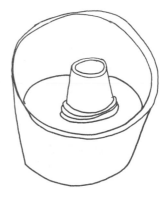

MEAT PIES

THE RITZ-CARLTON HOTEL ◆ MONTREAL, QUEBEC, CANADA

MAKES 6 MEAT PIES

1 cup small cubes of beef
1 cup small cubes of
  skinned and boned
  chicken
1 cup small cubes of veal
1 tablespoon finely
  chopped shallots
1 teaspoon chopped fresh
  thyme, or ½ teaspoon
  dried
1 tablespoon chopped
  fresh parsley
1 tablespoon chopped
  fresh basil, or
  1½ teaspoons dried
1 tablespoon chopped
  fresh chives
1½ teaspoons chopped
  fresh tarragon, or
  ¾ teaspoon dried
Salt and freshly ground
  black pepper, to taste
Pie dough to line and top
  6 large muffin cups
1 large Idaho potato,
  peeled and cut into small
  dice
1 egg, beaten

In 1910 a small group of very wealthy Montreal businessmen decided that their city needed a hotel in the grand European tradition. At first they planned to name the establishment after London's celebrated Carlton Hotel, but they soon realized that the most respected hotels of the period were those run by the great César Ritz. His Ritz Hotel in Paris had become the most fashionable place to stay. The Montrealers asked Ritz to lend his name to their new business. Ritz agreed but insisted on a series of conditions. Each room had to have its own bathroom (which was unusual and opulent for the time), each room had to have its own telephone—an unheard of luxury—each floor had to have its own kitchen, so room service would be perfect, and a valet was to be available twenty-four hours a day.

Ritz had a staircase in his Paris lobby specifically designed so that people could make a grand entrance into the public areas. He required that it be reproduced in Montreal. All the conditions were met, and on New Year's Eve of 1912 The Ritz-Carlton opened its doors.

1. Preheat the oven to 350° F.

2. Place each cup of meat in a separate bowl. Season each with shallots, herbs, salt, and pepper.

3. Roll out the pie dough and line 6 large nonstick muffin cups with it, reserving enough to make tops. If not using nonstick muffin cups, grease before lining with pie dough. Cut off overlap.

4. Make a layer of beef cubes at the bottom of each cup, followed by a layer of potato, then chicken cubes, more potato, and finally the veal cubes. Press down slightly to compact the filling. Dampen the top edge of the pie dough in each cup with water and top with a round of the pie dough. Press to make the dough adhere. Using a small paring knife, score the edge of each pie, without cutting through the dough. Make a hole in the center of each, so the steam can escape. Brush each with the beaten egg.

5. Place the muffin cups in the preheated oven and bake for 50 minutes. Remove pies to individual plates and serve warm.

EATING TO STAY COOL

Confucius, the ancient Chinese philosopher, suggested that we eat a low-fat diet during hot weather in order to stay cool, and he knew what he was talking about. Your body has to work harder to digest fat, and the extra work produces extra heat. In general, the lower the fat content of your diet during hot weather, the cooler you are going to be. And then there was Isador of Seville—you don't hear much about Izzy these days, but during the sixth century, Isador of Seville was a big deal. He suggested that a spicy diet would keep you cooler during hot weather, and he knew what he was talking about. A spicy diet will cause perspiration, and when the moisture on the surface of your body evaporates, that cools you down. It's also a good idea to avoid foods that are hot in temperature or cold in temperature. Your body has to do extra work to bring the temperatures of these foods into line with your own body temperature, and that extra work causes extra body heat. And finally, it's a really good idea to drink six to eight glasses of water each day during hot weather.

AGRICULTURAL FAIRS

Agricultural fairs have been part of farm life for almost as long as there has been agriculture. We had the first one in the colonies in 1810. A fair was a time when the entire farm community could get together. The harvest season had come to the end, people paid their debts and incurred new ones, young men and women met and married, ideas and techniques were exchanged. When our colonies broke free of Great Britain at the end of the Revolutionary War, we gained much, but we also lost much, and one of the things we lost was our access to good quality woolen cloth. We also lost our access to information on technological changes in agriculture.

People like George Washington and Thomas Jefferson were heads of state, but they were also farmers and they felt the need to have regular organized opportunities for the exchange of information about farming. Our state and county fairs became the vehicles for that exchange. At first, the prime objective was to improve sheep shearing so the colonists could improve their wool, but very soon every aspect of farming and farm life was included. As different food-related businesses were developed, they were incorporated into the local state fair.

MUSTARD

People have been making mustard for over 5,000 years. It is one of our earliest seasonings and its use is widely spread throughout the world. Freshly ground mustard seeds are tasteless, but when they are mixed with water, vinegar, or wine, they release their intense flavor.

As eighteenth-century Spanish missionaries made their way north along the coast of California, they sprinkled mustard seeds that took root and served to mark their path for other missionaries following them. The bright yellow bushes made an easy-to-see trail called the Mission Trail, parts of which are still visible.

Mustards do not spoil, but they lose their flavor over time. They keep best if refrigerated after they are opened. When cooking with mustard, remember this: Heat reduces its sharpness, and time allows it to blend with other flavors. If you add it early, it will be milder and blended throughout the dish. If you add it later, it will be sharper but will not dominate the other flavors.

PASTA AND RICE

PASTA, EGGPLANT, AND PECORINO
MEZZOGIORNO ◆ NEW YORK, NEW YORK

MAKES 4 SERVINGS

4 tablespoons olive oil
2 cloves garlic, thinly
  sliced
1 medium eggplant, cut
  into ½-inch cubes
1 cup canned Italian plum
  tomatoes, coarsely
  chopped, with their juices
2 tablespoons chopped
  fresh basil, or
  1 tablespoon dried
¾ pound penne pasta,
  cooked
Gratings of Pecorino
  Romano cheese

Little Italy is the result of an enormous wave of Italian immigrants that arrived in the United States between 1880 and 1914. Almost 4 million people came looking for a better life in a new world. The neighborhood acted as a buffer zone between the simple villages that they left behind and the madness of living in New York City. It gave them a sense of family, even if the family was just another guy from their old town in Italy.

Every day they ate the foods of their home country and reconfirmed their love of being Italian. And lucky for this country that they did that, too, because the Italians brought us great cheeses, great ice cream, great baking, and spaghetti. Where would this country be without spaghetti?

1. In a large sauté pan, heat the olive oil over medium heat. Add the garlic and sauté until golden, approximately 2 minutes. Add the eggplant and cook 7 to 8 minutes. Add the tomatoes and their juices and continue simmering for 15 minutes, stirring occasionally.

2. Add the basil and the cooked pasta and toss to combine.

3. Top each plate of pasta with a grating of Pecorino Romano cheese and serve.

PASTA, HAM, AND TOMATOES
EXCELSIOR HOTEL ◆ ROME, ITALY

1. In a stockpot, bring 4 quarts of water to a boil.

2. While the water is coming to the boil, heat the oil in a large sauté pan, over medium heat. Add the ham or bacon, cook for 4 minutes, stir often.

3. Add the pepper flakes, onion, tomatoes, and sugar, if used, to the sauté pan. Bring to a boil and cook for 10 minutes to thicken the sauce. Stir often.

4. Cook the pasta in the boiling water until it is cooked through but still has a firm texture when bitten. When the pasta is added to the water it will stop boiling; let the water come back to a rolling boil and then time the cooking for 10 minutes. Taste for doneness.

5. When the pasta is done, drain and add it to the sauce. Add the butter, Parmesan and Pecorino. Heat through, mix together, and serve.

NOTE: Cheeses like Parmesan and Pecorino should be measured after grating when the unit of measure called for in the recipe is in volume, e.g., cups. When the unit of measure is weight, e.g., ounces, the measuring should be done before grating.

MAKES 6 SERVINGS

1 tablespoon olive oil
½ pound prosciutto Italian ham, or bacon, minced
¼ teaspoon dried red pepper flakes
½ cup finely chopped onion
4 cups canned tomatoes, coarsely chopped, with their juices
1 teaspoon sugar, optional, depending on the sweetness of the tomatoes
1 pound bucatini, a form of spaghetti that is hollow, like a straw. (This recipe will also work well with 1 pound of any spaghetti. Bucatini is not essential.)
1 tablespoon butter, cut into small pieces
¼ cup grated Parmesan cheese
¼ cup grated Pecorino Romano cheese

RIGATONI PASTA WITH BROCCOLI
IL NIDO ◆ NEW YORK, NEW YORK

MAKES 4 SERVINGS

2 tablespoons olive oil
1 clove garlic, thinly sliced
½ cup chicken stock
1 tablespoon seasoned
  bread crumbs
Flowerets from 1 head of
  broccoli, blanched in
  boiling water for
  60 seconds
1 pound rigatoni pasta,
  cooked
Gratings of Pecorino
  Romano cheese

Il Nido is the name of one of the very best Italian restaurants in New York City. Il Nido means "the nest," and the owner, Adi Giovannetti, chose that name because he wanted to give his guests the feeling that they were coming to a little tender home, a place where they would be cosy, cared for, and protected.

1. In a large sauté pan, heat the olive oil over medium heat. Add the garlic and sauté until golden, approximately 2 minutes. Add the chicken stock and the bread crumbs to thicken the sauce. Mix well.

2. Add the broccoli flowerets and the cooked rigatoni and toss to coat with the sauce.

3. Top each serving with a grating of Pecorino Romano cheese.

NOTE: Using chicken stock and bread crumbs to make a sauce is an excellent low-fat technique. The pasta is packed with complex carbohydrates and the broccoli contains vitamins A, B, C, calcium, iron, and potassium. Broccoli is one of our most nutritious vegetables.

THE HISTORY OF PASTA

Traditionally it is believed that the Chinese introduced pasta to the Italians through the expeditions of Marco Polo. However, pasta historians at Italy's Museum of Spaghetti History contest this popular view, citing archival evidence that has the people of Rome eating ravioli in 1284, nine years before Marco Polo got back home.

What is undisputed is pasta's popularity, both in Italy and here in America. Thomas Jefferson is credited with introducing it to the United States. During his sojourn in Europe as ambassador to France, he grew so fond of spaghetti that he specially ordered the dies used to make it from Italy so his American cooks could duplicate the dish. Spaghetti was first produced commercially in the United States in 1848 and started becoming popular in the early 1900s, when large numbers of Italian immigrants began arriving on the East Coast.

The word "pasta" means more than just spaghetti. Pasta is a generic term that includes any of the thousand different forms of this food. Macaroni refers to hollow or pierced forms of pasta. Other names Italians have given to pasta usually describe its shape: cannelloni, "large reeds"; linguini, "small tongues"; vermicelli, "little worms"; capelli d'angelo, "angel's hair"; stelline, "little stars"; manicotti, "small muffs"; and ziti, "bridegrooms."

◆

PASTA COOKING TIPS

Use a large pot and at least four quarts of water per pound of pasta. Pasta should be cooked quickly, and the more hot water there is, the sooner it will come back to a rolling boil after the pasta has been added. Pasta should be added to the water all at once, and pushed under the water with a wooden spoon.

Fresh pasta can be ready in just a few seconds. Dried pasta usually takes from six to eight minutes to cook. The only way to know when it's done is to pull out a strand and taste it. It should be firm to the bite, not soft and mushy.

As soon as the pasta is cooked, drain it in a colander, shake out the water, and put it back into the pot with the sauce. Let the pasta and sauce warm together for a moment before serving.

◆

SESAME PEANUT BUTTER NOODLES
SHUN LEE ◆ NEW YORK, NEW YORK

MAKES 2 APPETIZER
SERVINGS

4 ounces fine egg noodles
4 teaspoons sesame oil
¼ cup sesame paste or
  smooth or chunky peanut
  butter
3 tablespoons hot water
1 teaspoon Szechuan chili
  paste or hot sauce
2 teaspoons sugar
1 tablespoon chopped
  garlic
2 tablespoons vegetable oil
3 tablespoons soy sauce
3 tablespoons red wine
  vinegar
Salt, to taste

Many of the food critics in New York City consider Michael Tong to be the city's outstanding Asian restaurateur. I have been a regular patron of Shun Lee since 1973. Early on, I fell in love with this dish and have always enjoyed it as an appetizer or a side dish.

1. In a large saucepan, bring 6 cups of water to a boil. Add the noodles and cook, stirring occasionally, until they are tender, 7 minutes or less. Drain noodles and run under cold water until they are thoroughly chilled and the strands are separated. Drain thoroughly. Turn the noodles into a bowl and toss with 1 teaspoon of the sesame oil. Set aside.

2. Spoon the sesame paste or peanut butter into a mixing bowl. Gradually add the hot water. Stir in the chili paste, sugar, garlic, vegetable oil, soy sauce, vinegar, salt, and 1 tablespoon sesame oil. Mix until well combined.

3. Arrange the noodles on a serving dish. Spoon the sauce over the noodles. Serve warm or cold.

Tortellini with Navy Bean Sauce
Waldorf Astoria ◆ New York

Bring together a legume, the beans, with a pasta, the tortellini, and the result is an improved nutritional bundle, an almost perfect balance of key elements. If you make this recipe with vegetable-filled tortellini, you can end up with a low-fat, low-calorie dish that makes a great first course for a big dinner or a light meal on its own.

1. Cover the beans with water and soak for at least 8 hours, overnight, or, if you are in hurry, boil the water-covered beans for 2 minutes, then set aside for 1 hour to soak. Drain the beans of the soaking water.

2. In a 3-quart saucepan, heat the olive oil over medium heat. Add the onion and cook, over medium heat, for 1 minute. Stir often. Mix in the garlic and cook for 30 seconds. Add the tomato and tomato paste, stir and cook for a moment. Add the beans, chicken broth, and pepper, bring to a boil, reduce the heat and simmer, uncovered, for 1½ hours.

3. Pour the bean mixture into the bowl of a blender or food processor and process into a puree. Adjust the consistency with more stock if necessary. The sauce should be the thickness of a rich tomato sauce. Return to the saucepan and keep warm.

4. Add the cooked tortellini and the basil to the sauce and toss to combine. Serve.

MAKES 10 SERVINGS

½ pound uncooked navy or white beans
2 tablespoons olive oil
1 cup finely chopped onion
1 tablespoon finely chopped garlic
1 cup chopped fresh tomato
2 tablespoons tomato paste
7 cups chicken broth
¼ teaspoon freshly ground white pepper
1 pound store-bought tortellini, with the filling of your choice, cooked
2 tablespoons chopped fresh basil

◆

PENNE PASTA WITH TOMATOES
IL NIDO ◆ NEW YORK, NEW YORK

MAKES 4 SERVINGS

2 tablespoons olive oil
1 small onion, finely
  chopped
¼ cup white wine or
  chicken broth
3 cups canned Italian plum
  tomatoes, coarsely
  chopped, and their juices
2 tablespoons chopped
  fresh basil
1 pound penne pasta,
  cooked
Pecorino Romano cheese

1. In a large sauté pan, heat the olive oil over medium heat. Add the onion and sauté until softened, approximately 3 minutes. Add the white wine or chicken broth and simmer about 3 minutes or until the alcohol has cooked off.

2. Add the tomatoes and their juices and cook for about 20 minutes over low heat.

3. Add the basil and the cooked pasta and toss to combine.

4. Garnish each serving with a grating of Pecorino Romano cheese.

ABOUT OLIVE OIL

Olive oil comes in three grades: extra virgin, virgin, and pure. Extra virgin is the best. It is the first crushing of the finest olives, it has the most flavor. The second best is virgin; that's the second crushing of second-quality olives, and it's okay, but not great. Pure is the least interesting, with the least flavor.

When you get olive oil home, you should store it in as close to an air-free environment as possible. When you pour some out of the bottle, pour water in. Since oil floats on top of water, the water just pushes it up to the top and puts the oil back into an air-free environment. You should also store olive oil in the refrigerator. It will stay fresh six months to a year.

Linguini with Red Clam Sauce
ALDO'S ◆ WYCKOFF, NEW JERSEY

Aldo's Restaurant, in Wyckoff, New Jersey, is a restaurant with a rather unusual clientele, including Michael Jackson, John Forsythe, Danny Aiello, Tim Conway, and Burt Young. Now what are all these celebrities doing at Aldo's? Simple: eating, talking, and thoroughly enjoying themselves at a classic down-home neighborhood Italian restaurant.

Aldo came to the United States from Italy. He's the kind of chef every neighborhood should have. His dishes are basic and simple, and they remind an Italian of his childhood kitchen. It's like eating Ma's cooking.

1. In a large sauté pan, heat the vegetable oil over medium heat. Add the garlic and sauté until golden, approximately 2 minutes. Add the parsley, pepper flakes, oregano, black pepper, and chopped clams. Stir to mix well.

2. Add the tomato sauce, cover, and simmer over low heat for about 10 to 12 minutes.

3. Add the cooked linguini to the sauté pan and stir to coat with the sauce.

4. Garnish with fresh parsley.

MAKES 4 SERVINGS

2 tablespoons vegetable oil
2 cloves garlic, thinly
  sliced
1 tablespoon chopped
  parsley
¼ teaspoon dried red
  pepper flakes
1 teaspoon dried oregano
¼ teaspoon freshly ground
  black pepper
One 6½-ounce can
  chopped clams
2 cups tomato sauce
1 pound linguini, cooked
Chopped parsley, for
  garnish

◆

PASTA WITH SCALLOPS
LA COSTA RESORT AND SPA ◆ CARLSBAD, CALIFORNIA

MAKES 4 SERVINGS

1 to 2 tablespoons Canola
  or other vegetable oil
16 sea scallops
¼ cup finely chopped
  shallots or onion
1 tablespoon finely
  chopped garlic
4 fresh plum tomatoes,
  skins on, chopped
1½ cups canned tomatoes,
  drained and chopped
Grated zest of 2 oranges
Juice of 2 oranges (1 cup)
Salt and freshly ground
  black pepper
¼ cup chopped fresh basil
1 pound angel's hair pasta

OPTIONAL GARNISH
Whole, small basil leaves

During the 1880s, a man named John Frazier discovered a mineral spring just outside of San Diego, California, and began to develop the area as a spa. Today, it is the home of one of the world's most famous spas: La Costa. The following low-calorie recipe is from their kitchen.

1. Heat the oil in a sauté pan over medium heat. When the oil is hot, add the scallops, without crowding, and sauté for 1 to 2 minutes on each side. When done, remove scallops and keep warm between two plates.

2. Add shallots or onion to the sauté pan, still over medium heat. Stir and sauté until they begin to soften. Add the garlic and sauté another minute. Don't allow the garlic to brown. Add the fresh and canned tomatoes and turn the heat up to high. Stir and cook until the tomatoes break down, about 4 minutes. Add the orange zest and juice and cook until the liquid is absorbed, about 5 minutes. Season with the salt and pepper, to taste. Add the chopped basil, stir, and remove from the heat.

3. While preparing the sauce, cook the pasta according to the package directions. Add the cooked pasta to the sauce. Toss to combine and divide among four plates. Spoon the scallops onto the pasta, and garnish with the whole basil leaves, if desired.

PASTA WITH SHRIMP AND ARTICHOKE HEARTS
GUAYMAS RESTAURANT ◆ TIBURON, CALIFORNIA

1. Heat the oil in a sauté pan over medium-high heat, sauté the red onion, stirring, for about 4 minutes. Add the garlic and stir for several seconds. Do not allow the onion or garlic to brown.

2. Add the tomatoes and salt and pepper, to taste. Turn up the heat to high, stir and cook for 2 minutes.

3. Add the shrimp, stir, reduce heat, and simmer for 2 minutes more. Add the artichokes and cook another 2 minutes. Stir while the sauce thickens slightly and the shrimp cook.

4. Combine the cooked pasta with sauce in the pan and, over low heat, toss until heated through. Divide among four plates and garnish with parsley. Serve immediately.

MAKES 4 SERVINGS

1 tablespoon vegetable oil
1 red onion, sliced
½ teaspoon chopped garlic
2 tomatoes, cut into bite-sized pieces
Salt and freshly ground black pepper
8 large shrimp, peeled and deveined
1 cup artichoke hearts, cooked and packed in water
½ pound pasta, cooked
Chopped parsley, for garnish

VEGETABLE FRIED RICE
TOMMY TOY'S RESTAURANT ◆ SAN FRANCISCO, CALIFORNIA

MAKES 4 SERVINGS

2 tablespoons vegetable oil
2 eggs, beaten
3 cups cooked rice
½ cup chopped celery
½ diced red bell pepper
½ cup chopped onion
½ cup diced carrot
Salt
1 teaspoon sesame oil
1 tablespoon soy sauce

The Chinese chefs were certainly among the earliest and most important influences on the cooking of San Francisco, but so were the French. The French opened the first really good restaurants that catered to the rising class of newly wealthy. They set the tone for fine dining in the town. A restaurant that combines the French and Chinese influences is Tommy Toy's. The dining room feels like a classic French restaurant, but it's actually patterned after the reading room of the Dowager Empress of China. The kitchen is definitely Asian, but the menu reflects both traditions.

1. Preheat a wok or large skillet over highest heat until very hot. Add the vegetable oil, tilt the wok or pan to coat, then quickly add the eggs and stir, scrambling the eggs.

2. Add the cooked rice, stir quickly. Add the vegetables and salt to taste. Stir and toss to blend quickly. Add the sesame oil and soy sauce, toss to combine flavors, for about 2 minutes.

COOKING PERFECT LONG-GRAIN WHITE RICE

1. Measure the rice by cupfuls and place it into a heavy-bottomed saucepan.

2. Add twice as much water as the volume of rice and bring to a boil.

3. Reduce the heat, stir the rice, and cover with a tight-fitting lid. Cook at a simmer for 15 minutes, or until all the water is absorbed by the rice.

MAKING PERFECT RICE IN THE MICROWAVE

Rice cooks beautifully in the microwave and can save you some time in cleaning up, since you can cook and serve in one dish.

1. For White Rice, combine 1½ to 2 cups of water or other liquid and 1 cup of rice. Microwave for 5 minutes on HIGH (100% power), then for 15 minutes on MEDIUM (50% power).

2. Brown Rice takes less time to cook in the microwave than on top of the stove. Combine 2¼ to 2½ cups of water or other liquid and 1 cup of rice. Microwave for 5 minutes on HIGH (100% power), then for 30 minutes on MEDIUM (50% power).

3. For Parboiled Rice, combine 2 to 2¼ cups of water or other liquid and 1 cup of rice. Microwave for 5 minutes on HIGH (100% power), then for 20 to 25 minutes on MEDIUM (50% power).

4. Reheat cooked rice by microwaving on HIGH (100% power) for 1 minute for each cup of rice. It's as good as fresh cooked!

◆

RISOTTO WITH ASPARAGUS
REMI RESTAURANT ◆ NEW YORK, NEW YORK

MAKES 6 SERVINGS

2 tablespoons olive oil
2 cups arborio rice, or
  short- or medium-grain
  rice, rinsed and drained
7 to 8 cups chicken broth,
  simmering
2 cups chopped fresh
  asparagus
¼ cup grated Parmesan
  cheese

1. In a large saucepan or stockpot, heat the olive oil over medium heat. Add the rice and stir to coat with the oil. Cook for 2 minutes, until the rice is opaque. Add the simmering chicken broth about ½ cup at a time. Simmer and stir constantly and let the rice absorb the broth before adding more. When about half the broth has been added (12 to 15 minutes), add the asparagus and stir. Continue adding broth. When the rice is soft, about 20 to 30 minutes since you started adding the broth, it is ready to serve.

2. Stir in the Parmesan cheese and serve immediately.

ABOUT ASPARAGUS

Asparagus, one of the oldest known vegetables, is classed in two groups—white, and green, although there are over 150 varieties.

White asparagus is white because it grows under the soil and is unable to darken in the absence of sunlight. Most white asparagus is sold canned. Green asparagus, which grows above the soil, is more flavorful, though slightly less tender.

The asparagus we eat is an immature sprout in the lily family. If uncut, it would grow into a large fernlike plant. A Swiss psychologist believed that eating asparagus will help you develop a sense of responsibility. The Romans were the first to cultivate asparagus, and Julius Caesar loved it with melted butter.

Asparagus is about 90 percent water, and 3½ ounces has about 52 calories, which makes it an ideal diet food. Asparagus spears are so tender because they grow so quickly, and can be harvested before they toughen. They can grow up to ten inches a day. Because they grow in the ground, the spears must be carefully washed to remove all grit.

VEGETABLES

ASPARAGUS WITH LEMON-HERB DRESSING

MAKES 6 SERVINGS

⅓ cup part-skim, no-salt
  ricotta cheese
2 tablespoons plain low-fat
  yogurt
¼ cup chicken stock
1 teaspoon no-salt Dijon-
  style mustard
¼ teaspoon freshly ground
  black pepper
Zest of 1 lemon, finely
  chopped (about
  1 tablespoon)
2 tablespoons fresh lemon
  juice
1 tablespoon red wine or
  tarragon vinegar
2 tablespoons chopped
  parsley
2 tablespoons minced
  chives, or 1 tablespoon
  dried
½ teaspoon dried tarragon
2 teaspoons minced
  shallots
1½ pounds fresh
  asparagus, trimmed,
  blanched and chilled

1. Place the ricotta cheese, yogurt, stock, mustard, pepper, lemon zest, lemon juice, and vinegar in a bowl and whisk together until smooth.

2. Add the parsley, chives, tarragon, and shallots. Mix well. Chill 1 hour.

3. Arrange the asparagus spears on a serving platter or individual plates. Pour the dressing over the asparagus.

BROCCOLI WITH OLIVES

1. In a large skillet, heat the oil and sauté the garlic for 15 to 30 seconds without browning. Add the tomatoes and cook, uncovered, for 10 minutes.

2. Add the broccoli and olives and season with the red pepper to taste. Cover and simmer until broccoli is tender, about 8 minutes. Serve.

MAKES 6 SERVINGS

3 tablespoons olive oil
2 cloves garlic, minced
1 cup coarsely chopped
  canned or fresh tomatoes
4 cups broccoli flowerets
½ cup pitted black olives
¼ to ½ teaspoon crushed
  red pepper

CALORIES AND CROSS-COUNTRY SKIING

The average woman cross-country skiing on a flat surface at about the same speed that you use for a normal walk will burn about seven calories in a minute, or about 420 calories in an hour. Men burn more calories with the same exercise, about eleven calories per minute, or about 600 per hour. If you cross-country ski for a few days in a row, you will set yourself up for some great eating. In the first two to four hours after each cross-country ski trip, your muscles will be ready to store up fuel for the next day. The foods that will do the best job are the complex carbohydrates: pasta with a low-fat sauce, beans, legumes, whole-grain rice, whole-grain breads, potatoes, and corn.

NEW YORK'S CHINATOWN

New York's Chinatown is a city within a city. The telephone booths are shaped like pagodas; movie theaters show Chinese films. The food shops are packed with ingredients and cooking equipment that comes here from Asia. There are hundreds of restaurants with every type of Chinese food, from Hunan to Szechuan. The first large group of Chinese to settle in New York City came here from the California goldfields, or after they'd finished their work building the transcontinental railroads. Today over 125,000 people of Chinese ancestry live in this neighborhood.

Much Chinese food is ideal from the point of view of good health, especially that cooked by the stir-frying method. In the best examples, small amounts of meat, fish, or poultry are cooked together with much larger amounts of vegetables and then served with rice. The food is cooked very quickly and doesn't spend much time exposed to high heat. That helps preserve the nutrients. And the cooking uses only a small amount of vegetable oil.

CHINESE TABLE MANNERS

At a traditional Chinese gathering, the food will always come to the table on a turning disk or what we call a "lazy Susan." At a Chinese meal conversation is extremely important, and it is thought to be impolite to interrupt that conversation to ask somebody to pass the stir-fried vegetables.

I was also curious as to why a society as sophisticated as the Chinese would invent chopsticks but not develop knives and forks to go on the table. I asked a leading Chinese historian and he told me that the Chinese had developed knives and forks thousands and thousands of years before Western society, but had decided that it was too impolite to continue butchering at the table.

ORIENTAL-STYLE STIR-FRIED VEGETABLES

The traditional cooking pot for stir-fried foods is the wok. The classic design has a round base because the ancient stoves of China had round holes for the wok to fit in. The system conserved energy, made it easy to turn and toss the ingredients, and allowed the cook to use different parts of the surface to get different heat levels at the same time. The area at the bottom of a wok is much hotter than the upper sides, and the angle of the wall is designed to hold food at each spot. Great piece of equipment. It can also be used to hold a steamer.

1. Heat the oil in a large skillet or wok over medium-high heat. Add the onion, gingerroot, and garlic. Cook, stirring often, for 2 minutes or until the garlic is golden. Remove the gingerroot and garlic and discard.

2. Add the broccoli, carrots, and red pepper. Cook for 2 minutes, stirring often, until the broccoli and carrots are tender-crisp.

3. Add the snow peas and teriyaki or soy sauce. Stir to combine.

MAKES 4 SERVINGS

1 tablespoon sesame oil
1 medium onion, sliced
3 slices fresh gingerroot
2 cloves garlic, cut in half
4 cups broccoli flowerets
2 carrots, thinly sliced on the diagonal
1 red bell pepper, cut into strips
2 cups snow peas
3 tablespoons teriyaki or soy sauce

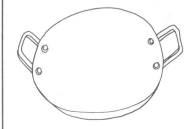

THE CASE FOR MORE VEGETABLES

The old parental cry of "eat your vegetables" has been taken up by almost everyone who is studying the relationship of food to good health, and there are sound historical and scientific reasons for the advice. Take a look at the history of how people have eaten, and you will see a story of diets high in vegetables.

In our earliest clan and tribal periods, we are described as hunters and gatherers. However, the truth of the matter is that most of our food came from gathering vegetables, fruits, nuts, and grains. Hunting produced only a small fraction of our nutritional needs. As our digestive system developed, it evolved the ability to digest a wide variety of foods, but the balance for most people on the planet was for large amounts of vegetables and fruits and small amounts of animal protein. The reason was very simple: It was (until recently in human history) much easier to gather vegetables and fruits than it was to catch wild animals. Think about it: Would you rather wander around your favorite patch of forest looking for some nice root vegetables to stew, or suit up for a little combat with a grizzly bear? Yes sir, nothing like hunting a saber-toothed tiger to bring out the vegetarian in you.

Modern technology has changed our capacity to produce food, but not our body's ability to digest it safely. The danger these days lies in too much tiger. Our best chance for continuing good health appears to reside in a diet higher in vegetables.

RED CABBAGE
GOLDENER HIRSCH HOTEL ♦ SALZBURG, AUSTRIA

1. In a large bowl, combine the cabbage, caraway seeds, 3 tablespoons lemon juice, and the vinegar. Marinate overnight (at least 10 hours) in refrigerator.

2. Place oil and sugar in a heat-proof casserole large enough to accommodate all ingredients. Cook over medium heat until sugar begins to turn brown. Stir to dissolve.

3. Add onion and stir.

4. Add the cabbage, apple juice, 2 tablespoons lemon juice, and grated apple. Stir and season with salt.

5. Lower heat, cover, and simmer for 1 hour, stirring occasionally.

MAKES 6 SERVINGS

10 cups shredded red
  cabbage (1 large head)
1 teaspoon caraway seeds
Juice of 1 lemon
  (approximately
  3 tablespoons)
2 tablespoons red wine
  vinegar
4 tablespoons vegetable oil
3 tablespoons sugar
½ cup finely chopped
  onion
2 tablespoons apple juice
2 tablespoons fresh lemon
  juice
1 cup grated apple
  (1 unpeeled Granny Smith
  apple)
1½ teaspoons salt, or to
  taste

EGGPLANT PARMESAN

MAKES 4 SERVINGS

Vegetable oil
1 cup flour
1 medium eggplant (about
  1½ pounds), peeled and
  sliced ¼ inch thick
1 cup tomato sauce
2 tablespoons chopped
  fresh basil, or 1 teaspoon
  dried basil, crushed
Salt and freshly ground
  black pepper, to taste
¾ pound mozzarella
  cheese, sliced ¼ inch
  thick
4 tablespoons freshly
  grated Pecorino Romano
  cheese
1 tablespoon olive oil

1. Preheat the oven to 375° F.

2. In a large skillet, heat ¼ inch of vegetable oil over medium heat.

3. Lightly flour the eggplant slices on both sides. Place 3 or 4 slices in the skillet and fry until golden brown, about 2 minutes per side. Place the fried eggplant on paper towels to drain. Continue until all the eggplant is used.

4. Spread one third of the tomato sauce in the bottom of a 4- to 5-cup-capacity heat-proof dish and sprinkle it with one third of the basil. Layer half of the eggplant in the dish. Sprinkle lightly with salt and pepper. Cover the eggplant with a layer of tomato sauce; sprinkle it with one third of the basil. Layer on half of the mozzarella cheese and sprinkle with 2 tablespoons of the Pecorino Romano cheese. Layer on the remaining eggplant, sprinkle lightly with salt and pepper, cover with the remaining tomato sauce, and sprinkle with the remaining basil. Top with the remaining mozzarella cheese, and sprinkle with the remaining Pecorino Romano and the olive oil.

5. Bake in the oven for 15 minutes. Remove the dish from the oven and place it under the broiler for 1 to 2 minutes, until the top is golden brown.

RICE-STUFFED PEPPERS

1. Preheat the oven to 350° F.

2. Trim off the tops of the peppers and set aside. Scoop out the cores, ribs, and seeds and discard. Be careful not to puncture the bottoms.

3. In a medium sauté pan, heat the olive oil over medium-high heat. Add the onion and garlic and sauté for 3 minutes. Add the rice and stir until translucent, approximately 1 minute. Add the tomato paste, tomatoes, parsley, oregano, salt, and pepper and simmer for 3 minutes.

4. Arrange the peppers in a baking dish and divide the rice mixture among them. Divide the water among the peppers, filling as needed to just cover the rice. Do not overfill. Replace the tops. Bake for approximately 1 hour, until water is absorbed and rice is tender.

MAKES 4 SERVINGS

6 medium or 4 large green or red bell peppers
2 tablespoons olive oil
1 small onion, chopped
3 cloves garlic, chopped
1 cup uncooked long-grain rice
2 tablespoons tomato paste
One 14½-ounce can Italian tomatoes, drained and coarsely chopped
2 tablespoons chopped fresh parsley
1 teaspoon dried oregano
1 teaspoon salt
¼ teaspoon freshly ground black pepper
1½ to 2 cups water

◆

WILD RICE AND POTATO PANCAKES
STAR'S RESTAURANT ◆ SAN FRANCISCO, CALIFORNIA

MAKES 4 SERVINGS

2 cups peeled, diced waxy
  potatoes
2 cups nonfat milk
Salt, to taste
3 cups cooked wild rice
Freshly ground black
  pepper, to taste
Vegetable oil
Four 4-ounce salmon fillets

GARNISHES
Cooked asparagus
½ cup chopped tomato
4 tablespoons low-fat
  mayonnaise flavored with
  curry powder or saffron

1. Place the potatoes and the milk in a heavy saucepan, adding more milk if needed to cover potatoes. Add salt to taste and bring to a simmer. Simmer for 20 minutes or until tender. Drain and place in a mixing bowl. Add the cooked wild rice, mix well, and adjust seasoning with salt and pepper.

2. Compressing the mixture firmly, form 4 large pancakes, about ½ inch thick. Heat enough oil to coat a large frying pan over medium heat and fry the pancakes until a golden crust forms, about 1 to 1½ minutes on each side. Drain on paper towels and keep warm.

3. Sauté the salmon in a little oil for 5 minutes on each side, carefully turning with a spatula.

4. Carefully place 1 pancake on each of 4 plates, place a fillet of salmon on top, and garnish each with asparagus, ¼ of the chopped tomato, and 1 tablespoon of the flavored mayonnaise.

WHY SAN FRANCISCO EATS WELL

Almost all frontiers in our country were settled by farmers: families that came in, cleared the land, settled down, and built a place for themselves a little bit at a time. Not so in San Francisco. When gold was discovered at Sutter's Mill, the population went from 850 to 25,000 in just three years. People came from all over the world, their only interest was in finding gold. It was the gold rush that set the tone for San Francisco. It was the single most important event in its history. In France they held lotteries for trips to the goldfields. Many Frenchmen first saw San Francisco as crew members of French cargo ships. Quite often these sailors would jump ship and head for the gold. If they didn't do well, they'd come back to town and open a restaurant.

A German arrived with a load of canvas to make tents for the miners, but he found he could do better making pants for them. His name was Levi Strauss, as in Levi's 501 jeans.

A hardworking prospector with a little luck could be wealthy beyond his wildest dreams in less than a month. Prices in San Francisco went through the roof—eggs were fifty dollars a dozen. These guys were rich and they wanted the best of everything. It was the gold rush environment that fostered the tradition for good food that you find in San Francisco today.

ABOUT WILD RICE

A number of years ago I demonstrated a wild rice recipe and got a letter from a viewer who said that he thought the wildest thing about wild rice was its price. In those days wild rice was about $14 a pound, but thanks to a group of growers in Northern California, today you can get top-quality wild rice for about $5 a pound. Wild rice is actually not a rice, it's really a grass that grows in water. It's a good source of vegetable protein, niacin, B vitamins, and potassium, with about 70 calories in a half-cup serving. To cook, mix one cup of wild rice together with three cups of boiling water, cover and simmer for 40 minutes. A cup of uncooked California Wild Rice will produce about three cups cooked. It has a nutty quality and a smoky taste. It goes well with vegetables, poultry, and pork, or any meat or fish that's been grilled or barbecued. Leave it to California to tame wild rice.

RICOTTA-STUFFED POTATO BOATS

MAKES 4 SERVINGS

4 Idaho potatoes, scrubbed
  clean and poked a few
  times on each side with
  the tines of a fork
¼ cup minced onion
4 cloves garlic, minced
½ pound low-fat ricotta
  cheese
¼ cup low-fat sour cream
  or plain low-fat yogurt
¼ cup fresh basil, chopped
1 bell pepper, chopped
4 teaspoons Parmesan
  cheese

1. Preheat the oven to 375° F.

2. Place the potatoes on the oven rack and bake until fork tender, about 1 hour. Set aside until they cool to a point where they are easy to handle.

3. In a small, nonstick skillet, sauté the onion with the garlic until barely browned.

4. In a large bowl, combine the onion and garlic with the ricotta, sour cream or yogurt, basil, and bell pepper. Stir until blended.

5. Cut a ½-inch slice off one end of each potato. Leaving a ½-inch wall on the sides and bottoms of the potato, scoop out the flesh. Add the potato flesh to the bowl with the other ingredients. Mix well, eliminating most of the lumps.

6. Fill the potato boats with the potato-cheese mixture and place on a baking tray or cookie sheet. Top each with 1 teaspoon of the Parmesan cheese and bake until the tops are lightly browned, about 15 to 20 minutes.

ABOUT RICOTTA CHEESE

Ricotta cheese is a fresh cheese similar to cottage cheese. It has a very mild flavor and delicate consistency and heats well in dishes like lasagna. It is made from whey or buttermilk, and comes in regular and part-skim varieties. At 4 and 2 percent fat, both are extremely low-fat cheeses.

OVEN-FRIED GARLIC POTATOES

1. Preheat the oven to 375°F.

2. In a large bowl, toss all of the ingredients together, coating the potatoes evenly.

3. Pour the mixture into a baking dish and bake, uncovered, until the potatoes can be easily pierced with a knife and are golden brown and crisp on the top, about 45 minutes.

MAKES 4 SERVINGS

4 Idaho potatoes, thinly
  sliced
2 tablespoons olive oil
4 cloves garlic, minced
2 teaspoons crushed
  rosemary

THE EXCELLENT NUTRITION OF THE IDAHO POTATO

In 1836, a missionary named Henry Harmon Spalding planted the first potato in the state of Idaho. He wanted to show the local Indians that they could provide nutritious foods for themselves through agriculture as well as by hunting and gathering. Henry could not have selected a better food to make his point. The potato that comes out of the rich volcanic soil of Idaho is a nutritional gold mine. It contains protein, iron, thiamine, niacin, potassium, and vitamin C. A 5-ounce baked potato has only 100 calories. It contains twenty-four grams of complex carbohydrates and is almost fat free. And there are only 4 milligrams of sodium in 5 ounces of baked potato, which makes it virtually sodium free. I can't think of a food that does a better job of meeting today's criteria for a healthful diet.

LEMONY IDAHO POTATOES

MAKES 4 SERVINGS

2 pounds Idaho potatoes
¼ cup olive oil
Juice of 1 lemon plus the
  grated zest
Salt and freshly ground
  black pepper
2 teaspoons dried oregano

These potatoes are easy to prepare and have a light and refreshing flavor. The taste of the lemon combines perfectly with the oregano.

1. Peel the potatoes, if desired. Cut them into 2-inch pieces. Cook the potatoes in plenty of boiling water until just tender. They must not overcook or they will be watery. Drain and return to the saucepan.

2. Over moderate heat, shake the saucepan with the potatoes to dry them out completely. Place them into a heated serving dish and keep warm.

3. Combine the other ingredients and beat until creamy. Pour over the potatoes, making sure to coat the slices well. Serve warm, at room temperature, or chilled.

A B O U T   Z E S T

Zest is the outer peeling of lemons, oranges, limes, and grapefruit. The best way to add zest to your cooking is to rub the whole fruit against the tiny holes on a small hand grater or a zester, or pare the outer rind from the fruit and cut the parings into very thin strips.

The zest, or outer rind, is more flavorful than the juice of the fruit because it has a very high oil content. Be sure to use only the colorful outer rind, because the white connective tissue right underneath is very bitter.

LAYERED IDAHO POTATOES
DUCK'S AMERICAN BAR & GRILL ◆ BOISE, IDAHO

Duck's American Bar & Grill in Boise, Idaho, is an informal eatery with a relaxed atmosphere. Things just flow together for the pleasure of patrons. The following recipe expresses this approach—the ingredients slide into each other and into the oven. The finished dish makes an excellent vegetable course for almost any meal.

1. Preheat the oven to 350° F. Lightly oil a 9-×-9-inch baking dish.

2. Layer the ingredients into the baking dish in the following manner: half of the potatoes, the eggplant, half of the basil, half of the goat cheese, the remaining potatoes, the fresh tomato, the sun-dried tomatoes, the remaining basil, the thyme, and the capers. Top with the remaining goat cheese and bake, uncovered, until the potatoes can be easily pierced with a knife, about 35 minutes.

MAKES 4 SERVINGS

2 Idaho potatoes, partially cooked and thinly sliced
1 small eggplant, sliced into thin rounds and sautéed in a little vegetable oil
½ cup fresh basil leaves, or 1 teaspoon dried
One 4-ounce log of goat cheese
1 medium-sized fresh tomato, thinly sliced
¼ cup sun-dried tomatoes in olive oil, cut into strips
1 teaspoon fresh thyme, or ½ teaspoon dried
2 tablespoons capers

SPECIAL SOIL FOR A SPECIAL POTATO: THE IDAHO RUSSET AND HOW TO BAKE IT

The geological history of Idaho has given it a fascinating collection of surface features. Idaho has more than two hundred mountains that go up over 8,000 feet. Ancient glacial ice formed lakes and seas that deposited valuable layers of sediment in the soil. River systems carved a web of canyons, including North America's deepest gorge, and lava flows have covered the surface.

Interesting information for a geologist or a tourist, but what does all that have to do with cooking? Well . . . quite frankly, everything if you love potatoes like I do. The volcanic soil, the abundance of clean water, and the fresh mountain air have created the perfect environment for growing what is probably the world's most famous potato—the Idaho Russet. And the perfect way to bake it is very simple.

1. Scrub the potato and dry it.

2. Prick it a few times with a fork, which will allow the steam to escape. That will result in a baked potato with a dry and fluffy texture.

3. Don't wrap it in foil. The foil will steam the potato.

4. Bake the potato in a preheated 375° F. oven for 1 hour. The internal temperature will be about 210° F. Your baked potato will have a dark, crispy skin and fluffy interior.

◆

GREEK SPINACH PIE

1. Preheat the oven to 350° F.

2. In a medium sauté pan, heat the olive oil over medium-high heat. Sauté the onion with the dill until translucent, approximately 3 minutes. Add the spinach and sauté 2 minutes more.

3. In a medium mixing bowl, combine the onion-spinach mixture, the feta cheese, egg whites, and Parmesan. Mix well.

4. On a cutting board, place one sheet of the filo dough and brush lightly with the melted margarine. Place a second sheet on top and repeat until there are 4 sheets, each brushed with margarine. In a 13½×8¾×1¾-inch baking dish, place the filo dough so it lines the bottom of the pan and overhangs the long sides so that it can be folded back over the filling. Repeat the process if necessary so that the bottom and long sides of the pan are covered. Spread the spinach filling on the filo lining and fold the dough over to cover. If necessary, trim some filo dough to make a 4-layer buttered strip to fill in between the folded edges. Trim 4 pieces of the remaining filo and make a 4-layer buttered lid to cover the entire surface. Score pie into 3-inch squares. Bake for approximately 1¼ to 1½ hours, until the dough is golden and crispy.

MAKES 12 SERVINGS

2 tablespoons olive oil
1 medium onion, chopped
2 tablespoons chopped dill
Four 10-ounce packages
   frozen spinach, cooked
   and well drained
½ pound feta cheese,
   crumbled
6 egg whites
1½ cups grated Parmesan
   cheese
12 sheets frozen filo dough
   (about ¼ pound), thawed
4 tablespoons margarine,
   melted

BUTTERNUT SQUASH AND WINTER PEAR BAKE

THE RITZ HOTEL ◆ PARIS, FRANCE

MAKES 4 SERVINGS

1 medium butternut
  squash (about 3 pounds)
2 Bosc pears, or any other
  firm variety
⅓ cup slivered almonds
½ cup brown sugar
2 tablespoons butter or
  margarine

1. Preheat the oven to 350° F. Butter a baking dish or casserole.

2. Peel the squash, cut it into quarters, and clean out the seeds and fibers. Slice the quarters into pieces about ½ inch thick. Set aside.

3. Peel and core the pears and slice about the same thickness as the squash.

4. In the casserole or baking dish, alternate the squash and the pears. You will have approximately 3 layers of alternating slices. Sprinkle the top with the almonds, then the brown sugar, and finally, dot with the butter.

5. Bake, uncovered, for approximately 35 minutes, until the squash is tender and cooked through.

ABOUT FIBER

There are two basic types of fiber: soluble and insoluble. Soluble fiber dissolves in water, and you find it in fruits, vegetables, beans, and oats. Insoluble fiber does not dissolve in water, and you find that in the skins of fruits and vegetables and in whole wheat products. Medical authorities feel that we need both types of fiber and, together, they can improve your digestion, help with weight loss, and reduce the risk of heart disease.

BAKED APPLE-STUFFED ACORN SQUASH
THE RITZ HOTEL ◆ PARIS, FRANCE

1. Preheat the oven to 350° F. Put about 1 inch of water in a baking dish. Set aside.

2. Wash the acorn squash and cut them in half. Scoop out the seeds and slice a thin piece off of the bottom of each half, being careful not to make a hole in the squash. (This slice will give the squash a flat base so it will sit upright in the baking dish.) Place the squash in the baking dish and set aside.

3. Peel and core the apples and cut into thin slices.

4. In a large skillet, combine the wine or water and the sugar over moderate heat. Add the apples and cook until they are crisp-tender and the liquid is slightly reduced, about 2 minutes. Sprinkle the cinnamon on top of the apples, swirl in the butter and continue to cook until the sauce is thick, about 2 to 3 minutes.

5. Place an equal portion of the apple mixture into each of the 4 squash halves and bake until a knife easily pierces the meat of the squash, about 1 hour. With 10 minutes to cook, sprinkle 1 teaspoon of the almonds on top of the apple mixture in each squash half.

MAKES 4 SERVINGS

2 medium acorn squash
2 Golden Delicious apples, or any other baking variety
¼ cup white wine or water
¼ cup sugar
½ teaspoon cinnamon
2 tablespoons butter
4 teaspoons ground almonds

DRY-FRIED STRING BEANS
SHUN LEE ◆ NEW YORK, NEW YORK

MAKES 4 SERVINGS

1½ pounds string beans
1 cup vegetable oil
1 tablespoon chopped
  scallions
1 teaspoon chopped garlic
½ teaspoon Szechuan chili
  paste or hot sauce
2 tablespoons soy sauce,
  low-sodium if possible
1 tablespoon dry sherry or
  rice wine
1 tablespoon sugar

Part of the art of Chinese cooking consists of being able to take a few common ingredients and prepare them in a way that lets each individual flavor element improve all the other ingredients. The following string bean recipe will illustrate the approach.

1. Wash the beans under running water. Drain the beans well on paper towels.

2. In a wok or skillet, heat the oil until just before it smokes. Add the beans, standing back to avoid being spattered with oil. Cook the beans over high heat, stirring and turning frequently, until they are wrinkled and lightly browned, about 7 minutes. Remove the beans with a slotted spoon and place in a colander to drain. Set aside.

3. Discard all but about 2 tablespoons of oil from the skillet. Over high heat, reheat the remaining oil. Add the scallions, garlic, and Szechuan paste and stir-fry for 20 seconds. Add the soy sauce and stir.

4. Put the string beans back into the skillet. Add the wine and sugar and stir until well mixed, about 1 minute. Remove from skillet and serve.

TOMATOES STUFFED WITH RAISIN-NUT RICE

1. Slice off the top of each tomato. Scoop out the pulp and reserve. Salt the insides of each tomato and let drain upside down for 20 minutes.

2. Meanwhile, heat the oil in a skillet. Sauté the onion until lightly golden. Add the carrot and rice and sauté for 1 minute more. Add the remaining ingredients to the skillet and set aside.

3. Preheat the oven to 350° F.

4. In the container of a blender or food processor, puree the reserved tomato pulp and add about 1 cup of it to the rice mixture in the skillet. Bring the rice mixture to a boil, lower heat, cover, and cook for 20 minutes or until rice is cooked. Add more tomato puree if the rice is not done and continue too cook until all the liquid is absorbed. Remove from the heat.

5. Stuff the tomatoes with the rice mixture and arrange in a baking dish. Pour remaining tomato puree around the tomatoes. Bake for 30 minutes or until tomatoes are tender. Serve hot or cold.

MAKES 6 SERVINGS

6 large, firm tomatoes
¼ teaspoon salt
¼ cup olive oil
½ cup finely chopped onion
½ cup finely chopped carrot
½ cup uncooked rice
¼ cup chopped walnuts
¼ cup raisins
¾ cup chicken stock or broth
2 tablespoons chopped fresh mint, or 1 teaspoon dried
¼ cup chopped parsley
2 teaspoons sugar

VEGETABLE PIE
LE CIRQUE ◆ *NEW YORK, NEW YORK*

MAKES 8 SERVINGS

10 tablespoons olive oil
2 cups sliced onions
8 ounces fresh spinach
  leaves, blanched and well
  drained
½ pound mushroom caps
2 tomatoes, peeled and cut
  into wedges
2 teaspoons minced garlic
3 red bell peppers, peeled,
  halved, and seeded
1 pound eggplant, peeled
  and sliced into ¼-inch-
  thick discs
1½ pounds zucchini, cut
  lengthwise into
  approximately ¼ inch
  thick slices

Le Cirque is French for "The Circus," and that's a pretty good description of this restaurant. The ringmaster is Sirio Maccioni, who is probably the most skillful restaurateur in America. At Le Cirque, everyone is treated like royalty, and some people actually are.

1. Preheat broiler. Over moderate heat, in a large skillet, heat 2 tablespoons of the oil. Add the onions and sauté until lightly browned. Transfer to a bowl and set aside.

2. Sauté the spinach leaves in 2 tablespoons of oil until wilted. Transfer to a bowl and set aside.

3. Sauté the mushroom caps in 2 tablespoons of oil until lightly browned. Transfer to a bowl and set aside.

4. Sauté the tomatoes and garlic in 2 tablespoons of oil. Transfer to a bowl and set aside.

5. Sauté the bell peppers in 2 tablespoons oil. Transfer to a bowl and set aside.

6. Place a single layer of eggplant slices on a baking sheet. Place under preheated broiler about 4 to 6 inches from the heat. Cook until both sides are golden, turning once. Repeat with remaining eggplant.

7. Repeat with zucchini slices, but browning only one side.

8. Line a round cake pan, 8 inches in diameter and 2 inches deep with plastic wrap.

9. Line the bottom and sides of the pan with the zucchini slices, browned side up, overlapping, with an inch hanging over the edge of the pan (like wheel spokes).

10. Place a layer of the peppers over the zucchini, then a layer of the onions, then a layer of the mushroom caps. Drain tomatoes and layer next. Follow with spinach and eggplant.

11. Fold over zucchini flaps and press down gently. Cover with plastic wrap and weight with plate on top for 30 minutes.

12. Invert pie onto a plate. Remove plastic wrap. Serve and cut pie into wedges.

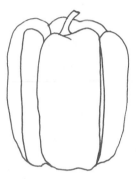

VEGETABLE MOLD BROOKE SHIELDS
THE PENINSULA HOTEL ◆ NEW YORK, NEW YORK

MAKES 4 SERVINGS

MARINATED VEGETABLES

1 tablespoon Dijon-style
  mustard
¾ cup water
1½ cups freshly squeezed
  lemon juice
¼ cup white wine vinegar
Salt and freshly ground
  black pepper, to taste
¾ teaspoon dried thyme
3 cloves crushed garlic
  (optional)
3 cups thinly sliced fresh
  mushrooms
1 cup thinly sliced zucchini
1 cup thinly sliced yellow
  summer squash
1 cup thinly sliced fresh
  plum tomatoes

PESTO

1 cup fresh basil leaves,
  washed and patted dry
1 clove garlic
1 tablespoon pine nuts
  (pignoli)
⅔ cup olive oil
⅓ cup grated Parmesan
  cheese

Brooke Shields was only eleven months old when she got her first paying modeling job as the Ivory Soap baby. At eleven years of age she had her first major film role in Pretty Baby. *Since then she has become one of the world's most sought-after models, appearing on hundreds of magazine covers. Because her physical well-being has been at the center of her occupation, she has spent a considerable amount of time studying the relationships between good health and good food and exercise.*

Vegetables are Brooke's favorite food, so Chef Adam Odegard at New York's Peninsula Hotel prepared this mold of marinated vegetables.

TO MARINATE THE VEGETABLES:

1. In a large bowl, whisk together the mustard, water, lemon juice, and vinegar until well blended. Season with salt and pepper. Add the thyme and garlic.

2. Add the vegetables to the marinade. Cover the bowl and refrigerate and allow vegetables to marinate for 12 to 24 hours.

TO MAKE THE PESTO:

3. Combine all the pesto ingredients except the Parmesan cheese in the container of a food processor or blender. Process until smooth. Add the Parmesan and mix in thoroughly. Set aside.

TO MAKE THE YELLOW PEPPER PUREE:

4. Heat the oil in a sauté pan over medium heat and add the peppers. Stir and sauté until the peppers are softened and have a nice golden color. Season with salt and pepper. Place in the container of a blender or food processor and process until pureed. Thin, if needed, with a small amount of water or oil. Set aside.

TO ASSEMBLE THE MOLDS:

5. Set out 4 salad plates. If desired, for ease in decorating, fill one plastic squeeze bottle with the pesto and another with the puree. Drizzle the pesto decoratively on each plate. Center a small pastry ring or an empty 8-ounce can with both top and bottom removed on plate. Layer the marinated vegetables, one at a time, inside each ring. (Be aware of the color combinations.) Example: start with the green zucchini, go on to red tomatoes, then yellow squash, and the mushrooms on top. Lift off rings very carefully and garnish plates with the cubed vegetables, the yellow pepper purée, and some fresh basil leaves.

YELLOW PEPPER PUREE

1½ tablespoons olive oil
2 yellow bell peppers, seeded and peeled with a vegetable peeler and cut into strips
Salt and freshly ground black pepper, to taste

GARNISHES

Carrot, cucumber, and zucchini, cut into very small cubes
Fresh basil leaves

GOOD HEALTH TIP

Broccoli, Brussels sprouts, cauliflower, and kale are in the cabbage family. They are high in vitamin C, and contain calcium and phosphorous. They also contain a substance called beta-carotene, which our bodies use to make vitamin A.

ABOUT SCALLIONS

Scallions, also called green or spring onions, are actually adolescent onions, harvested before the bulb has a chance to develop. To buy the best scallions, look for those with crisp, green unwithered tops and clean white bottoms. At home, cut off any brown tops or edges and store the scallions in a plastic bag in the refrigerator for not more than five days.

Many people find it difficult to chop scallions with a knife. Line up two or three scallions on a cutting board. Holding them in row with one hand, chop them into tiny rounds, going all the way into the dark green portion.

Another technique is to take the scallions in one hand, and with clean, dry scissors, snip them into small pieces.

◆

SALADS

ABOUT TURKEY

The Thanksgiving holiday commemorates the first harvest in the Plymouth Colony, which took place in 1621. The governor of the colony, William Bradford, wished to give thanks for the group's survival . . . and did so with a feast that included most of the foods that we now consider essential to Thanksgiving dinner —cranberries, pumpkins, corn, and, of course, turkey.

Over two hundred years ago, Ben Franklin, one of America's founding fathers, wrote a letter to his daughter, in which he said he wished that the bald eagle had not been chosen as the symbol of our country: "He is a bird of bad moral character. The turkey is a much more respectable bird and a true native of America."

Franklin certainly knew what he was talking about when it came to the turkey. The turkey is an excellent source of protein . . . and one of the best buys in poultry. But in spite of its growing popularity in the kitchen, it is having a difficult public relations problem. You've got the beavers and bears, colts, cardinals, dolphins, and rams, but not a single sports team in the entire world is named after the turkey. You've even got a bunch of guys with the razorback hog as their namesake, but no turkeys take the field—at least no turkeys who put that name on their jerseys. And no wonder.

The turkey's negative image goes all the way back to certain American Indian tribes who thought the turkey was cowardly. They avoided the bird's meat for fear of being infected with the same trait.

Then during the 1930s, Americans began to use the word "turkey" to describe a person who could be easily tricked, and today we use the word as a small insult. I have seen movies that were turkeys, read books that were turkeys, and met more people who were turkeys than I'd like to think about. But we also eat more turkey than ever before. So public relations aren't everything.

◆

ALL-AMERICAN IDAHO POTATO AND TURKEY SALAD

The area of the Andes Mountains in South America is the original home of the potato. It was first cultivated there by the ancient Incas of Peru. The turkey was originally domesticated by the Aztec Indians of Central America, where the bird had been wild for centuries. Both the potato and the turkey clearly originated in the New World. Put potatoes and turkey together in the same dish and you have an all-American recipe. And that's exactly what a few friends of mine did. They happen to be Idaho potato farmers, so they called their dish All-American Idaho Potato and Turkey Salad.

1. In a large skillet over low heat, heat the oil and sauté the onion until soft, about 5 minutes.

2. Add the potatoes. Sprinkle with the thyme and oregano, partially cover, and cook for 15 to 20 minutes over medium heat, turning often, until potatoes are lightly browned.

3. Add the turkey, peas, tomatoes, chilies, vinegar, salt, and pepper and cook 3 minutes more or until heated through and the peas are cooked. Serve warm or cold on lettuce leaves.

MAKES 6 SERVINGS

¼ cup olive oil
1 onion, chopped
4 cups frozen Idaho hash
   brown potatoes, (not the
   shredded kind), or
   4 medium Idaho potatoes,
   cooked, peeled and cut
   into ½-inch pieces
¼ teaspoon thyme
¼ teaspoon oregano
½ pound cooked turkey,
   diced
1 package (10 ounces)
   frozen peas, thawed,
   drained
2 cups cherry tomatoes,
   halved
1 can (4 ounces) chopped
   green chilies, drained, or
   1 tablespoon chopped
   fresh green chilies
2 tablespoons cider
   vinegar, or more to taste
½ teaspoon salt
½ teaspoon freshly ground
   pepper
Lettuce leaves, for serving

WARM CHICKEN SALAD
THE SEA GRILL ♦ NEW YORK, NEW YORK

MAKES 4 SERVINGS

1 pound warm cooked
  chicken, skin removed
  and discarded, meat
  pulled into bite-sized
  pieces
½ cup chopped celery
½ cup sliced mushrooms
1½ tablespoons Dijon-style
  mustard
2½ tablespoons prepared
  white horseradish
3 tablespoons olive oil
1½ tablespoons vinegar
Favorite fresh seasonal
  fruit cut into bite-sized
  pieces, for fruit kabobs

1. Place the warm chicken in a mixing bowl. Combine with the celery and mushrooms.

2. In a small bowl, mix the mustard, horseradish, olive oil, and vinegar until combined. Add to the chicken mixture. Let marinate for 20 minutes.

3. Make kabobs by threading an assortment of fruit on bamboo skewers.

4. Garnish each serving of the chicken salad with a fruit kabob.

VIENNESE POTATO SALAD
HOTEL IMPERIAL ◆ VIENNA, AUSTRIA

1. Place the potatoes in a large pot and cover by 2 inches with cold water. Bring to a boil and add salt, to taste. Turn down heat to a simmer and cook the potatoes until tender, about 10–15 minutes. Don't overcook. Test with the point of a knife. When done, drain, then set aside until just warm.

2. When potatoes are cool enough to handle, but still warm, peel and slice them into ¼-inch rounds. Place in a mixing bowl.

3. Splash the potatoes with the hot broth and toss gently with your fingers. Add the vinegar and toss again. Add the remaining ingredients, except the parsley, in the order given and toss gently, still using your fingers to prevent the potatoes from breaking up.

4. Allow the potato salad to marinate for at least ½ hour at room temperature so the flavors can meld and develop.

5. Before serving, toss in the parsley.

MAKES 6 SERVINGS

2 pounds small new
  potatoes, scrubbed
Salt
3 tablespoons *hot* beef
  broth
1 tablespoon red or white
  wine vinegar
3 tablespoons vegetable oil
½ teaspoon freshly ground
  black pepper
1 teaspoon salt
½ teaspoon confectioners
  sugar
1½ teaspoons prepared
  Dijon-style mustard
½ cup finely chopped red
  onion
2 tablespoons finely
  chopped parsley

LOW-CALORIE POTATO SALAD

MAKES 6 SERVINGS

3 pounds new potatoes,
  scrubbed
1 tablespoon caraway
  seeds
1 clove garlic
1 tablespoon fresh lemon
  juice
⅓ cup buttermilk (made
  with skim or low-fat milk)
½ cup low-fat cottage
  cheese
½ cup low-calorie
  mayonnaise
Freshly ground black
  pepper, to taste
2 tablespoons dried dill
Lettuce leaves and tomato
  wedges, for garnish

In my search for those foods that can help me con-trol my blood pressure, I've been particularly pleased with potatoes. They are high in potassium, which is proving to be of some importance in help-ing to prevent high blood pressure. A single potato will supply about 20 percent of my daily need for potassium. Potatoes are also sources of protein, vi-tamin C, vitamin B$_6$, phosphorus, magnesium, and fiber. But how do you take this nutritionally valu-able food and make it into potato salad without destroying its nutritional balance by adding a se-ries of high-fat ingredients? This recipe provides a delicious answer.

1. In a large saucepan, combine the potatoes, caraway seeds, and garlic. Add water to cover and cook over moderately high heat for 20 minutes or until the potatoes are tender. Drain and cool.

2. Meanwhile, make the dressing. In a blender container, combine the lemon juice, buttermilk, cottage cheese, and mayonnaise. Blend for about 5 seconds.

3. Quarter the partially cooled potatoes and place them in a mixing bowl. Add the pepper and stir in the dressing and the dill.

4. Line the serving bowl with lettuce leaves, add the potato salad, and garnish with tomato wedges.

PAPAYA AND SHRIMP SALAD

1. Shell and devein the shrimp. Cook in boiling water for 2 to 3 minutes until they turn slightly pink and lose their translucent look. Refresh in ice water, pat dry and refrigerate.

2. Peel and seed the papaya. Cut it into ½-inch cubes.

3. Seed the bell pepper, remove the ribs, and cut the pepper into ½-inch cubes.

4. In a small mixing bowl, combine all of the dressing ingredients and whisk.

5. Place all of the salad ingredients in a large mixing bowl and pour the dressing over them. Toss to combine.

P A P A Y A

The papaya is easily bruised and requires careful handling; it is a bit harder to judge for quality than other fruits, but those people who like it, love it.

Look for papayas that are golden yellow to orange and yield to gentle pressure. This fruit is ripe for eating. Avoid papayas that are quite soft (and mushy) with any dark patches, which are signs of age and decay.

MAKES 4 SERVINGS

SALAD
¾ pound shrimp
1 ripe papaya
1 red bell pepper
½ cucumber, split lengthwise and sliced into half circles
1 small bunch radishes, trimmed and sliced
2 scallions, thinly sliced
3 cups fresh spinach, thoroughly washed, stems removed, and torn into bite-sized pieces
¼ cup pine nuts, toasted at 350° F. until golden, about 15 minutes

DRESSING
Juice of 2 limes, strained
1 teaspoon low-sodium soy sauce
4 tablespoons vegetable oil
2 drops Tabasco sauce, or more to taste
2 teaspoons grated ginger
1 tablespoon chopped cilantro (coriander) or Chinese parsley
¼ teaspoon freshly ground black pepper

FIVE BEAN SALAD
LA CITÉ ◆ NEW YORK, NEW YORK

MAKES 12 SERVINGS

1 cup dried (½ pound)
  black beans, soaked
  overnight, or 1½ cups
  canned black beans
1 cup dried (½ pound)
  white beans, soaked
  overnight, or 1½ cups
  canned white beans
1 cup dried (½ pound) red
  kidney beans, soaked
  overnight, or 1½ cups
  canned red kidney beans
2 cups green string beans,
  washed and ends
  snapped off
2 cups yellow string beans,
  washed and ends
  snapped off
6 teaspoons olive oil
½ teaspoon freshly ground
  black pepper
Leaves of one branch
  of fresh thyme, or
  1 teaspoon dried thyme
2 fresh tomatoes, chopped
3 small heads of your
  favorite greens, cleaned
  and torn into bite-sized
  pieces
3 tablespoons red wine
  vinegar

La Cité is somewhere between a big French bras-serie and a bright upscale New York restaurant. It is the creation of Alan Stillman, who has opened some of New York's more interesting restaurants, including Smith & Wollensky, The Manhattan Ocean Club, and The Post House.

The Five bean Salad below is served as a first course at La Cité. It has an excellent flavor, it's a light way to start a meal, it's low in calories and high in complex carbohydrates. I've put in a recipe that makes twelve servings because it is a good dish for the beginning of a dinner party, and it's great as a leftover.

1. Rinse and drain the black, white, and red dried beans. Place each in a separate medium saucepan and cover with water. Cook according to directions on the packages, until tender. Drain well. (If using canned beans, rinse well and drain.)

2. Blanch the green and yellow string beans in separate pots of boiling water for about 1 minute. Drain and rinse in cold water to stop the cooking.

3. In a large bowl, toss together all five beans. Add the olive oil, pepper, and thyme. Stir well. Add the tomatoes and toss. Refrigerate for at least 1 hour.

4. Just before serving, arrange the mixed greens on salad plates. Add the red wine vinegar to the beans and toss again. Serve the beans on the greens.

ABOUT BEANS

Beans are the seeds of plants in the legume family. About a dozen major varieties have been grown for thousands of years in various countries around the world.

When shopping for beans, remember that dried beans are much more nutritious, firm, and flavorful than canned or frozen beans.

Beans are nutritional gold mines. One cup of cooked beans supplies about a quarter of your body's daily protein requirements, can lower cholesterol, gives you a quarter of the daily iron that most of us need, and a lot of B vitamins. Four ounces of cooked dry beans have only about 115 calories. One cup of beans supplies more fiber than equal amounts of celery, carrots, or rice.

The cannellini bean is very popular with Italians, particularly the cooks from Tuscany. It is a small white bean similar to a navy bean.

Beans should be presoaked, or they will take many hours to cook. There are two ways to soak beans. The preferred method (because fewer nutrients are lost) is to cover the beans with three times their volume of water, remove the beans that float, which are bad, and bring the water to a rapid boil. Then remove the pot from the heat and let it sit, covered, for one hour. The other method is just to let them soak in water for six to ten hours.

◆

RED CABBAGE, WALNUT, AND GOAT CHEESE SALAD
STAR'S RESTAURANT ◆ SAN FRANCISCO, CALIFORNIA

MAKES 4 SERVINGS

6 cups thinly sliced red
 cabbage
1 tablespoon vegetable oil
1 tablespoon red wine
 vinegar
1 tablespoon fresh thyme,
 chopped
½ cup shelled walnuts
Salt and freshly ground
 black pepper
One 8-ounce log of goat
 cheese, cut into 4 equal
 portions
1 cup dry bread crumbs
Chopped Italian parsley,
 for garnish

Star's, one of San Francisco's most popular restaurants, was opened in 1984 by Chef Jeremiah Tower, who was to a great extent responsible for our country's renewed interest in our own regional cooking. Each day before the restaurant opens, Jeremiah conducts a briefing on the foods and the operational game plan for the meal. Every dish is tasted, evaluated and improved. The following recipe was prepared by Star's sous chef David Robins.

1. Toss the cabbage with the oil, vinegar, thyme, walnuts, salt, and pepper, to taste.

2. Heat the cabbage mixture in a large nonstick skillet; toss for 2 minutes or longer in order to wilt the cabbage. Remove to a bowl and set aside. Preheat the broiler.

3. Coat the cheese sections with the bread crumbs and set them in a heat-proof dish with low sides. Place cheese under broiler until crumbs begin to turn golden and the cheese is soft to the touch.

4. Divide the cabbage among 4 plates. Using a spatula, place one piece of cheese on top of each and garnish with the parsley.

ABOUT WALNUTS

The ancient Romans believed that the walnut was a physical model of the brain. The hard shell was the skull, the papery partition was the membrane, and the nut itself represented the brain's two hemispheres. The ancient Greeks traded walnuts throughout the Mediterranean. They were a symbol of fertility and a very important gift at wedding parties. For many centuries they were ground up and used as a thickening agent in sauces. They were also chopped up and used as ingredients to give body to a dish or as a garnish.

During the thirteenth and fourteenth centuries, walnuts were so important that there were many cities that had government officials whose job it was to make sure that people got an honest count when they bought walnuts. The Franciscan Fathers brought walnut trees to the first missions in California, and that was the beginning of the California walnut industry. Today the state produces 98 percent of the walnuts eaten in America. The walnut is an excellent food, especially for people who are cutting down on animal protein and substituting vegetable protein. Walnuts are rich in copper, potassium, and magnesium. A quarter cup provides four grams of protein and two grams of fiber. Walnuts will hold in the shell for several months, or they can be frozen for a year.

◆

LOW-CALORIE COLESLAW

MAKES 10 SERVINGS

1 cup low-calorie
  mayonnaise
½ cup plain low-fat yogurt
¼ cup prepared mustard
3 tablespoons white wine
  vinegar
1½ teaspoons dried
  tarragon
¼ teaspoon celery seed
Freshly ground black
  pepper, to taste
2 large heads green
  cabbage, shredded (about
  10 cups)

The real trick in turning cabbage into coleslaw is to do it in a way that doesn't add lots of calories, fat, cholesterol, and sodium. Here's the way I do that.

1. In a large bowl, combine the mayonnaise, yogurt, mustard, vinegar, tarragon, celery seed, and black pepper.

2. Add the cabbage to the dressing and mix until all the cabbage is evenly coated.

3. Cover and refrigerate briefly before serving.

CABBAGE AND GOOD HEALTH

The world "coleslaw" comes from the Dutch word **koolsla. Kool** *means cabbage and* **sla** *means salad, so that's a pretty descriptive name. Coleslaw shows up in American cooking as early as 1792. All cabbage dishes were popular with settlers because cabbage keeps crisp and fresh well into the winter, long after most other vegetables have been lost to frost. These days, a good reason to love cabbage is its relationship to good health. Cabbage is a cruciferous vegetable. That means that when you look at the base of the vegetable, you can see a cross formed by the ribs. Cruciferous vegetables appear to have a cancer-blocking effect. Cabbage is also high in vitamin C and low in calories.*

HEALTHFUL CAESAR SALAD

The most popular salad in the United States is Caesar salad. It was invented in 1920 by a man named Caesar Cardini who had a restaurant in Tijuana, Mexico. Cardini was an Italian immigrant, and so the salad is basically Italian in nature. It's traditionally made with romaine lettuce, olive oil, lemon juice, Parmesan cheese, garlic, anchovies, and raw eggs. Now you could easily think that these ingredients are quite safe, but that might not be true. As you may know, many of the chickens sold in the United States contain salmonella bacteria, which can cause food poisoning. Salmonella bacteria can also be found in raw eggs. Those uncooked eggs in the Caesar salad could be as dangerous as Brutus was to Julius. In the interest of good food and good health, I've modified all my recipes that previously used raw eggs. Here's my Healthful Caesar Salad.

1. In a salad bowl, blend together the hard-boiled egg whites, anchovies, mustard, garlic, and lemon juice to make a paste.

2. Add the vinegar and slowly blend in the vegetable oil.

3. Add the remaining ingredients and toss to coat thoroughly.

MAKES 4 SERVINGS

2 hard-boiled egg whites, finely chopped
2 anchovy fillets, chopped
2 tablespoons prepared mustard
2 cloves garlic, chopped
Juice of ½ lemon
1 tablespoon red wine vinegar
¼ cup vegetable oil
1 large head of leaf lettuce, washed, dried, and chopped into bite-sized pieces
1 cup garlic croutons (see following recipe)
3 tablespoons grated Parmesan cheese
3 drops Tabasco sauce
5 drops Worcestershire sauce

GARLIC CROUTONS

MAKES 2 CUPS

3 cloves garlic, finely
  minced
⅓ cup olive oil
6 slices bread, crusts
  removed, cut into ½-inch
  cubes

1. In a small bowl, combine the garlic and oil. Cover and let marinate for 3 hours or longer.

2. Preheat the oven to 400° F.

3. Place the bread cubes in a single layer in a sauté pan or baking pan. Pour the garlic and oil mixture over the bread and stir to coat.

4. Bake for 10 minutes, or until golden brown.

NOTE: The croutons can be stored in a covered container in the refrigerator for 2 weeks.

SALAD

Richard II was a monarch of England during the fourteenth century. The earliest recorded recipe for a tossed salad appeared in a cookbook that was written for Richard's household. It reads: "Pluck into small pieces by hand, parsley, sage, garlic, onions, leeks, herbs, mint, fennel and mix well with raw oil and vinegar." Things haven't changed much in the last five hundred years.

Green leafy lettuce is packed with nutrients; the darker the green, the greater the nutritional value. Lettuce with loose leaves has high levels of vitamins C and A. Most loose-leaf lettuce, as well as chicory, spinach, watercress, and collard greens, are good sources of fiber, calcium, and iron. Iceberg lettuce, in comparison, has about as much nutritional value as an iceberg.

STEAK SALAD
OLD EBBITT GRILL ◆ WASHINGTON, D.C.

1. Marinate the steak in the ½ cup Italian dressing overnight in the refrigerator, covered, turning occasionally.

2. In a bowl, whisk together the mustard, Worcestershire sauce, and shallots. Whisk in the vinegar, and then slowly whisk in the oil, drop by drop, until the dressing is emulsified. (May be done in a food processor.) Set aside.

3. Preheat a charcoal grill, stovetop grill, or broiler. Allow it to get very hot. Blot the excess marinade from the steak. Place the steak on the grill and cook about 5 to 8 minutes on each side, depending on the thickness of the steak and desired doneness. When cooked, remove the steak to a cutting board and loosely cover with foil. Allow steak to rest for about 5 minutes. Carve the steak against the grain, into thin slices.

4. Toss the greens with additional Italian dressing. Arrange on four plates. Sprinkle with the red onion, carrots, cucumber, cheese, and tomato. Add slices of steak to each plate on top of the greens and serve.

MAKES 4 SERVINGS

1½ pounds flank steak or London broil
½ cup Italian dressing
2 teaspoons prepared mustard
½ teaspoon Worcestershire sauce
2 teaspoons finely chopped shallots or onion
2 tablespoons red wine vinegar
½ cup vegetable oil
6 to 8 cups cleaned fresh salad greens
Additional Italian dressing, to taste
2 tablespoons chopped red onion
2 carrots, peeled and sliced
1 cucumber, peeled, seeded, and cubed
½ cup cubed feta cheese
1 large, ripe tomato, cut into wedges

THE NUTRITIONAL VALUE OF THE LONG-DISTANCE TOMATO

Fifty years ago most of the fresh foods in our markets had a very specific season. A fruit or vegetable came to market when its harvest time began and vanished a month or so later when its harvest season was over. Because many fruits and vegetables did not ship well, most produce came from farms that were quite close to the market. But the invention of the humidity- and temperature-controlled railroad car, the long-haul truck, and overnight air freight changed all that.

Today our markets are packed with foods that come from fields that are thousands of miles away. In most cases the farmers and shippers have been able to work out techniques that keep the food as good tasting and nutritious as it would be if the growing fields were right behind the supermarket.

In some cases, however, our desire to have the produce available every day throughout the year has led to some compromises. An example is the tomato. The long-distance tomato looks good and feels good, but usually doesn't have the taste that you'd find in a local vine-ripened tomato. There is, however, some good news on the nutritional front. Studies have shown that the early harvest, long-distance tomato has almost the same nutritional value as the vine-ripened tomato. It has lots of beta-carotene, vitamin C, B vitamins, iron, and fiber.

◆

SAUCES

COCKTAIL SAUCE

MAKES 2¼ CUPS

1 cup ketchup
1 cup chili sauce
¼ cup white horseradish
3 drops Tabasco sauce
Juice of ¼ lemon
Salt and freshly ground
  black pepper, to taste

The word "cocktail" is used to describe a variety of drinks that often contain alcohol, juices, bitters, and soda water . . . Martinis, Screwdrivers, and Scotch and soda are three well-known examples. There are many theories as to where the word came from, but its significance is widely accepted. William Safire, an editorial writer for The New York Times *pointed out: "Were it not for this word, nobody could put on a cocktail dress, go to a cocktail party, put feet up on a cocktail table, listen to a cocktail pianist or order a nonalcoholic bitters— much less shrimp cocktail." Or for that matter, serve the shrimp cocktail with an appropriate cocktail sauce.*

In a medium bowl, whisk together all of the ingredients and serve.

HORSERADISH CREAM

This is an excellent sauce for cold meat, poultry, or fish. I have also enjoyed it as a dip for fresh vegetables.

In a bowl, blend all the ingredients together.

MAKES 1 CUP

1 cup plain low-fat yogurt
1 teaspoon sugar
1 teaspoon white vinegar
4 tablespoons grated white
   horseradish

> ## HORSERADISH
>
> *Horseradish is the pungent root of a member of the cabbage family. It's called horseradish because it looks like a giant beige-colored radish. Native to southeastern Europe and western Asia, most of the horseradish grown in the United States comes from Illinois farm country, just across the Mississippi River from St. Louis.*

PICO DE GALLO RELISH

MAKES 4 CUPS

½ cup chopped green
  onion
1 fresh or canned jalapeño,
  serrano, or other hot
  pepper, finely chopped
  (adjust the amount of
  pepper for desired
  spiciness)
1 tablespoon corn oil
2 fresh tomatoes, chopped
2 medium avocados,
  chopped
Juice of 1 large lemon
6 sprigs cilantro
  (coriander), chopped
Salt and freshly ground
  black pepper, to taste

In a small bowl, combine all ingredients. Chill for 1 hour before serving.

ABOUT HOT PEPPERS

Spicy foods are eaten in hot-weather countries, where the spiciness stimulates appetites dulled by the heat. Spicy recipes also cool you off by making you sweat. Hotness in peppers is caused by a chemical, capsicum, stored mostly in the inside membranes. The insides can be scooped out of the pepper to remove the real fire while keeping the pepper's flavor. Take care in handling peppers; keep them and your fingers away from your eyes, nose, and mouth. Wash your hands thoroughly after handling hot peppers.

RAVIGOTE SAUCE
ANTOINE'S ◆ NEW ORLEANS, LOUISIANA

Mix all of the ingredients together and chill.

MAKES 1¼ CUPS

1 cup mayonnaise
1½ tablespoons minced
   red bell pepper
1½ tablespoons minced
   green onion
1½ tablespoons minced
   anchovies
1½ tablespoons minced
   pimiento

REMOULADE SAUCE
BRENNAN'S RESTAURANT ◆ NEW ORLEANS, LOUISIANA

MAKES 1½ CUPS

6 tablespoons prepared
  Creole or other hot and
  spicy mustard
1 teaspoon prepared white
  horseradish
3 tablespoons chopped
  garlic
⅓ cup chopped celery
⅓ cup chopped dill pickles
3 tablespoons chopped
  fresh parsley
⅓ cup chopped scallions
⅔ cup vegetable oil
⅓ cup white wine vinegar
Dash of Worcestershire
  sauce
5 drops of Tabasco sauce

Brennan's Restaurant on Royal Street in the French Quarter of New Orleans has been a landmark for decades. Owen Brennan, the patriarch of the Owen Brennan restaurant family, opened his first restaurant in 1945. His idea was to merge top-quality ingredients with the home-style cooking of southern Louisiana and to present it in a first-class establishment. It was Brennan's that introduced the idea of an elegant breakfast in a restaurant. Breakfast at Brennan's is a tradition in New Orleans. The following sauce is often served on freshly boiled shrimp as a brunch starter.

In a mixing bowl, combine the mustard, horseradish, garlic, celery, pickles, parsley, and scallions. Blend together. Whisk in the remaining ingredients.

MANGO SALSA

This sauce is ideal as an accompaniment to grilled meats, fish, or poultry.

1. Cut the flesh off both sides of each mango, as close to the large flat seed as possible. Trim any extra flesh from around the edge of the seed. Chop finely.

2. In a medium bowl, combine the mangoes and remaining ingredients. Refrigerate.

MAKES 2 CUPS

2 ripe mangoes, peeled
2 scallions, thinly sliced
2 tablespoons chopped
    cilantro (coriander) or
    Chinese parsley
1 tablespoon grated fresh
    ginger
Juice of one lime, strained
½ teaspoon low-sodium
    soy sauce
2 drops Tabasco sauce

MANGOES

Mangoes have a truly exotic taste . . . somewhat like an effervescent peach. The best way to prepare them is to remove the peel and slice the meat off the large center pit. Or you can mark a band down one side of the mango with a sharp knife and peel back skin as necessary. The pulp can be eaten right out of the skin with a spoon.

When ready to eat, a mango will have an orange-yellow to red surface skin and flesh that yields slightly to pressure. They can be bought green and allowed to ripen at room temperature.

SALSA
ZARELA ◆ NEW YORK, NEW YORK

MAKES 5 CUPS

4 large ripe tomatoes,
  peeled and coarsely
  chopped
½ cup finely chopped
  scallions
1 medium clove garlic,
  finely chopped
¼ cup chopped cilantro
  (coriander)
1 jalapeño pepper or more,
  to taste, trimmed,
  seeded, ribs removed,
  and finely chopped
1 teaspoon dried oregano
Juice of ½ lime

Zarela is the creation of Zarela Martinez, who is also responsible for the cooking. Many consider this establishment to be the best Mexican restaurant in New York. The salsa, which is served with nacho chips, is one of her specialties.

Both the fresh tomatoes and scallions provide small amounts of folic acid, and the tomatoes also contribute a welcome quantity of vitamin C. The fresh chilies have beta-carotene, which your body converts to vitamin A.

In a medium bowl, combine all ingredients. Serve well chilled.

LIME DRESSING

1. In a mixing bowl, combine all the ingredients.

2. Whisk together thoroughly and serve over your favorite salad.

MAKES 1½ CUPS

¼ cup honey
1 cup vegetable oil
⅓ cup lime juice
2 tablespoons lime zest,
   grated
1 teaspoon fresh ginger,
   grated
Salt and freshly ground
   pepper, to taste

LOW-FAT SALAD DRESSINGS

The popularity of the salad has never been higher. With more than half of the people in the United States on a weight-loss program, a filling but low-calorie salad has become a frequent choice at lunch and dinner. The basic ingredients for most salads—lettuce, vegetables, beans, and herbs—are usually excellent from the nutritional point of view. The dressings, however, are a different story. Dressings are often packed with fat in the form of oil, mayonnaise, cheese, and cream. The common two-ounce dressing ladle can add a quick 300 to 500 calories to your plate. A single tablespoon of oil has about 100 calories.

One of the best ways to reduce the calorie content of your salad dressings is to use low-fat yogurt, the new light (or reduced-calorie) mayonnaise products, pureed vegetables, or buttermilk made from skim milk as the basis for the dressing. Buttermilk is usually made from skim milk and is therefore low in calories.

FLORA DANICA BLUE CHEESE DRESSING
D'ANGLETERRE HOTEL ◆ COPENHAGEN, DENMARK

MAKES 1⅓ CUPS

½ cup blue cheese,
 crumbled
Freshly ground black
 pepper, to taste
½ cup chopped onion
2 tablespoons chopped
 chives
Juice of ½ lemon, strained
1 cup plain low-fat yogurt

One of the world's most amazing sets of dishes is on exhibit at Christiansborg Palace in Denmark. It's called the Flora Danica service. originally Flora Danica was a set of books illustrating the plants and flowers of Denmark. In 1790, King Christian VII of Denmark ordered a set of dinnerware with paintings of these plants as a present for Empress Catherine of Russia. It took twelve years to finish making the service, and by then Catherine had died. So King Christian kept it for himself. Good move, because today the set is considered a Danish national treasure.

Today Flora Danica is also the name of a cheese that has become a national treasure. It's a blue cheese with a rich intense flavor, and it makes an interesting salad dressing. Some of the flavors that we love are actually the result of bacteria working on the food. Cheese, buttermilk, yogurt, and sauerkraut are some examples of foods perfected in what is actually a process of controlled aging.

In a small bowl, blend all ingredients. Serve well chilled.

RED PEPPER DRESSING
VISTA HOTEL ◆ NEW YORK, NEW YORK

Serve as a dressing with salad, as a sauce with fish, or as a dip with raw vegetables.

MAKES 1 CUP

1. Place the peppers over the flame on your stove or under the broiler. Turn the peppers until the skin blisters and blackens. After removing from the heat, rub the skin off the peppers under cold running water.

2. Cut the peppers open, remove the seeds and ribs, and dice the peppers.

3. In the container of a blender or food processor, puree the peppers until they form a smooth paste.

4. Pour the puree into a large bowl and whisk in the vinegar, olive oil, salt, pepper, and lemon juice, to taste.

2 red bell peppers
4 tablespoons red wine
  vinegar or more, to taste
½ cup olive oil
Salt and freshly ground
  black pepper
Juice of ½ lemon

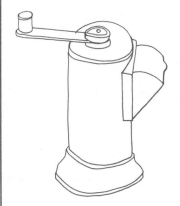

THE WARING BLENDER

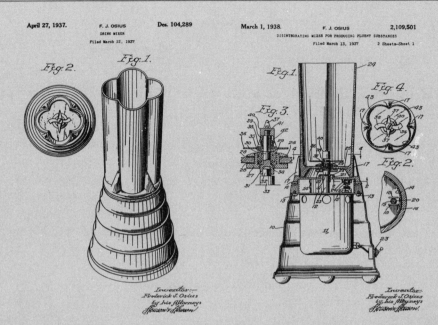

The above drawings are part of a patent that was registered in the mid-1930s by a man named F. J. Osius. It describes a "mixer for producing fluent substances." The device that eventually came out of these drawings was the first Waring Blender.

Osius had gone to Fred Waring, a famous bandleader of the period. Waring put up the money, directed the technical development, and formed the company that would market the invention. Waring then traveled around the country with his band and a trunk that opened up into a bar so he could demonstrate his mixer. In 1938, he introduced the blender everywhere he went.

The blender's original popularity was as a drink mixer. Waring once used it to make over four hundred Daiquiris at a single cocktail party. He also liked to make fruit-flavored milk shakes. Everyone was fascinated with the machine's ability to liquify fruit. And not all that much has changed. The Waring Blenders are modernized and more powerful, but they still have their primary employment in the making of drinks.

SALSA VERDE DIP

*Salsa **is a Spanish word meaning "sauce" and is applied especially to a sauce made with chili peppers that is much used in Mexican-American cookery.***

The following salsa gets its green color from the inclusion of chopped parsley. It can be used for dipping, as a flavoring ingredient, or as a sauce for fish or poultry.

1. In a large bowl, place the garlic, parsley, pimientos, capers, and vinegar. Blend thoroughly.

2. Slowly add the oil and blend until all the oil is absorbed. Season with the pepper.

MAKES 2 CUPS

4 large cloves garlic, finely chopped
2 bunches parsley, stems removed, finely chopped
One 4-ounce jar sliced pimientos, drained and finely chopped
1 tablespoon capers
¼ cup red wine vinegar
¾ cup vegetable oil
¼ teaspoon freshly ground black pepper

CUCUMBER GARLIC DIP

MAKES 3 CUPS

1 medium cucumber,
  peeled, seeded, and
  chopped
8 ounces feta cheese,
  crumbled
½ cup thinly sliced
  scallions
¼ cup light (reduced-
  calorie, cholesterol-free)
  mayonnaise
¼ cup plain low-fat yogurt
1 teaspoon dried oregano
3 tablespoons chopped
  fresh parsley
3 cloves garlic, finely
  minced

The use of reduced-calorie mayonnaise and nonfat yogurt give this traditional recipe a low-calorie twist. I serve it with a plate of freshly sliced vegetables for dipping (carrots, celery, broccoli, cauliflower, cherry tomatoes, etc.) and wedges of toasted pita bread.

In a medium bowl, combine all the ingredients and mix well. Refrigerate for at least 2 hours.

EGGPLANT DIP

Most people remember Lindsay Wagner for her Emmy Award—winning role as the Bionic Woman. Since that time, Lindsay has established herself as one of Hollywood's brightest stars. Her unique ability and talent for playing a diversity of roles has established her as one of the most sought-after stars in made-for-TV movies. The following recipe is from her collection of vegetarian dishes.

1. In a large skillet, heat the oil over medium heat. Add the onion and sauté for 2 minutes. Add the garlic and sauté for 1 minute more. Add the eggplant and green pepper and sauté for 10 minutes. Stir occasionally.

2. Add the tomatoes, parsley, salt, pepper, paprika, rosemary, oregano, and basil. Stir to combine. Add the water and cook, uncovered, for 30 minutes. Stir often.

3. Remove from heat, place in the container of a food processor or blender, and pulse until dip is the desired texture.

4. Return to skillet and cook, covered, for 30 minutes more. Stir occasionally.

MAKES 6 CUPS

1 tablespoon olive oil
1 medium onion, chopped
2 cloves garlic, chopped
1 large eggplant, unpeeled, cut into ½-inch cubes
1 green bell pepper, seeded, ribs removed, and julienned
2 cups chopped tomatoes
¼ cup chopped fresh parsley
½ teaspoon salt
½ teaspoon freshly ground black pepper
¼ teaspoon paprika
¼ teaspoon dried rosemary
¼ teaspoon dried oregano
¼ teaspoon dried basil
1 cup water

GUACAMOLE
ROSA MEXICANO ◆ NEW YORK, NEW YORK

MAKES 3 CUPS

1 small onion, chopped
½ teaspoon salt
½ jalapeño pepper or
  more, to taste, seeded,
  ribs removed, and minced
2 ripe Haas avocadoes,
  peeled and pits removed,
  cut into bite-sized pieces
1 medium tomato, chopped
Taco chips, for serving

Legend has it that the first person to eat an avocado was a Mayan princess, around 290 B.C. The ancient Aztecs believed that avocados had mystical and romantic powers. The following recipe is a classic guacamole recipe from Chef Josephina Howard.

1. In a small mixing bowl, combine the onion and salt. Add the jalapeño, avocadoes, and tomato. Stir to combine.

2. Serve with taco chips.

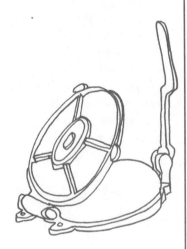

CAROLINA-STYLE BASTING SAUCE

1. In a medium saucepan, sauté the onions in the oil until they are soft and translucent.

2. Add all other ingredients.

3. Bring to a boil and simmer for 20 minutes.

4. Remove from the heat and cool; store in the refrigerator.

MAKES 10 CUPS

2 medium onions, pureed
  (about 3 cups)
¼ cup vegetable oil
3 bay leaves
1½ tablespoons cayenne
  pepper
½ cup hot sauce
⅛ tablespoon salt
¾ tablespoon freshly
  ground black pepper
5 cups tomato puree
3 cups water
1 cup brown sugar
1½ ounces fresh lemon
  juice

HOW TO REDUCE THE FAT AND COOKING TIME FOR RIBS

You can reduce the cooking time for ribs as well as their fat content by parboiling them before grilling. Place the ribs in a pot, cover them with cold water, heat until the water comes to the boil, reduce the heat to simmer, and simmer the ribs for thirty minutes. Remove the ribs from the water and set them on the grill for the final barbecuing.

◆

TIPS FOR A BETTER BARBECUE

1. Your grill should be steady and secure when it is standing in place. It should have sturdy handles that are heat resistant in the area where you grip them.

2. The grill rack should raise and lower. This will give you the ability to control the degree of heat reaching your food.

3. The unit should be set up in a draft-free place or protected with a guard. A slight breeze can cut in half the effectiveness of the heat.

4. Never set up your barbecue grill indoors or in a garage. The fire will produce carbon monoxide gas, which is deadly. Opening the doors and windows will not protect you.

5. As a general rule, you will need about six briquets per person. Pile the briquets in a pyramid, they will get hot faster. When the edges of the coals turn gray, spread out the pyramid. Spread the coals out so they cover an area that is about an inch bigger, all around, than the food that is going to be cooked on top. When the coals have a gray ash all over them, with no black showing, they are ready for cooking.

6. Take the foods out of the refrigerator about an hour before you are going to cook them. They will cook faster and better if they start cooking when they are at room temperature.

7. Rub a little vegetable oil on the grill just before you put on your food. The oil will help prevent the food from sticking to the grill while it's cooking.

8. *Keep a spray bottle filled with water near your grill. A quick burst of spray will help keep flare-ups to a minimum. Remember, it's the smoke that comes up from the dripping fat that flavors the food, the flames that are part of the flare-ups just burn the food.*

9. *Fresh herbs or dried herbs soaked in water and placed on top of the coals will add their flavor to the food. Rosemary, basil, thyme, bay leaves—any herb flavor that you enjoy.*

10. *Closing the cover of your grill will help the smoke flavor the food.*

11. *Long tongs should be used to turn meat during cooking; forks will make holes in the meat and let the juices drain out.*

12. *It's not easy to tell when your foods are properly done when you are cooking on an outdoor grill. The temperature of your food, the temperature of the air, the degree of wind—all have an effect on the cooking. The best way to tell when your meat is cooked to the degree of doneness that you like is to check the internal temperature of the meat with a tiny instant-reading thermometer.*

Insert the thermometer into the meat at its thickest point. Keep the probe away from any fat or bone, which can throw off your reading.

Keep a record of the internal temperature for the foods that you enjoy and use that as your future guide.

13. *After meat has been cooked to the degree of doneness that you like, take it off the grill and let it sit for three minutes before carving. That will allow the juices in the meat to settle; the final pieces will be juicier.*

◆

CHILI BARBECUE WET BASTING SAUCE

MAKES 3 CUPS

½ cup vegetable oil
1 medium onion, peeled
  and chopped
2 cloves garlic, peeled and
  finely minced
20 ounces canned tomatoes
Dash Tabasco sauce
3 tablespoons chili powder
¼ cup red wine vinegar

1. Heat 2 tablespoons of the oil in a saucepan.

2. Add the onion and sauté until browned, about 5 minutes.

3. Add the garlic, tomatoes, Tabasco, chili powder, and remaining oil.

4. Bring to a boil and cook over low heat for 15 minutes. Add the vinegar and cook for 10 minutes more. Use as a basting sauce.

BBQ FOLKLORE

The word "barbecue" is traditionally used to describe an outdoor cooking method in which the food is prepared over an open fire, with no pots or pans between the food and the flame. Barbecuing was probably the first form of cooking: lightning hit a tree, a fire started, and a few cavemen and women marched over with some meat on a stick. Except for the addition of briquets and beer, things haven't changed very much. The word "barbecue" itself comes from the old Caribbean word barbacoa, *which means "framework of sticks." It was used to describe the structure that held the meat over the flames.*

In North America barbecuing was already a big deal in the 1700s. In the southern part of the United States it became a standard type of outdoor social event, particularly favored by politicians and almost mandatory on the Fourth of July. In order to get more votes, Southern politicians would hold an Independence Day Barbecue: all the beef you could eat, lots to drink, a marching band, and an agonizingly boring speech. Thanks to the development of television, the political speeches are being sent to us on TV, and you can turn them off. Most barbecues are now boredom free and still filled with good eating.

RIO GRANDE-STYLE BARBECUE MARINADE

Mix all ingredients together in a 2- or 3-quart saucepan. Simmer, uncovered, for 10 minutes. Use as a marinade or basting sauce.

MAKES 2 CUPS

One 8-ounce can tomato
  sauce
1 teaspoon dry mustard
1 teaspoon sugar
1 tablespoon
  Worcestershire sauce
1 tablespoon white vinegar
½ cup red wine
1 clove garlic, minced
Tabasco sauce, to taste
½ cup vegetable oil

SOY SAUCE MARINADE

MAKES 1¼ CUPS

½ cup soy sauce, regular
 or low-sodium
¼ cup sherry
½ cup vegetable oil
2 cloves garlic, minced
1 tablespoon ground ginger
Zest and juice of 1 orange

Mix all of the ingredients together. Use as a marinade.

BARBECUE-FLAVORING GRILLED FOODS

In general, there are three basic techniques for flavoring grilled foods: marinating, basting, and dry rubbing.

Marinating a food consists of letting it soak in a mixture of an oil, an acid, and a flavoring agent. The oil is there to keep the food moist during the cooking time, the acid—which is usually vinegar, citrus juice, wine, or beer—acts as a tenderizer, breaking down the fibers of the meat during the marinating time. Herbs, spices, Worcestershire sauce and Tabasco sauce are often the flavoring agents. A time guide for marinating meat that usually works is three hours of marinating time for every inch of thickness.

Basting is a simple method of flavoring food by painting it with sauce during cooking. Basting usually does not tenderize the food. It can, however, keep it moist during the cooking time and add flavor and a glaze to the surface. Basting sauces with ketchup, tomatoes, or sugar as a major ingredient should be brushed on near the end of cooking time or they will scorch.

Dry rubbing, or dry spicing, is a technique that consists of making a paste from a little oil and a blend of dry herbs and spices. The paste is thoroughly rubbed into the meat before grilling.

BREADS, PANCAKES, WAFFLES, PIZZA, MUFFINS, STUFFINGS, AND A SCONE

CHERRY TEA BREAD

MAKES 6 TO 8 SERVINGS

½ cup walnuts, coarsely
  chopped
2¼ cups all-purpose flour
1 teaspoon double-acting
  baking powder
¾ teaspoon baking soda
¼ teaspoon salt
1¼ cups sweet canned
  cherries, drained and
  pitted
8 tablespoons (1 stick)
  unsalted butter, softened
¾ cup sugar
¼ cup honey
2 large eggs
⅓ cup fresh orange juice

One cup of cherries has about eighty-five calories. They are high in complex carbohydrates, high in vitamin C and potassium, and low in sodium and fat. Like all red-colored fruits, they contain some vitamin A, which appears to be a blocker of cancer.

1. Preheat the oven to 300° F.

2. Toast the chopped walnuts in a baking pan in the oven for 15 minutes. Remove from the oven and set aside.

3. Raise oven temperature to 350° F.

4. Sift the flour, baking powder, baking soda, and salt together into a bowl. In a second bowl, combine the cherries and the nuts.

5. In the bowl of an electric mixer, cream the butter until it is light and fluffy; add the sugar and honey gradually, beating the mixture until it is very light. Add the eggs, one at a time. With mixer at lowest speed, add the flour mixture (reserving ¼ cup), alternating it with the orange juice.

6. Toss the cherry-nut mixture with the reserved ¼ cup flour, and fold it into the batter. Turn the batter into a buttered and floured loaf pan, approximately 9 × 5 × 3 inches. Bake the bread in the center of the oven for 1 hour.

7. Cool the loaf for 15 minutes in the pan; unmold the bread on a rack to cool completely. Wrap it in plastic wrap and keep it a day before serving.

HOW THE CROISSANT CAME TO BE

When the Turks attacked Vienna in the 1680s, they permanently changed the way people eat. At the time of the siege, the city of Vienna was totally surrounded; nothing was going in, nothing was going out. Things were not looking too good. Then a baker who had a shop near the city wall got up early one morning to start working on his bread. While he was working on it, he realized something was going on underneath his shop . . . the Turks were trying to tunnel under the city wall. He notified the guards, the guards counterattacked, the Turks fell back, and the city was saved. The ruler of Vienna rewarded the baker by giving him a patent to produce a bread in the shape of a design on the Turkish flag. It was to remind the people of Vienna that they had devoured the Turks. The symbol was the shape of the crescent moon, and the bread was the first croissant. So next time you start your day with a croissant, or have one offered to you as part of a sandwich, remember you owe it all to a Viennese baker of the 1600s.

◆

ABOUT DANISH PASTRY

The Danish Bakers' Guild, which has been around for hundreds of years, has its own symbol, a pretzel-shaped pastry with a crown on top. It hangs above the door of every bakery. Danish pastry is certainly well known in the United States, but here in Denmark it's called Viennese pastry. That's because about a hundred years ago, the Danish bakers went on strike. They wanted to get paid money as well as just receiving room and board. The bakeries brought in Viennese workers to do the baking. After the strike was over, the people loved the Viennese pastry so much that the Danes began to bake it themselves. The Americans learned about it from the Danes, and that's why we call it Danish pastry, but strictly speaking, from an historical point of view, it's more accurate to order a coffee and a cheese Viennese.

◆

JARLSBERG TWIST BREAD
GRAND HOTEL ◆ OSLO, NORWAY

MAKES 2 LARGE LOAVES

1 package (¼ ounce) dry
  yeast
1 tablespoon sugar
1 cup water
4 cups all-purpose flour
1 teaspoon salt
⅓ cup milk
¼ cup (½ stick) butter,
  melted
1 egg
3 cups (about 1 pound)
  shredded Jarlsberg
  cheese
⅔ cup parsley

Count Gustav Wihelm Jarlsberg of Norway (1641–1717) lived on a fabulous farm near Oslo. Descendants of his family still live there, and it's the largest farm in Norway. Jarlsberg cheese is literally the national cheese of Norway. It is used in hundreds of recipes. One of my favorites is a Jarlsberg Twist Bread. Chef Namdal, at Oslo's Grand Hotel, is a master at the Jarlsberg Twist.

1. In a small bowl, place the yeast and sugar and add ½ cup warm water. The water should not be hot, the ideal temperature is between 100° F. and 115° F., about the temperature of a baby's formula. Stir to mix and set aside.

2. In a second bowl, combine the flour and the salt. Set aside.

3. In a small saucepan over medium-low heat, combine the milk, melted butter, and the remaining ½ cup water. Heat to lukewarm.

4. Pour the yeast mixture into the dry ingredients and gently mix. Add the lukewarm milk mixture and the egg and 1 cup of the cheese and mix thoroughly until the dough pulls together into a ball.

5. Turn the dough out onto a floured surface and knead until the dough becomes smooth and elastic, approximately 5 to 6 minutes. Cover and let rise until doubled, about 45 minutes.

6. Punch down the dough and divide in half. Roll out two rectangles of dough approximately 12 × 15 inches and sprinkle each with half the parsley and half the remaining cheese.

7. Beginning at the short end of the rectangle, roll the dough up into a very tight roll, smoothing it out as you go. Slice in half lengthwise, but stop about 1 inch from one end, as below:

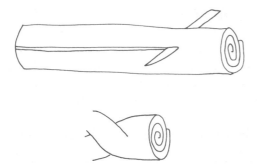

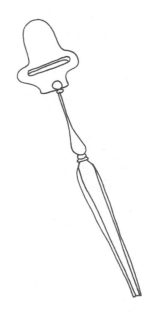

Twist each half around the other to make a braided loaf and smooth out the ends. Repeat with the second rectangle to form the second loaf. Place on a cookie sheet and let rise until double, approximately 30 minutes.

8. Preheat the oven to 400° F.

9. Place the cookie sheet in the oven and bake loaves for 18 to 22 minutes. Immediately remove to a rack to cool.

PALATSCHINKEN (SWEET PANCAKES)
GOLDENER HIRSCH HOTEL ◆ SALZBURG, AUSTRIA

MAKES 12 PANCAKES,
OR 6 SERVINGS

1¾ cups unbleached all-
  purpose flour
2 cups 1% milk (99% fat
  free)
1 tablespoon confectioners
  sugar
Pinch of salt
1 whole egg
4 egg whites
Vegetable oil
1 cup apricot preserves,
  heated
Confectioners sugar, for
  garnish

The leading culinary guidebooks to Europe regularly recommend the Goldener Hirsch restaurant as having some of the best and most authentic of Austrian food, and classic examples are found in the work of their pastry chefs. A perfect example is a dessert called Palatschinken—"sweet pancakes." Traditionally, whole eggs go into whole milk, flour is added and mixed into a light batter, which is pan-fried in butter into pancakes. But the times they are a changing; these days many Austrians are lightening up. Four of the eggs have been replaced with egg whites, and the whole milk has become skim milk. Instead of being cooked in butter, it's in a pan with just a little vegetable oil. Tradition also calls for Palatschinken to be filled with apricot preserves. They still are, but health-conscious Austrians are using preserves with high fruit content and much less sugar than standard preserves. They use fruits that are picked in the Austrian Alps, which have a very short growing season. The result is that the fruit has a very concentrated flavor. More taste for the calories. The brand that is available in the United States is called DARBO.

1. Whisk the flour, milk, 1 tablespoon confectioners sugar, and the salt until smooth, about 3 minutes. If mixture isn't smooth, add more milk, a little at a time. It should look like the consistency of very heavy cream. Then whisk in the whole egg and the egg whites.

2. Place a 9-inch crêpe pan or nonstick frying pan over medium heat. Lightly oil pan with vegetable oil and pour about 2 ounces (¼ cup) of the batter into the pan, turning pan quickly to cover the surface. The pancake should cover the entire surface of the pan and not be thick. If batter seems too thick to do this, add more milk and whisk batter until smooth.

3. Allow the pancake to brown slightly, turn it with the help of a spatula, and brown slightly on the other side. Remove from the pan when done and stack between two heated plates to keep warm. Oil pan lightly before cooking each pancake.

4. When all pancakes are done, begin filling with apricot preserves. Place about 1 tablespoon of preserves in the middle of each pancake and fold into thirds. Place 2 pancakes on each serving plate and sift some confectioners sugar over each.

LINGONBERRY PANCAKES
GRAND HOTEL ◆ STOCKHOLM, SWEDEN

MAKES 8 PANCAKES

½ cup all-purpose flour
1 cup milk
2 eggs
4 tablespoons melted
  butter
Dash salt
1 10-ounce jar
  lingonberries in syrup, or
  1 cup fresh lingonberries
  tossed with 1 to 2
  tablespoons sugar
Whipped cream or
  confectioners sugar, for
  garnish (optional)

For centuries, the lingonberry has been treated as one of the national treasures of Sweden. This recipe, which uses lingonberries as the topping for dessert pancakes, is based on one from the Grand Hotel in Stockholm. The dish is Scandinavia's answer to France's crêpes suzette.

1. Place the flour in a bowl. Add the milk and combine, using a whisk, until the batter is smooth. Add the eggs, 3 tablespoons of the butter, and the salt; beat until well blended.

2. Heat an 8-inch nonstick skillet or crêpe pan over medium heat. Lightly grease the pan with some of the remaining butter. Add ¼ cup of the batter to the heated pan. Immediately tilt the pan to spread the batter over the entire bottom of the pan. Cook 1 to 2 minutes or until bottom of the pancake is lightly golden. Use a spatula or a fork to flip the pancake over. (The first pancake may stick to the pan. If it does, discard it.) Cook the other side until golden. Fold the pancake in quarters and keep warm.

3. Continue to make pancakes until all of the batter is used.

4. To serve, place 2 pancakes on each plate. Alongside the pancakes, place 1 to 2 tablespoons of the lingonberries in sugar or ¼ cup of the fresh lingonberries. Serve with whipped cream or sprinkle the pancakes with confectioners sugar, if desired.

APPLE PANCAKES
OLD EBBITT GRILL ◆ WASHINGTON, D.C.

Washington is a town that loves to start work over breakfast . . . and one of the best spots to do that is the Old Ebbitt Grill. Just a few blocks from the White House, the Old Ebbitt Grill was founded in 1856, and its regular guests included presidents McKinley, Grant, Jackson, Cleveland, and Theodore Roosevelt. And it still draws a crowd of Capitol cronies. There's a Victorian quality to the main dining room: lots of antiques from the period, lots of natural wood and high ceilings, and a good breakfast menu. One of my favorite dishes is Chef Paul Muller's Apple Pancakes.

1. In a mixing bowl, combine the flour, salt, and egg whites. Whisk until well blended, then whisk in the milk. Cover with plastic wrap and allow to sit overnight in the refrigerator.

2. Preheat the oven to 400° F.

3. Heat the oil in a 12-inch ovenproof frying pan over medium heat. When the oil is very hot, pour in all the batter. Let the pancake form a bit of a crust and then top with the apple slices, sugar, cinnamon, and nutmeg.

4. Place the pan in the oven and bake for 15 to 20 minutes, until the pancake is puffed and golden and the apples have softened. Slide the pancake onto a platter, cool for 2 minutes and slice and serve.

MAKES 4 SERVINGS

1 cup all-purpose flour
Pinch of salt
8 egg whites
¾ cup low-fat milk
2 tablespoons vegetable oil
1 Granny Smith apple, peeled, cored, and thinly sliced
1 to 2 tablespoons sugar
¼ teaspoon cinnamon
⅛ teaspoon nutmeg

DIETARY FIBER AND GOOD HEALTH

Scientists are continuing to study the relationship between dietary fiber and good health. And though the research is complex and there are many questions that still need to be answered, it's become evident that a diet low in fat and rich in dietary fiber is a diet that promotes good health.

There are two basic types of dietary fiber. The first is called soluble fiber because it dissolves in water. Some particularly good sources are dried beans, oats, and some fruits. The second form—insoluble fiber—does not dissolve in water. Good sources of insoluble fiber are wheat brans, whole grains, and vegetables.

The research indicates that soluble and insoluble fibers have different functions, however, between the two, we find there are many possible benefits. High fiber foods promote a feeling of fullness, help in weight control, prevent constipation, colon cancer, hemorrhoids, and varicose veins. High fiber foods can also help reduce fat absorption, smooth sugar surges for diabetics, and can lower cholesterol.

Foods that are high in fiber include high fiber breakfast cereals, bran products, whole wheat products, oatmeal, cabbage, carrots, apples, raspberries, and strawberries.

The more I see of the research on dietary fiber, the more I'm personally convinced of its importance in our diet.

◆

OATMEAL WAFFLES

Researchers are telling us that eating oatmeal can lower our cholesterol levels and help prevent heart disease. Oatmeal contains a form of soluble fiber. When the fiber gets inside you, it forms a gel. As the gel moves through your body, it appears to affect your cholesterol level. Research at Northwestern University indicates that two ounces of oatmeal each day can reduce your cholesterol level by almost five percent. One of my favorite ways of keeping the oat bran in my diet is with this recipe.

1. Lightly oil and preheat a waffle iron.

2. In a bowl, beat the egg whites until stiff.

3. In a second bowl, mix together the oatmeal, whole wheat flour, cornmeal, and white flour. Mix in the baking powder. Add the buttermilk and vanilla extract and fold in the beaten egg whites.

4. Pour half the batter into the waffle iron and bake until done. Repeat.

NOTE: I often serve these waffles with a puree of strawberries that I make by running a 10-ounce package of frozen strawberries through a blender for 30 seconds.
   This batter also works for pancakes.

MAKES 2 BELGIAN-STYLE WAFFLES

2 egg whites
½ cup uncooked quick or
   old-fashioned oatmeal
½ cup whole wheat flour
½ cup cornmeal
½ cup enriched white flour
1 tablespoon baking
   powder
1½ cups buttermilk
1 teaspoon vanilla extract
Frozen strawberries, for
   topping (optional)

PIZZA WITH ARTICHOKES, MUSHROOMS, EGGPLANT, AND LEEKS
SPAGO'S ◆ HOLLYWOOD, CALIFORNIA

MAKES 4 PIZZAS

½ cup olive oil
1 small eggplant, thinly
  sliced lengthwise
8 ounces fresh
  mushrooms, thinly sliced
20 ounces pizza dough,
  divided into 4 equal
  pieces
3 cups (12 ounces)
  shredded mozzarella
  cheese
One 6-ounce jar artichoke
  hearts, drained and sliced
1 medium leek, white part
  only, thinly sliced
4 plum tomatoes, thinly
  sliced
1 teaspoon dried oregano
1 teaspoon dried thyme

Pizza came from Naples to New York City. Like the early moviemakers, pizza headed West, and when it got to Tinseltown, like everything else in Hollywood, it needed an agent. Somebody to make it rich and famous, powerful, beautiful, sought after . . . a celebrity. The star-maker for pizza, the Goldwyn of goat cheese, the Zanuck of zest, is Chef Wolfgang Puck.

California Dreaming cuisine became a reality when Wolfgang opened Spago's in 1982. Sitting pretty on top of the Sunset Strip, this star-studded bistro quickly became the home of Hollywood's rich and famished.

1. Preheat the oven to 500° F.

2. In a sauté pan, heat 2 tablespoons of the olive oil over high heat. Sauté the eggplant for 2 to 3 minutes. Remove and add 2 more tablespoons of olive oil to the pan. Sauté the mushrooms for 1 minute.

3. Roll or stretch the dough into four 8-inch circles. Place the pizzas on 2 lightly floured baking sheets. Brush each circle of dough to within 1 inch of the edge with 1 tablespoon olive oil. Top each with a quarter of the cheese, eggplant, mushrooms, artichokes, and leeks. Finish with the tomato slices. Sprinkle with the oregano and thyme. Bake for 10 to 12 minutes or until the crust is golden brown.

ABOUT ARTICHOKES

The artichoke has a rather interesting history, with beautiful women playing a part in its story from the beginning. The ancient Greeks had a legend that told of an angry god turning a radiant maiden into a thistlelike plant—the first artichoke. Then there was Catherine de' Medici of Italy. She married King Henry II of France in the 1500s. She loved artichokes and ate them all the time, but artichokes were thought to be an aphrodisiac, and she created quite a scandal. And most recently we have Marilyn Monroe, who was the first artichoke queen. Quite a past for these little thistle plants.

Artichokes grow best in an area that is cool but frost free and has lots of fog. That's why the very heart of the artichoke-growing industry in the United States is a place south of San Francisco, California, called Castroville.

Artichokes first came to the United States with French settlers who arrived in the area near New Orleans and with Spanish missionaries who came to California. They're low in calories, low in fat, low in sodium, and high in vitamins A, B, C, iron, iodine, and potassium. For convenience, they're available throughout the year, packed in vegetable oil or water or frozen.

GARLIC AND GOOD HEALTH

One of the earliest American cookbooks is called New England Cookery. It was published in 1808. The section on garlic has the following note: "Garlic is used by the French, but it is better used in medicine than in cookery." People have talked about the medicinal benefits of garlic for hundreds of years.

During the Black Death of the fourteenth century, people noticed that the garlic sellers didn't come down with the plague as often as other people. Since everyone believed vampires spread the plague, they assumed vampires were afraid of garlic.

That is how we came to believe that wearing garlic around your neck scared off vampires. What was actually going on is quite interesting. The garlic sellers were poor, so they ate a lot of their own garlic. Garlic can act as a very mild antibiotic and that protected many of the garlic sellers.

Scientists are now telling us that garlic is back in the health business. It looks like garlic lowers the bad form of cholesterol and increases the good form. One study covered a group of people who ate the equivalent of ten cloves of garlic a day. After eight months they showed an 18 percent drop in their total blood cholesterol level. Garlic also seems to be valuable in preventing and treating arteriosclerosis. And it helps the blood flow more freely.

So after three thousand years of folklore . . . garlic is finally getting its scientific confirmation in the world of medicine.

TOMATO-GARLIC TARTS
THE SHERMAN HOUSE ◆ SAN FRANCISCO, CALIFORNIA

MAKES 6 LARGE OR 12
SMALL TARTS

1 cup peeled garlic cloves
  (about 3 heads)
½ to ¾ cup milk (enough
  to cover garlic)
¼ cup honey
1 teaspoon chopped fresh
  thyme, or ½ teaspoon
  dried
Salt and freshly ground
  black pepper, to taste
Pie dough, rolled to a
  thickness of ⅛ inch and
  cut into six 5-inch disks
  or twelve 2-inch disks
4 ripe tomatoes, thinly
  sliced, seeds removed

1. Place the garlic, milk, honey, thyme, salt, and pepper in a small, heavy saucepan. Set over high heat until mixture comes to a boil. Lower the heat to simmer and cook for about 30 minutes. The garlic should be completely tender and the liquid should be thick and golden. Mash the mixture into a paste. Preheat the oven to 375° F.

2. Line a baking sheet with parchment paper and place the disks of pie dough on it. Spread each with garlic paste, top with overlapping tomato slices.

3. Bake the tarts for 25 minutes. Serve the large tarts as a first course and the small tarts as appetizers.

PIZZA WITH PROSCIUTTO, GOAT CHEESE, THYME, AND RED ONIONS
SPAGO'S ◆ HOLLYWOOD, CALIFORNIA

1. Preheat oven to 500° F.

2. Roll or stretch the dough into four 8-inch circles. Place the pizzas on 2 lightly floured baking sheets. Brush each pizza to within 1 inch of the edge with 1 tablespoon of the olive oil and sprinkle with a quarter of the dried red pepper flakes. Arrange a quarter of the Monterey Jack and mozzarella cheeses on each, and sprinkle with a quarter each of the red onion, goat cheese, and prosciutto. Sprinkle with the thyme. Bake for 10 to 12 minutes or until the crust is golden brown.

MAKES 4 PIZZAS

20 ounces pizza dough, divided into 4 equal pieces
¼ cup olive oil
1 teaspoon dried red pepper flakes, or more to taste
1 cup (4 ounces) shredded Monterey Jack cheese
2 cups (8 ounces) shredded mozzarella cheese
½ medium red onion, very thinly sliced
1 cup (4 ounces) cubed goat cheese
4 ounces prosciutto or cooked ham, very thinly sliced
1 tablespoon fresh thyme, or 1 teaspoon dried

◆

PIZZA PECORINO
MEZZOGIORNO ◆ NEW YORK, NEW YORK

MAKES TWO 13-INCH PIZZAS

SAUCE
2 tablespoons olive oil
1 medium onion, chopped
1 clove garlic, crushed
One 28-ounce can Italian
  tomatoes, with their
  juices
¼ teaspoon freshly ground
  black pepper
⅛ teaspoon crushed red
  pepper

DOUGH
2 cups all-purpose flour
1 cup whole wheat flour
1 package (¼ ounce) rapid-
  rising yeast (*Do not* use
  active dry yeast for this
  recipe.)
1½ teaspoons salt
1 cup water
2 tablespoons olive oil
Vegetable oil spray
Cornmeal

TOPPING
1 medium onion, thinly
  sliced
8 ounces Pecorino Romano
  cheese, grated

1. Preheat oven to 400° F.

FOR THE SAUCE:
2. In a sauté pan, heat the olive oil over medium heat. Add the onion and the garlic and cook until translucent, about 3 minutes. Stir in the tomatoes and the black and red pepper. Simmer until the sauce has thickened, about 30 minutes, stirring occasionally. Using a food processor or blender, puree to desired smoothness.

FOR THE DOUGH:
3. In a bowl, mix 1 cup of the all-purpose flour, 1 cup of the whole wheat flour, the yeast, and salt. Heat the water and olive oil until hot to the touch. (125° F. to 130° F.). Stir into the dry mixture. Add enough of the remaining flour to make a stiff dough. Knead lightly until smooth and elastic, about 5 minutes. Cover and let rest 10 minutes.

4. Divide dough in half. Roll and stretch each piece into a 13-inch circle. Place on 2 round pizza pans or baking sheets sprayed with vegetable oil spray and sprinkled with cornmeal, or on a baking stone. Shape edge into rim.

FOR THE TOPPINGS:
5. Top each circle with tomato sauce, sliced onion, and grated Pecorino Romano cheese. For a really crispy crust, use only a third of the sauce on each pizza and reserve a third for later use. Bake until crust is golden, about 20 to 30 minutes.

◆

PECORINO ROMANO CHEESE

The ancient Romans made dozens of different cheeses, and records clearly show that they used many of them as cooking ingredients. Pecorino Romano cheese was a regular part of the diet of the Roman legions. The soldiers carried the cheese with them as a convenient source of energy and inspiration. Italy soon became the center of cheese making.

Today Pecorino Romano is produced in Sardinia. It is a hard-grained cheese made entirely of fresh sheep's milk. It is firm enough to grate and yet soft enough to cut in slivers. The production of Pecorino Romano starts with the gathering of the flock and the milking. The milk is processed in modern Pecorino Romano facilities. When the milk reaches the plant it is placed in containers and heated. Negative bacteria are destroyed while at the same time those microorganisms essential to the making of the cheese are allowed to flourish. A starter enzyme is introduced into the milk, and a short time later, the rennet is added. The entire process is monitored by a complex computer system. The solid curds are allowed to form, after which they are broken up into small pieces. The liquid whey is then pressed out. The cheese is cut into large rectangular blocks and placed in perforated stainless-steel molds. Weights are set on top, to press out additional whey and compress the curds into their traditional shape. The cheeses are then removed from the steel containers and wrapped in a flexible form that incorporates the seal of the authentic Pecorino Romano maker. It is the stylized head of a sheep with the words Pecorino Romano *underneath. This emblem is pressed into the surface of every cheese and signals to the consumer that the product being purchased is authentic Pecorino Romano.*

Once the cheese has been removed from the mold, it goes into the ripening cellar for a six- to eight-month period. Each of the cheeses can weigh up to seventy pounds. Eighty percent of the Pecorino Romano produced in Italy is consumed by people in the United States. It is used primarily as an ingredient in cooking or as a grating cheese at the table. It supplies taste, texture, and valuable nutrients.

◆

TOMATO PIZZA
MARCH OF DIMES GOURMET GALA ◆ NEW YORK, NEW YORK

MAKES TWO 13-INCH PIZZAS

Juice of ½ lemon
2 teaspoons olive oil
¼ teaspoon cumin
¼ teaspoon oregano
Salt and freshly ground
  pepper, to taste
¼ teaspoon red pepper
  flakes
1 boneless, skinless
  chicken breast, cut into
  strips 2 inches long
½ cup cornstarch
½ cup vegetable oil

PIZZA DOUGH
1 package (¼ ounce) active
  dry yeast
¾ cup warm water (110° F.
  to 115° F.)
½ teaspoon sugar
1⅔ cups all-purpose flour
1 teaspoon salt
1 tablespoon olive oil

In 1938, President Franklin Delano Roosevelt established the National Foundation for Infantile Paralysis. The organization quickly became known as the March of Dimes, and for over fifty years it has been raising money to protect the health of people all over the world. Much of the fund raising takes place at gourmet galas, where famous folks from movies, theater, and sports cook in competition. A recent competitor was Dinah Shore. Dinah's been famous in the world of entertainment for more than half a century, and for most people, she's thought of in terms of her singing career. Well, somewhere along the way, while she was singing for her supper, she learned to cook, and some of her best cooking takes place while she's helping to raise money for the March of Dimes.

1. In a bowl, combine the lemon juice, 2 teaspoons olive oil, the cumin, oregano, salt, pepper, and the ¼ teaspoon red pepper flakes. Add chicken strips and toss to coat. Let chicken marinate for 1 hour.

2. Place the cornstarch on a plate. In a large skillet, heat the vegetable oil over medium-high heat. Dip the chicken strips in the cornstarch and fry them quickly in the oil until lightly golden on both sides. Remove the chicken from the pan, drain the pieces on paper towels, and set aside.

3. To make the pizza dough, in a bowl, combine the yeast, water, and sugar. Place the bowl in a warm place until the mixture is doubled in bulk.

4. In the container of a food processor, using the metal blade, place the flour, salt, olive oil, and yeast mixture. Process until the dough forms a soft ball.

5. Remove dough from the food processor and place on a lightly floured board. Knead for a minute or two until smooth. Cover the bowl with plastic wrap and place it in a warm place. Let the dough rise until doubled in bulk.

6. Preheat oven to 450° F.

7. Brush two 13-inch pizza tiles or 2 baking sheets with a very light coating of olive or vegetable oil. Divide the dough in half. Place half the dough on a tile or baking sheet and stretch or roll it into a circle 13 inches in diameter. Repeat with the other half of the dough. Make a small lip on the outer edge so filling will not run over.

8. Cover each pizza crust with approximately 1 cup of tomato sauce. (You can add any or all of the optional toppings listed above and dot lightly with more tomato sauce, if you like.) Sprinkle generously with mozzarella and Parmesan or Romano cheese and red pepper flakes. Dot very lightly with olive oil.

9. Bake for approximately 12 minutes or until the cheese is bubbly. Remove the pizza from the oven. Arrange the cooked chicken slices on top of the pizza. Return pizza to oven. Reduce the heat to 400° F. Bake another 5 minutes or until crust is brown and crisp.

TOPPING
Tomato Sauce (see following recipe)
Finely shredded mozzarella cheese
Finely grated Parmesan or Romano cheese
Red pepper flakes
Olive oil

OPTIONAL TOPPINGS
Green, red, and/or yellow bell peppers, thinly sliced
Fresh mushrooms, thinly sliced
Sliced pepperoni
Italian sausage, cooked, drained, and crumbled
Greek olives, pitted and thinly sliced
Capers
Finely chopped fresh basil

PIZZA WITH SMOKED SALMON AND CAVIAR

SPAGO'S ◆ HOLLYWOOD, CALIFORNIA

MAKES 4 PIZZAS

20 ounces pizza dough,
   divided into 4 equal
   pieces
¼ cup olive oil
½ medium red onion, very
   thinly sliced
½ cup sour cream
4 ounces smoked salmon
4 tablespoons black caviar
Fresh dill, for garnish

1. Preheat the oven to 500° F.

2. Roll or stretch the dough into four 8-inch circles. Place the pizzas on 2 lightly floured baking sheets. Brush each pizza crust to within 1 inch of the edge with 1 tablespoon of olive oil and sprinkle with a quarter of the red onion. Bake for 8 to 10 minutes or until the crust is golden brown.

3. Spread each crust with 2 tablespoons of the sour cream. Divide the salmon, arranging it decoratively on top. Place 1 tablespoon of the caviar in the center of each pizza and garnish with fresh dill.

OATMEAL MUFFINS

1. Preheat oven to 375° F.

2. In a bowl, combine the oats and the skim milk. Set aside for 10 minutes.

3. Add egg whites, brown sugar, melted margarine, and vanilla to soaked oat mixture. Stir to combine.

4. In a smaller bowl, combine the remaining dry ingredients. Stir the dry ingredients into the oat mixture.

5. Divide batter into 12 muffins cups sprayed with a nonstick vegetable oil spray. Bake for 20 to 25 minutes or until golden and cooked through. A toothpick or knife inserted in the center of the muffin should come out clean. Cool on a wire rack.

MAKES 12 MUFFINS

1½ cups rolled oats
1½ cups skim milk
3 egg whites
½ cup brown sugar
½ cup melted unsalted
  margarine
2 teaspoons vanilla extract
1½ cups whole wheat flour
2 teaspoons baking powder
½ teaspoon baking soda
Dash salt
¼ teaspoon cinnamon

BANANA-ORANGE MUFFINS

MAKES 12 MUFFINS

3 egg whites
½ cup brown sugar
¼ cup melted margarine
2 small ripe bananas,
  mashed
¾ cup orange juice
1½ cups whole wheat flour
2 teaspoons baking powder
½ teaspoon baking soda
Dash salt
⅛ teaspoon nutmeg

1. Preheat the oven to 375° F.

2. In a bowl, combine the egg whites, brown sugar, melted margarine, bananas, and the orange juice.

3. In a second bowl, combine the remaining dry ingredients. Stir the dry ingredients into the orange-banana mixture.

4. Divide the batter into 12 muffin cups sprayed with a nonstick vegetable oil spray, like Pam. Bake for 20 to 25 minutes until golden and cooked through. A toothpick or knife inserted in the center of the muffin should come out clean. Cool on a wire rack.

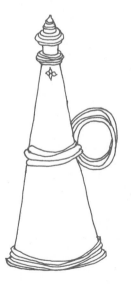

APPLE CORN MUFFINS

Kim Alexis—Her fabulous face has graced the covers of over four hundred magazines, but supermodel-actress Kim Alexis is more than just a pretty face. She's the fashion commentator for "Good Morning, America" and the host of her own television program, "Healthy Kids." But giving birth and mothering her two small sons have been her most challenging and rewarding roles.

One of Kim's favorite recipes is for Apple Corn Muffins. They contain vitamin B, folic acid, and fiber, and they're jam-packed with flavor.

1. Preheat the oven to 425° F.

2. In a large mixing bowl, combine the cornmeal, flour, baking powder, sugar, cinnamon, and salt. Mix well. Stir in the eggs, honey, and margarine. Stir just to combine. Do not overmix. Stir in the apple.

3. Fill paper-lined muffin tins two-thirds full. Bake for 20 to 25 minutes.

MAKES 12 MUFFINS

⅔ cup cornmeal
1⅓ cups unbleached
  all-purpose flour
1 tablespoon baking
  powder
2 tablespoons sugar
1 teaspoon cinnamon
½ teaspoon salt
2 eggs, lightly beaten
⅓ cup honey
⅓ cup margarine, melted
1 cup grated unpeeled
  apple

AN APPLE A DAY

There's an old saying: An apple a day keeps the doctor away. Wonder why? Well, for one thing, recent studies indicate that a single serving of fresh fruit every day can reduce your risk of stroke by up to forty percent. Also apples are high in pectin, a type of fiber that can reduce your risk of heart disease.

CORNBREAD STUFFING
AMERICAN FESTIVAL CAFÉ ◆ NEW YORK, NEW YORK

MAKES 10 CUPS

1½ cups cornmeal
2 cups all-purpose flour
2 tablespoons sugar
1 teaspoon salt
4 teaspoons baking powder
2 eggs, lightly beaten
2 cups milk
6 tablespoons vegetable oil
1 pound sausage meat
3 cups chopped onions
4 stalks celery, chopped
½ teaspoon dried sage
½ teaspoon dried thyme
½ teaspoon salt
½ teaspoon pepper
1 cup chicken broth or
  water

1. Preheat oven to 450° F.

2. Grease two 8-inch-square baking pans. In a mixing bowl, combine the cornmeal, flour, sugar, salt, and baking powder together, then stir in the eggs, milk, and 4 tablespoons of the vegetable oil until well mixed. Spread this batter in the baking pans and bake for 30 minutes. Cool, then crumble the cornbread.

3. Reduce oven temperature to 325° F.

4. In a skillet, over medium-low heat, cook sausage meat until golden and cooked thoroughly. Break up pieces with a fork. If you use link sausage, chop the sausage before cooking. Sauté onions and celery in the remaining 2 tablespoons vegetable oil until tender, about 5 minutes.

5. In a bowl, combine sausage meat, onions and celery, crumbled cornbread, sage, thyme, salt, and pepper. Use this mixture to stuff a turkey, or place the stuffing in a 9-×-13-inch baking pan or an ovenproof casserole. If you are baking the mixture in a pan or casserole, sprinkle it with chicken stock or water and bake for 30 minutes.

CHESTNUT AND APPLE STUFFING
AMERICAN FESTIVAL CAFÉ ◆ NEW YORK, NEW YORK

The idea of stuffing one food inside another goes back as far as gastronomic history has been able to trace. In the United States, the most common stuffings have been made with bread, and the customary place for them to be stuffed is in the cavity of a turkey. During the 1880s, modest Victorians suggested that the word "stuffing" carried vulgar overtones and replaced it with the word "dressing."

1. Preheat oven to 325° F.

2. Cook the bacon in a skillet over medium heat until crisp. With a slotted spoon, remove the bacon to a bowl. Pour all but 2 tablespoons of bacon fat from the skillet. Add the celery, scallions, and chestnuts and cook over medium heat until vegetables are softened, about 5 minutes.

3. Place bacon and sautéed vegetables in a bowl. Add the cider, egg yolks, and pepper. Mix. Add bread and toss until liquid is absorbed. Mix in the apples.

4. Place in a 9-×-13-inch baking pan or an ovenproof casserole and bake for 45 minutes.

MAKES ABOUT 8 CUPS

5 thick slices bacon, cut into ½-inch pieces
1 cup diced celery
½ cup sliced scallions
1 cup canned chestnuts, coarsely chopped
3 cups apple cider
2 egg yolks
½ teaspoon freshly ground black pepper
10 cups of bite-sized pieces of stale bread
2 unpeeled apples, cored and coarsely chopped

ABOUT BLUEBERRIES

The first settlers that came to the Northwest arrived in the late fall. The growing season was over and the trees and bushes were empty, so the settlers didn't get to see all the wonderful foods that nature made available until the next spring. But when they did get a look at what was growing in their valley they thought they had truly come to the Garden of Eden. The Native American tribes that had been here for thousands of years already knew they were in Eden and had a vast collection of stories about the natural foods. They were particularly fascinated with the blueberry because of the five-pointed star on top. They believed that the Great Spirit had sent the blueberry down from the skies to help their people get through a difficult time.

Blueberries are still an important crop in the Northwest. Popular too. Wash them and they're ready to eat; or put them into a container, seal it, and store in a 0° F. freezer. They'll last up to two years. They're a good source of vitamin C and have about ninety calories in a cup.

The only problem that the early settlers had with the wild blueberries came from bears. Bears love blueberries and they would compete with the farmers for the crop. Nothing like coming face to face with a six hundred-pound grizzly to give you a thrill on blueberry hill.

BLUEBERRY SCONES
B. MOLOCH/HEATHMAN BAKERY & PUB ◆ PORTLAND, OREGON

1. Preheat the oven to 375° F.

2. In a mixing bowl, combine the flour, sugar, cornmeal, and baking powder. Cut up the margarine or butter into ¼-inch cubes and, using your fingertips, squeeze the butter into the dry ingredients until you have a well-blended mealy mixture.

3. Add the buttermilk or yogurt to the mixture. Add the blueberries, mixing to incorporate. The dough will be slightly sticky. If it is too sticky to handle, add a small amount of flour.

4. Divide the dough in half, shape into 1-inch-thick disks. Place on a buttered baking sheet. Brush with the beaten egg, then cut a deep X into the top of each scone. Bake for 20 to 30 minutes until golden brown.

MAKES 8 SCONES

1 cup all-purpose flour
¼ cup sugar
½ cup yellow cornmeal
1 tablespoon baking
  powder
⅔ cup chilled margarine or
  butter
⅓ cup buttermilk or yogurt
¾ cup fresh or frozen
  blueberries
1 egg, beaten

BREAKFAST CAN MAKE YOU SMARTER

There's a study that clearly indicates that children who have a well-balanced breakfast do much better on standard intelligence tests than kids who don't.

HOW COFFEE CAME TO EUROPE

For one thousand years, Vienna has been a bridge between Europe and the Near East. Its culture and its cuisine have been influenced by both areas. Coffee is a perfect example of what I mean. Coffee originated in Ethiopia, in a town called Kaffa. By the sixth century, Arab communities in the area were cultivating coffee. The Muslim sect called the Dervishes loved the stuff. They discovered that when they drank coffee, they had more energy and they were able to stay up longer. That gave them more time at prayer, so they assumed it was a gift from their god. They called it kahveh.

In 1683, Muslim armies attacked Vienna. When their siege failed and they headed back to the Near East, they left behind sacks and sacks of coffee beans. The Viennese discovered them, figured out how to brew the coffee, and set up their first coffeehouse right then and there.

After a while, the Indonesian port city of Java became a major export point and Americans took up the word "java" as a slang expression for what became our national drink. We consume over a half-billion cups of coffee every single day.

◆

MAKING A PERFECT CUP OF TEA

Tea experts agree that there are a number of things you should do to make a good cup of tea. First of all, you want fresh water. Water that has been standing around for a long time or that comes out of the hot water tap doesn't have very much oxygen, and it is oxygen that gives tea it's excellent flavor. Second, when you put the water and the tea together, you don't want it to stay together for more than three minutes. Longer than that and the water will draw out bitter tannins and acids that don't taste good and are unhealthful. Finally, if you use a tea infuser or a tea bag, don't bounce it up and down. That will make the tea bitter. And if you're going to use a tea bag, please don't use it more than once.

◆

DESSERTS

PEACH MELBA
THE RITZ HOTEL ◆ *PARIS, FRANCE*

MAKES 8 SERVINGS

RASPBERRY SAUCE
One 10-ounce package
  frozen raspberries,
  thawed
2 tablespoons sugar
3 tablespoons raspberry
  liqueur (optional)

One 16-ounce can halved
  peaches, well drained, or
  fresh pitted peaches, if
  available
2 pints vanilla ice cream

Nellie Melba was a famous singer in the late 1800s. One of her regular roles was in Wagner's opera Lohengrin. A particular scene in this work presented a sculpture of a swan floating across the stage with Miss Melba sitting on top. This part of the opera was much beloved by a distinguished chef of the time by the name of Auguste Escoffier, and it inspired him to create a dessert for the great Nellie. In its original presentation, the dessert consisted of a swan made of ice, supporting peaches and vanilla ice cream, topped with berries. Nellie loved it and ordered it quite often. Eventually it took its toll on poor Nellie's figure, which led Escoffier to develop Melba Toast, as a low-calorie counterbalance. For many years, Escoffier worked at The Ritz Hotel in Paris. Located in the majestic Place Vendôme, it is one of the most sumptuous hotels in the world, and as befits an institution of such standing, it has had in residence some of France's leading chefs.

1. To make the sauce, puree the raspberries and sugar in the container of a food processor. Add the liqueur and chill, or use immediately.

2. In a single-serving dish, place a half a peach, cut side up.

3. Top the peach with a scoop of vanilla ice cream and pour some of the raspberry sauce on top. Serve immediately.

DIALOGUE OF FRUITS
HOTEL NASSAUER HOF ◆WIESBADEN, GERMANY

This is a very refreshing low-calorie dessert that comes from the kitchens of Hans Peter Vadat at the Hotel Nassauer Hof in Wiesbaden, Germany.

1. Choose 3 or 4 of the fruits that contrast in color, such as mangos, pears, and strawberries.

2. In the container of a food processor or blender, separately puree each type of fruit until it is smooth. Wash out the container between fruits. If apples, bananas, or pears are used, add 1 teaspoon of lemon juice to the fruit while pureeing to prevent discoloration.

3. Place about ¼ cup of each fruit puree side by side in a shallow, single-serving dish. Lightly tap the bottom of each dish to settle the purees. With a knife or a chopstick, swirl the fruit purees into a colorful pattern. Garnish each serving with a whole berry.

MAKES 6 SERVINGS

ANY 3 OR 4 OF THE FOLLOWING FRUITS:

2 large ripe mangos, peeled and pitted

2 large ripe papayas, peeled and seeded

4 ripe kiwis, peeled and seeded

3 apples, peeled, cored, and poached until tender

3 ripe bananas, peeled

3 ripe pears, peeled and cored

3 cups berries (strawberries, blueberries, or raspberries)

Fresh lemon juice

6 whole berries, for garnish

CITRUS TERRINE
THE PLAZA HOTEL ◆ NEW YORK, NEW YORK

MAKES 12 SERVINGS

Two 1-ounce envelopes of
  unflavored gelatin
⅜ cup cold water
One 26-ounce jar citrus
  salad, drained on paper
  towels, 1 cup of liquid
  reserved
¼ cup orange juice
Juice of 2 lemons
5 tablespoons sugar

1. Sprinkle the gelatin on the surface of the ⅜ cup cold
water to soften.

2. In a medium saucepan, bring the reserved citrus salad
liquid, the orange juice, the lemon juice, and the sugar to a
boil. Remove from the heat and stir in the gelatin until
dissolved.

3. Arrange decoratively the drained citrus salad in an
8½-×-4½-×-2½-inch loaf pan. Carefully pour the gelatin
mixture over the fruit. Place the pan in the refrigerator,
covered, overnight.

4. To unmold, slide a knife around the edge to release the
vacuum. Place a serving platter on the top of the pan and
invert. If the gelatin does not release, place a warm towel
around the inverted pan. Cut the terrine in slices and serve.

STUFFED APPLES
LE CIRQUE ◆ NEW YORK, NEW YORK

1. Preheat the oven to 350° F.

2. Core the apples. Hollow out the center from 4 of them, reserving their tops. Peel the remaining 2 apples and slice into rings. Place the rings on a baking sheet that has been sprayed lightly with vegetable oil. Place the 4 hollowed-out apples, with their tops in place, on the baking sheet. Bake the apples for 45 minutes.

3. When the apples are ready, in a large sauté pan, heat the margarine over medium-high heat. Add the walnuts, dates, figs, vanilla extract, brown sugar, and apple juice. Stir until the sugar dissolves and the mixture begins to boil. Cook for 2 minutes more.

4. Divide the apple rings among 4 dessert plates and arrange in a circle. Place a whole apple in the center of each plate. Spoon some of the fruit-nut filling into each hollowed-out apple. Replace the tops. If there is additional filling, spoon over the slices.

MAKES 4 SERVINGS

6 yellow or other baking
  apples
1 tablespoon margarine
½ cup chopped walnuts
½ cup chopped dates
½ cup chopped dried figs
¼ teaspoon vanilla extract
¼ cup brown sugar
¼ cup apple juice

NORWEGIAN HOT APPLE DESSERT
SAS HOTEL ◆ OSLO, NORWAY

MAKES 4 SERVINGS

Juice of 1 lemon
3 large Golden Delicious
 apples
½ cup water
½ cup sugar
1 teaspoon cinnamon
½ cup raisins
4 tablespoons (½ stick)
 butter or margarine
Basic Vanilla Sauce, for
 serving (see following
 recipe)

1. Place the lemon juice in a large bowl.

2. Peel, core, and slice the apples about ½ inch thick and place them in the bowl with the lemon juice. Toss well and set aside.

3. In a large skillet, combine the water, sugar, cinnamon, and raisins. Over high heat, stir this mixture constantly so that the sugar will caramelize without sticking to the pan. This will take approximately 5 to 7 minutes. The mixture will thicken and be caramel in color.

4. Whisk in the butter and add the apple slices, stirring gently but constantly. The apples will give off some juice and cause the liquid to thin out. After about 6 minutes, the juice will evaporate and the sauce will thicken again.

5. On a dessert plate, place a portion of Basic Vanilla Sauce and arrange a quarter of the apple slices in a fanned-out wheel on top of the sauce. Drizzle a little of the caramel over the apples and top with some of the raisins. Serve warm.

BASIC VANILLA SAUCE

1. In a small saucepan over medium heat, bring the milk to a simmer.

2. Meanwhile, in a medium bowl, whisk the egg yolks and the sugar together until a ribbon forms when the whisk is lifted from the mixture.

3. Whisk constantly while slowly pouring the hot milk into the yolk-sugar mixture.

4. Return the mixture to the saucepan. Over low heat, stir constantly with a wooden spoon until the mixture thickens. Be careful not to overcook or the eggs will scramble. The sauce is finished when you can dip a spoon into it, then draw your finger over the back of the spoon and have a track remain that is almost free of sauce.

5. Remove the sauce from the heat and stir in the vanilla. Serve, or chill and use later.

MAKES 1 CUP

1 cup milk
3 egg yolks
8 tablespoons sugar
1 tablespoon vanilla extract

IRISH APPLE CRUMBLE
JURY'S HOTEL ◆ DUBLIN, IRELAND

MAKES 8 SERVINGS

Pastry dough to fit an
  8-inch pie pan
4 medium Granny Smith or
  Red Delicious apples,
  peeled, cored, and
  coarsely chopped
¾ cup plus 1 tablespoon
  sugar
½ teaspoon cinnamon
½ cup all-purpose flour
4 tablespoons (½ stick)
  unsalted butter, softened

1. Preheat the oven to 350° F.

2. Line an 8-inch pie pan or heatproof baking dish with the pie dough. Prick the dough with the tines of a fork.

3. In a bowl, mix together the apples, ¼ cup of the sugar, and ¼ teaspoon of the cinnamon.

4. In a second bowl, mix together the flour, ½ cup of the sugar, and the butter. Work these ingredients together with a fork until you have a crumbly mixture.

5. Fill the pie crust with the apple mixture and smooth over the surface. Spoon the crumble over the apple mixture so that the apples are completely covered. Sprinkle the remaining tablespoon of sugar and ¼ teaspoon of cinnamon over the crumble

6. Bake for 25 minutes.

STICKY MEASURING

When you have to measure honey, molasses, corn syrup, or other sticky liquids, coat the surface of the measuring tool with a little butter, margarine, or corn oil. The sticky liquid will all pour out easily, and you will have a more accurate measure.

BAKED OREGON APPLES
COLUMBIA GORGE HOTEL ◆ COLUMBIA RIVER GORGE, OREGON

Oregon's Columbia Gorge Hotel, built in 1921, remains one of America's finest country inns. It sits on a cliff overlooking a spectacular landscape, and it keeps up a hundred-year-old gastronomic custom.

The early pioneers who settled in this part of the country had a life filled with heavy work. The time pressure of the day pretty much did away with a lunch break. Breakfast became the most important meal, and that tradition lives on. If you watch people eat breakfast around here, you get the feeling that they are on their way to a day on the trail. The Columbia Gorge breakfast consists of fruits, fritters, oatmeal, biscuits with honey, eggs, smoked pork chops, bacon, sausages, potatoes, pancakes, and their famous Baked Oregon Apples. And that's not a list you choose from; you get it all.

MAKES 6 SERVINGS

¾ cup light brown sugar
1 teaspoon cinnamon
¼ teaspoon nutmeg
⅓ cup raisins
⅓ cup cinnamon red-hot candies
1 tablespoon butter or margarine, for buttering the baking pan
6 unpeeled baking apples, cored
½ cup maple syrup

1. Preheat the oven to 350° F.

2. Mix together the sugar, cinnamon, nutmeg, raisins, and red-hot candies. Set aside.

3. Lightly butter a baking pan and place the apples in it. Divide the filling mixture in 6 parts and fill each apple. Pour the maple syrup over the apples and bake for 35 to 40 minutes or until tender.

VIENNESE APPLE STRUDEL
HOTEL IMPERIAL ◆ VIENNA, AUSTRIA

MAKES 2 STRUDELS,
12 SERVINGS

2 pounds McIntosh apples,
   peeled, cored, and sliced
   thin
½ cup granulated sugar
1 tablespoon cinnamon
Juice of 1 lemon
1 cup golden raisins
½ cup chopped walnuts
12 sheets phyllo dough,
   defrosted, if frozen
6 tablespoons melted
   margarine or butter
1 cup cookie crumbs
   (ground vanilla wafers)
Confectioners sugar

Vienna's Hotel Imperial is situated on the main street that rings the old city. A magnificent structure on the outside, it is even more impressive on the inside. The grand staircase invites you up to the imperial chambers; Old World luxury on the surface, modern technology underneath. The royal suite gives you a clear idea of what life was like at the tippy-tippy top.

The hotel's restaurant is a favorite dining spot for serious eaters, and the chef has given a light creative touch to traditional Austrian fare. What could be more traditional for Vienna than a piece of Viennese Apple Strudel? Strudel is at the heart of Austrian cooking, and what a sweet heart it is too.

1. Preheat the oven to 375° F. and grease a baking sheet (or spray with nonstick spray).

2. In a large bowl, combine the apples, granulated sugar, cinnamon, lemon juice, raisins, and walnuts. Mix well and set aside.

3. Unwrap the phyllo, but keep it covered with plastic wrap or a damp towel to avoid drying out. On a sheet of plastic wrap or wax paper, lay down one sheet of phyllo, with the narrow end facing you. Brush with melted margarine or butter, working as quickly as possible. Top with 5 more sheets of phyllo, brushing each with margarine or butter. Sprinkle about ¼ cup of the cookie crumbs over the entire surface of the dough. Place half the apple mixture along the narrow end of the dough facing you. It should only cover about a quarter of the entire surface. Leave a 1-inch margin on each of three sides. Sprinkle another ¼ cup of the crumbs over the apples.

4. Using the plastic wrap or wax paper, roll the strudel up and away from yourself. You should be able to roll it over about 3 times. Roll it onto half the baking sheet. Press the ends together to seal.

5. Repeat this process with the remaining phyllo, apple mixture, and cookie crumbs.

6. Brush strudel with melted margarine and bake for 35 minutes or until golden.

7. Allow to cool slightly on cooling rack, then sift confectioners sugar over strudel and serve.

VIENNA'S SWEET TOOTH

To understand how the people of Vienna feel about sweets, all you have to do is look into a classic old Viennese cookbook. You'll find that about twenty percent of the recipes are devoted to appetizers, soups, and main dishes; the other eighty percent are for sweets, baked goods, and desserts. In the old days of the Austrian Empire, every household that could afford one had a woman who baked sweet goods and that's all. Even today, Vienna is the center of the world of pastry.

GRANOLA FLAN WITH FRESH FRUIT SAUCE
CHÂTEAU WHISTLER RESORT ♦ WHISTLER, BRITISH COLUMBIA, CANADA

MAKES 4 SERVINGS

2 cups granola, pulsed in
   food processor to break
   down lumps
½ cup honey
1 cup sliced strawberries
1 ripe papaya, peeled,
   seeded, and cut into
   chunks
2 small bananas, peeled
   and cut up
⅓ cup orange juice

GARNISHES
Whole strawberries
Papaya slices
Sprigs of mint

Located at the base of two world-class ski mountains, the Château Whistler is the ideal splash-down area when returning to earth. The château takes you back to a time when hotels were built by people in love with their craft. Included in the Château Whistler's works of art are the creations of Executive Chef Bernard Casavant. The following is his recipe for a Granola Flan with Fresh Fruit Sauce.

1. Preheat the oven to 350° F. Grease an 8-inch pie pan.

2. Combine the granola and honey in a bowl. Mix thoroughly and press into the pan firmly to obtain an even, compact layer. Bake for 10 minutes. Remove the pan to a rack to cool.

3. Combine the fruit and orange juice in the container of a food processor and puree. Press through a strainer to make the sauce as smooth as possible. Chill until ready to serve.

4. Place some of the sauce on a serving plate and place a slice of the granola flan on top. Garnish with whole strawberries, papaya slices, and a sprig of mint.

APPLE OAT CRISP

1. Preheat the oven to 350° F. Butter an 8-×8-inch baking dish. In a medium mixing bowl, combine all the filling ingredients. Pour into the baking dish.

2. In a second medium mixing bowl, combine all the topping ingredients. Cover the filling with the oat mixture.

3. Bake for 40 minutes or until the topping is lightly browned and the apples are tender.

MAKES 8 SERVINGS

FILLING
6 apples, peeled, cored, and sliced
1 cup raisins
½ cup apple or orange juice
3 tablespoons fresh lemon juice
2 tablespoons all-purpose flour
1 teaspoon cinnamon

TOPPING
1½ cups rolled oats
½ cup all-purpose flour
½ cup brown sugar
½ cup melted unsalted butter
2 teaspoons cinnamon
½ teaspoon salt

ABOUT BROWN SUGAR

Brown sugar, in most cases, is white refined sugar with molasses added to it. In England, it is common to find turbinado, West Indian, or Barbados sugar. All these are coarse granulated brown sugar in which some molasses is naturally present.

The best way to store leftover brown sugar is in an airtight container. Add a slice of apple or a lettuce leaf to it before closing it up. The moisture in the apple or lettuce will help keep the moist texture that you find in fresh brown sugar.

You can also use this technique to soften brown sugar that has hardened. You can soften hard brown sugar immediately in a blender or food processor.

For most recipes, pack brown sugar firmly when you measure it.

THREE BERRY COBBLER
JAKE'S RESTAURANT ◆ PORTLAND, OREGON

MAKES 4 SERVINGS

1 cup strawberries
1 cup blueberries
1 cup raspberries
3 tablespoons sugar
2 tablespoons cornstarch
  mixed with 2 tablespoons
  cold water
1 tablespoon fresh lemon
  juice
Prepared pie dough to
  yield one 9-inch pie crust

GARNISHES
Whipped cream, ice
  cream, or low-fat frozen
  yogurt

Jake's Restaurant in downtown Portland was named after Jake Freiman, a deeply beloved waiter who worked here during the early years of this century. The place has a fascinating collection of memorabilia from its past, dating back to 1892. The kitchen specializes in dishes prepared from the local products of the Northwest. When it comes to desserts, their principal attraction is their Three Berry Cobbler.

1. Preheat the oven to 350° F.

2. Combine the berries and the sugar in a saucepan over medium heat. Cook for about 10 minutes or until juices are released.

3. Add the cornstarch mixture and blend. Stir in the lemon juice.

4. Ladle into 4 individual custard cups or one 9-inch pie pan or casserole. Cut out pie dough disks, or one large disk, to fit over the berry mixture. Place the disk of pie dough on top of the berry mixture and put the dish on a baking sheet to catch any spills. Bake for 20 minutes or until the crust is golden. Before serving, top with any of the garnishes.

BERRY COBBLER
RHETT'S RESTAURANT ◆ NASHVILLE, TENNESSEE

Audiences worldwide have loved "Little Miss Dynamite," Brenda Lee, ever since her first hit single "Jambalaya." She's delighted fans at a royal command performance for Queen Elizabeth and played to standing-room-only crowds in Japan for seventeen years. She's a megastar whose worldwide record sales have surpassed the one hundred million mark. Brenda Lee has single-handedly sold more albums than any other female vocalist. We were invited along to sample one of Brenda's sweet Southern recipes, Berry Cobbler, at Rhett's Restaurant.

MAKES 4 SERVINGS

2 cups fresh or frozen, thawed, strawberries, sliced
2 cups fresh or frozen, thawed, blueberries
1 cup all-purpose flour
1 teaspoon baking powder
1 cup sugar
1 cup buttermilk
2 tablespoons margarine, melted
Frozen yogurt and fresh berries, to garnish

1. Preheat the oven to 350° F.

2. In a sauté pan over high heat, combine the strawberries and blueberries and cook until warm, approximately 2 minutes. Divide among 4 buttered ramekins or ovenproof dishes, about 4½ inches in diameter.

3. In a mixing bowl, combine the flour, baking powder, sugar, buttermilk, and margarine. Stir until combined. Spoon evenly over the berry mixture.

4. Place the ramekins on a cookie sheet and bake for 45 minutes.

5. Serve topped with frozen yogurt and fresh berries.

◆

CHOCOLATE BREATHLESS
WINDSOR COURT HOTEL ◆ NEW ORLEANS, LOUISIANA

MAKES 12 SERVINGS

MOUSSE
1 pound semisweet
  chocolate, broken into
  pieces
4 large eggs, separated
⅓ cup water
⅓ cup dark rum
3 cups heavy cream
⅓ cup granulated sugar

MERINGUE
7 large egg whites
¾ cup granulated sugar
1 heaping cup plus 2
  tablespoons confectioners
  sugar
¾ cup unsweetened cocoa
  powder

FOR THE MOUSSE:

1. Place the chocolate in the top half of a double boiler over simmering water to melt. Place the 4 egg yolks in a large bowl, add the water and the rum and whisk to blend thoroughly. Stir in the melted chocolate.

2. Whip the cream until it forms stiff peaks. Set aside.

3. In a medium bowl, beat the 4 egg whites until foamy. Add the sugar and continue to beat until the mixture forms stiff peaks. Fold the beaten egg whites into the chocolate mixture, then fold in the whipped cream. Refrigerate until ready to serve.

FOR THE MERINGUE:
4. Preheat the oven to 150° F.

5. In a large bowl, beat the 7 egg whites until foamy. Add the granulated sugar and continue to beat until the mixture forms stiff peaks. Sift together the heaping cup of confectioners sugar and the cocoa, then fold gently into the egg whites. Do not overmix. Spoon the mixture into a pastry bag fitted with a plain ½-inch tube. (If a pastry bag is unavailable, use a tablespoon).

6. Line 2 baking sheets with parchment or wax paper. Pipe thirty-six 2-inch disks, or place heaping tablespoonfuls of meringue onto the sheets, about an inch apart. Pipe long lines with the rest of the meringue. Place in the preheated oven, with the oven door left open 1 inch, and bake for about 1½ hours or until firm. Remove from the oven and let cool. (The chocolate meringues can be made a day in advance and stored in a dry, airtight container until ready to serve.)

7. Chop the meringue lines into ½-inch pieces and set aside.

8. Place a meringue disk on a flat work surface and top with a layer of chocolate mousse. Add another meringue disk, then more mousse. Complete the stack with another meringue. Frost the top and sides of the stack with mousse, then sprinkle chopped meringue pieces on top. Repeat the assembly with the remaining meringue disks, making 12 servings in all.

9. Place one Breathless on each of 12 individual-serving plates and dust the tops lightly with the remaining 2 tablespoons confectioners sugar. Serve immediately.

CHOCOLATE AND HEALTH

From our earliest contact with chocolate, we have thought of it as a food or drink that fortifies the gastronomic soul. But from time to time it has gotten an unfair rap. For many years, skin specialists thought that there might be some sort of relationship between skin problems like acne and chocolate. Not so, say researchers from the University of Pennsylvania School of Medicine.

And as far as chocolate and tooth decay is concerned, the most recent studies show that cocoa may actually have an inhibiting effect on the formation of dental cavities.

◆

RICE PUDDING WITH FRESH FRUIT

THE CULINARY INSTITUTE OF AMERICA ◆
HYDE PARK, NEW YORK

MAKES 8 SERVINGS

1 cup converted rice
3 cups water
1 cup raisins
¼ teaspoon nutmeg
¼ teaspoon cinnamon
⅓ cup sugar
1 tablespoon fresh lemon
  juice
¾ cup part-skim ricotta
  cheese, pureed
2 teaspoons vanilla extract
3 cups sliced fresh fruit

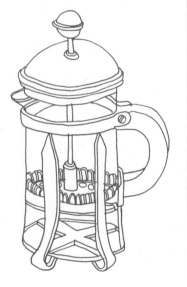

The Culinary Institute of America, in Hyde Park, New York, is one of the leading schools for the training of professional chefs. Each year their graduates are taken into the kitchens of great restaurants throughout the world. Francis Lopez is a chef instructor at the institute, and the following is his family recipe for Rice Pudding with Fresh Fruit.

1. In a large saucepan, combine the rice, water, raisins, nutmeg, cinnamon, sugar, and lemon juice. Stir to combine. Cover and bring to a simmer. Cook until the rice is tender, approximately 30 to 40 minutes. Remove from the heat and let stand, covered, for 5 to 10 minutes until the water is absorbed. Let cool. Fold in the ricotta cheese and vanilla extract.

2. Mold in individual molds and turn out onto a serving plate, or place a ½-cup mound in the center of 8 dessert plates. Surround with fresh fruit.

SUMMER PUDDING

THE EMPRESS HOTEL ◆ VANCOUVER ISLAND, BRITISH COLUMBIA, CANADA

1. Combine the sugar and water in a heavy saucepan, bring to a simmer over high heat. Simmer until liquid is clear and all the sugar has dissolved.

2. Place all the berries in another saucepan. Pour the sugar syrup over the fruit and bring to a simmer over high heat.

3. Drain the berries, reserving the liquid. Quickly chill ¼ cup of the liquid, either over ice or in the freezer. Reserve the remaining fruit juice.

4. Sprinkle the gelatin over the ¼ cup chilled fruit juice and let it dissolve. Combine with the reserved fruit juice.

5. Line a 4- to 6-cup bowl with plastic wrap. Dip the slices of bread, one at a time, into the fruit juice-gelatin liquid and, starting with the bottom of the bowl, line the inside of the bowl with them, overlapping slightly.

6. Fill the center with the berry mixture, fold the dipped bread over the top of the filling, using more bread (dipped in the fruit juice-gelatin liquid) to completely cover the top of the berry mixture. Fold the plastic wrap over the top of the bread and press lightly to compact the filling. Refrigerate for at least 8 hours.

7. Unmold the pudding, peel off the plastic wrap. Glaze with the strained, warm strawberry jam.

MAKES 6 SERVINGS

1 cup sugar
3 cups water
1 cup fresh or frozen strawberries
2 cups fresh or frozen raspberries
1 cup fresh or frozen blueberries
Two 1-ounce envelopes Knox unflavored gelatin
10 to 12 slices white bread, cut in half, crusts removed
½ cup strawberry jam, heated and strained

◆

ABOUT CANEBERRIES

When the first wagon trains crossed the continent and arrived in the Northwest, the farmers soon realized that they had come into one of the world's most unique agricultural environments. The soil is extremely fertile, but it also drains well. Good spring rains come at just the right time in the growing cycle; summer days are warm, but summer nights are cool. It's an unusual collection of environmental factors that produces one of the few places on the planet where caneberries can grow.

Each year a caneberry plant will produce a long leafy cane. The following year that cane will be covered with berries. The most common caneberries are raspberries, blackberries, boysenberries, loganberries, and marionberries.

A cup of these berries has an average calorie content of about sixty. That same cup will also have fifty percent of the recommended daily allowance for vitamin C, and the raspberry gives you more fiber for the calories than any of our common foods.

The more research that comes in from the scientific community, the more we see how important fiber is to our good health. The caneberry is a food you can lean on to help you increase your fiber intake.

◆

LEMONY BANANA FROZEN YOGURT

1. In the container of a blender or food processor, combine the very ripe bananas and the brown sugar and puree.

2. Add the banana puree and lemon zest to the yogurt.

3. Cut the just-ripe bananas into quarters lengthwise and then into ¼-inch-thick slices. Add the slices to the yogurt mixture.

4. Refrigerate for 1 hour, then freeze in an ice cream freezer according to the manufacturer's instructions.

MAKES 1 QUART

2 very ripe bananas
½ cup loosely packed dark
  brown sugar
1 tablespoon grated lemon
  zest
1 quart plain low-fat yogurt
2 just-ripe bananas

THE SWEET TASTE OF SURVIVAL

There is an interesting historical reason why most people like sweets. In the wild, most things that taste sweet are safe to eat; most things that taste bitter are dangerous. So those of our early ancestors who loved sweets, in moderation, had a better chance of survival, and we have descended from them.

CHOCOLATE TRUFFLES

MAKES ABOUT
24 TRUFFLES

⅓ cup heavy cream
2 tablespoons unsalted
  butter
6 ounces milk chocolate,
  coarsely chopped
4 ounces bittersweet or
  dark chocolate, coarsely
  chopped
Unsweetened cocoa
  powder, finely chopped
  nuts, or confectioners
  sugar

1. In a small saucepan or the top of a double boiler over simmering water, heat the cream and butter until the butter is melted and the mixture just starts to come to a boil. Remove from the heat and add the milk chocolate. Stir until the chocolate is melted.

2. Cover and chill in the freezer until firm, approximately 1 hour.

3. With a pastry bag, or with two spoons, form small balls of the chilled chocolate mixture and place on a parchment-paper-lined cookie sheet. Let chill in the refrigerator for 1 hour until firm.

4. In a small saucepan over simmering water, melt the bittersweet chocolate. Dip the truffles in the melted chocolate and roll in the cocoa powder, chopped nuts, or confectioners sugar. Return the coated truffles to the cookie sheet and refrigerate for 30 minutes. Serve immediately, or store in an airtight container until needed.

ABOUT CHOCOLATE

The Mayans believed that after the demise of a good person, his spirit would dwell in the gentle shade of the cacao tree, and chocolate would be available to drink forever. Cortés was the first European to taste chocolate, and he quickly sent it back to Spain, where it became a drink of major importance. The Spanish loved it so much and valued it so highly that they kept chocolate a secret for over a hundred years.

The cacoa tree thrives in the hot, moist climate of the jungle. The beans develop inside a pod that hangs from the bark of the tree. The ideal spot is at the edge of a tropical rain forest. There you have the heat, the humidity, and the rich soil that are necessary. The tree grows to twenty or thirty feet, but is very delicate.

The pod is harvested, opened, and the beans removed. They ferment for a while in the heat of the jungle; then they're dried and shipped off to a chocolate factory. The beans are roasted, cracked into small nibs, and pureed into a liquid. The liquid is put under an enormous amount of pressure—six thousand pounds per square inch. That separates the liquid cocoa butter from the solids, which are now called cocoa. Mix the cocoa powder together with lots of cocoa butter and some sugar and you've got a chocolate paste. Smooth that chocolate paste out with rollers, mix it together to a nice consistency in the conching process, and you're ready to make a chocolate bar.

◆

A GOOD WORD ON MILK

Archaeological evidence suggests that cattle were domesticated some eight thousand years ago, and that dairying has been going on for about five thousand years.

Milk is an unusual food. Like eggs and seeds, milk is designed to sustain life during an early growth period. It contains the essential elements for survival.

Recently, however, various questions have been raised about milk and milk products. Almost all of the talk surrounds cholesterol. Cholesterol is a fatty acid that can build up in your circulatory system and cause heart disease, and milk contains cholesterol.

Taken at face value, that information could drastically reduce your milk consumption . . . which would be a shame since milk is really packed with valuable nutrients, especially calcium, which is so important in protecting us from the bone disease osteoporosis. The solution to the problem is very simple: use milk and milk products that have had the fat removed.

Low-fat milk products are skim milk, buttermilk, 1% milkfat milk, skimmed-milk cheeses, uncreamed low-fat cottage cheese, and low-fat yogurt.

With skim milk products, you get all of the valuable nutrients in milk, with very little fat or cholesterol. A cup of skim milk has only ninety calories and so does an equal amount of apple. Low-fat milk and milk products can still be a very important part of a good diet.

ABOUT CALCIUM

Children need calcium. It's essential for building strong bones and teeth during the growth years of childhood and beyond. Since our bodies don't manufacture calcium, it must be replenished every day through the foods we eat. Calcium is readily available in foods like macaroni and cheese, pizza, milk, and ice cream. It's also available in some fruit juices like Citrus Hill orange juice. Which is good news for parents who struggle with ways to give children good nutrition in foods they like.

CAKES

SWEDISH APPLE CAKE
OPERAKALLAREN RESTAURANT ◆ STOCKHOLM, SWEDEN

MAKES 8 SERVINGS

3 tablespoons milk
3 large eggs
1 teaspoon almond extract
½ teaspoon vanilla extract
1½ cups all-purpose flour
¾ cup granulated sugar
1 teaspoon baking powder
¼ teaspoon salt
¾ cup (1½ sticks) butter
2 large baking apples,
  peeled, cored, and cut in
  half horizontally
½ cup lingonberry jam
Confectioners sugar, for
  dusting

Stockholm is packed with excellent hotels, great shopping, and some of the best restaurants in Europe. The Operakallaren Restaurant was opened a little over two hundred years ago and has been a gastronomic landmark from the start. Operakallaren is home to one of Europe's leading chefs . . . Werner Vogeli, and this is his recipe.

1. Preheat the oven to 350° F.

2. In a bowl, combine the milk, eggs, and the almond and vanilla extracts.

3. In a second bowl, combine the dry ingredients. Add the butter and half of the milk-egg mixture. Using an electric mixer at low speed, blend until the dry ingredients are moistened, about 1½ minutes. Using a spatula, scrape down the sides of the bowl. Add the remaining milk-egg mixture. Mix at medium speed for 2 minutes.

4. Butter a 9-inch cake pan and lightly dust with flour.

5. Pour the batter into the pan. Carefully place the apple halves, flat side down, in the pan. Spoon out cake batter from the holes left by the removal of the apple cores and add it to the batter in the pan. Spoon 2 tablespoons of jam into each of the holes.

6. Bake the cake for 45 minutes or until golden brown.

7. Let cool. Lightly dust the cake with confectioners sugar before serving.

ABOUT THE APPLE

From our earliest colonial days, the apple has been an important fruit for Americans. We eat them raw, baked, stewed, juiced, and pureed.

The apple has a long and special history. It is a member of the rose family and often used as a symbol for all other fruits. Very often when new fruits were discovered they were called apples until they were given their own names. Among the foods that were once called apples are the avocado, the cashew, the date, the eggplant, the lemon, the melon, the orange, the peach, the pineapple, and the potato. The French word for potato is pomme de terre, *which translates to "apple from the earth."*

Although most people do not realize it, there is no mention of the apple in the Genesis chapter of the Bible, which says only that Eve tempted Adam with the fruit of the tree of knowledge. Artists, not knowing how to paint the fruit of the tree of knowledge, decided to paint an apple.

It was not until he was hit on the head by a falling apple that Sir Isaac Newton was able to formulate his theory of gravity, in 1666. The tree from which this apple fell was in his own orchard in Woolsthorpe, England. Its remains are still preserved.

Johnny Appleseed, the American folk hero, was based on the life of pioneer John Chapman. Chapman did not wander the countryside tossing apple seeds along the road. He was a sophisticated seedmaster who established a series of complex forest nurseries that extended from Pennsylvania to Ohio. Sylvester Stallone's famous movie character is named after John Chapman's favorite apple, the Rambo.

An average apple has less than ninety calories, is an excellent source of fiber, a good source of vitamin A, and is very low in fat.

◆

SPICED APPLE CAKE
LA COSTA RESORT AND SPA ◆ CARLSBAD, CALIFORNIA

MAKES 12 SERVINGS

Vegetable oil spray, for
  greasing pan
2 cups unsweetened
  applesauce
1 peeled or unpeeled red
  apple, core removed, cut
  into small dice (about
  2 cups)
1 peeled or unpeeled green
  apple, core removed, cut
  into small dice (about
  2 cups)
1 teaspoon vanilla extract
4 egg whites
½ cup raisins
2 cups whole wheat flour
1 cup granulated or
  fructose sugar
1 tablespoon baking
  powder
2 teaspoons cinnamon
1 teaspoon nutmeg

This recipe is very low in fat and totally free of in-gredients that contain cholesterol. There are about fifty calories in a two-by-two-inch piece, along with a rich sweet taste.

1. Preheat the oven to 325° F. Grease a standard 17-×-11-×-1 inch jelly roll pan.

2. In a bowl, blend the applesauce, apples, vanilla, egg whites, and raisins until well combined. Set aside.

3. In a second bowl, combine the flour, sugar, baking powder, cinnamon, and nutmeg.

4. Fold the wet ingredients into the dry ingredients until combined. Use a spatula to evenly spread the batter in the pan. Bake for 30 minutes. Cool the cake in the pan on a wire rack. Slice and serve.

HOW DO THE PROS KNOW WHEN A CAKE IS DONE?

There are three ways: You can put a toothpick in, and if it comes out clean, the cake's done. You can press the center of the cake, and if it bounces back, it's done. Or you see that the cake has pulled away from the sides of the pan. It pulls in when most of the moisture has been baked out, which happens when the cake's done.

ABOUT NUTMEG

The island of Grenada originally rose from the sea in a volcanic eruption. Its inner harbor is actually formed from the open mouth of that long-dormant crater. The capital city and major port is St. George's, which has become famous for its picturesque beauty, and it's easy to see why. The blue lagoon is surrounded by English Georgian and French provincial homes that reflect the town's colonial past. Just behind the harbor is the town's market square: a typical open-air Caribbean affair with a substantial selection of locally produced fruits, vegetables, and spices, including nutmeg, which is the national spice of the island. Grenada produces about thirty percent of the world supply. It's actually the kernel of the fruit of the nutmeg tree. There is a fibrous lattice covering that grows on the outside of the seed, and when that lattice is removed, dried, and ground up it becomes a second spice, mace. But don't overuse nutmeg; it's kind of potent and too much of it can be dangerous. Use it in terms of quantity the way you'd use black pepper. Grenada is the major spice-growing island of the Western hemisphere. In addition to nutmeg and mace, it produces cinnamon, cloves, and bay leaves. The streets are peppered with women who place their spices in home-made baskets and offer them for sale.

◆

ABOUT RAISINS

Raisins are grapes that have been dried to a point that prevents the development of enzymes that cause spoilage.

In 1873 a California grape grower had his entire crop scorched by very hot sun. Instead of throwing out the dehydrated grapes, he brought them to a local grocer and convinced him that he was selling raisinated grapes, a rare Persian delicacy. That was our first California raisin crop.

To store raisins properly, remove them from the carton they come in, and place them in an airtight container in the refrigerator. To plump out raisins that have become too dry, soak them in water or fruit juice.

◆

CONNIE'S CHEESECAKE
ALDO'S RESTAURANT ◆ WYCKOFF, NEW JERSEY

MAKES 10 SERVINGS

CRUST
1⅓ cups graham cracker
  crumbs
3 tablespoons sugar
3 tablespoons unsweetened
  cocoa powder
⅓ cup butter or margarine,
  melted

FILLING
12 ounces cream cheese,
  softened
¾ cup sugar
2 eggs
1 tablespoon vanilla extract
1 tablespoon coffee-
  flavored liqueur or rum
  (optional)
8 ounces sour cream
1 ounce unsweetened
  chocolate, coarsely grated

TO MAKE THE CRUST:

1. Preheat the oven to 350° F. In a bowl, blend together the crumbs, sugar, cocoa, and butter. Press this mixture firmly onto the bottom and sides of a 9-inch springform pan. (Crumbs will go only about halfway up the sides of the pan.)

2. Bake for 10 minutes. Set aside to cool.

TO MAKE THE FILLING:

3. In a bowl, beat cream cheese with an electric mixer at high speed until light and fluffy. Gradually beat in the sugar. Add the eggs, one at a time, beating well after each addition. Add vanilla and coffee liqueur. Pour filling into the baked crust.

4. Bake for 45 minutes or until golden. Remove from the oven and cool on a wire rack for 10 minutes.

5. When the baked layer is sufficiently cool, spread sour cream over the top. Sprinkle with grated chocolate.

TO MAKE THE TOPPING:

6. In the top of a double boiler, dissolve the instant coffee powder in 2 tablespoons of hot, not boiling, water. Add the semisweet chocolate and stir until melted and blended.

7. In a medium-sized bowl, beat the egg yolks with an electric mixer until thick. Gradually add the sugar. Add a tablespoon of the chocolate mixture from the double boiler to the egg mixture; beat well. Continue adding small amounts of the chocolate mixture to the egg mixture, beating until all of the chocolate has been added. Add the vanilla extract and the coffee liqueur.

8. In another bowl, with clean beaters, beat egg whites until stiff. Gently fold into chocolate mixture. Spread the mixture over cooled baked layer.

9. Refrigerate until firm (at least 4 hours).

10. When ready to serve, loosen the sides of the pan and remove cake. Place cheesecake on serving plate. Garnish with whipped cream, if desired.

TOPPING

1½ teaspoons instant
  coffee powder
2 tablespoons hot water
4 ounces semisweet
  chocolate, coarsely
  chopped
4 eggs, separated
⅓ cup sugar
½ teaspoon vanilla extract
1 tablespoon coffee-
  flavored liqueur or rum
  (optional)
1 cup whipped cream, for
  garnish (optional)

CHEESECAKE

Cheesecake is a rich dessert that is made with cream cheese, cottage cheese, or ricotta cheese. Cheesecakes have been made since the time of the ancient Romans.

The three main types of cheesecakes in America are the cottage cheese with graham cracker crust cake, popular in the Midwest; the cream cheese cheesecake, also known as New York cheesecake; and Italian cheesecake, made with ricotta cheese. Midwestern cheesecakes are often topped with sweet cherries in syrup or with chocolate. New York and Italian cheesecakes are usually flavored with the zests of oranges and lemons.

NO-CHOLESTEROL LIGHT CHOCOLATE CAKE

THE RAINBOW ROOM ◆ NEW YORK, NEW YORK

MAKES 8 SERVINGS

8 egg whites
1 cup granulated sugar
½ cup unsweetened cocoa
  powder
3 tablespoons vegetable oil
½ cup toasted almonds
½ cup toasted walnuts
8 sliced strawberries and
  1 teaspoon confectioners
  sugar, for garnish
  (optional)

1. Preheat the oven to 350° F.

2. In a dry bowl, using an electric mixer, beat 6 egg whites until stiff and dry, set aside.

3. In another bowl, combine the sugar, cocoa, oil, and remaining egg whites.

4. Combine the toasted almonds and walnuts in the container of a food processor or blender and process until finely chopped. Add to the sugar-cocoa mixture.

5. Add a quarter of the beaten egg whites to the sugar-cocoa-nut mixture. Gently mix together. Fold in the remaining whites until no white appears. Pour into a greased and floured 9-inch springform pan. Bake for 30 to 35 minutes or until firm in the center.

6. Cool in the pan. Remove from the pan and divide into 8 servings. Garnish each slice with a sliced strawberry and sprinkle with confectioners sugar.

THE FIRST SQUARE
CHOCOLATE CAKE

The Austrian Empire was really serious about managing through marriage, so when things got a little tense with the Prussians during the 1860s, the Austrian Archduke Albrecht arranged for a marriage between his daughter and a member of the Prussian royal family, Duke Philip of Württemberg. The young couple married, set up housekeeping, and settled down in Vienna. But after a while, Phil got tired of living in one place and moved on. You know, dukes can be that way. Good thing too, because at the time the city was getting ready for the World Exhibition of 1873, and the Emperor of Austria, Francis Joseph, needed an imperial and royal building to house all of the imperial and royal guests that would be coming to the city. And that's how Vienna's Imperial Hotel came to be.

The night before the Emperor himself was to inaugurate the hotel, an apprentice cook set about preparing a cake that he wanted to offer to his beloved monarch: five extra-thin layers of almond paste interspersed with chocolate, topped with marzipan, and finished with chocolate icing. It was the first square chocolate cake in culinary history, and the Emperor loved it. That's how the world-famous Imperial Torte was invented. It shares its name with the hotel in which it was created.

◆

GRAHAM CRACKERS, THE LINK
BETWEEN DIETARY FIBER AND
MORAL FIBER

Graham crackers are sweet whole-wheat crackers made from graham flour. Graham flour is whole-grain wheat flour with the husk, or bran, and center, or germ, left in. The Reverend Sylvester Graham (1794–1851) gave his name to the flour because of his rigid views on temperance and the virtue of eating whole-grain and unadulterated foods. Reverend Graham, who lived in Connecticut, believed that a healthy diet would produce better citizens of superior moral fiber.

◆

BROWN-AND-WHITE POUND CAKE
CLUB MED 1

MAKES 1 LOAF

2 cups plus 2 tablespoons
  all-purpose flour
½ teaspoon salt
2 teaspoons double-acting
  baking powder
¼ teaspoon mace
¾ cup (1½ sticks) butter or
  margarine, room
  temperature
1½ cups sugar
4 eggs, room temperature
1 teaspoon vanilla extract
½ cup milk
¼ cup unsweetened cocoa
  powder, sifted

1. Preheat the oven to 325° F. Grease and flour a
9-×-5-×-3-inch loaf pan, using the 2 tablespoons of flour,
shaking out the excess flour.

2. Sift the remaining 2 cups of flour with the salt, baking
powder, and mace.

3. In a bowl, using an electric mixer, cream the butter or
margarine, adding sugar gradually. Cream until very light.

4. Add the eggs, one at a time, incorporating one before
adding the next.

5. Mix the vanilla into the milk and add it alternately with
the flour mixture to the creamed mixture. Stir only until
blended.

6. Divide the batter in half and fold the cocoa into one half.

7. Carefully place the chocolate batter in one side
(lengthwise) of the pan and the plain batter in the other
side.

8. Bake for 1 hour. Cool on a wire rack, removing the cake
from the pan after about 10 minutes.

Vermont Maple Syrup Upside-Down Cake

Shelburne Farms ◆ Vermont

1. Preheat the oven to 400° F.

2. In a small saucepan, bring the maple syrup to a boil over medium-high heat. Pour the syrup into a greased 8-×-8-inch baking pan.

3. In a bowl, using an electric mixer, cream together the sugar, butter, and egg until fluffy. Add the milk and blend in.

4. In a separate bowl, sift together the flour, baking powder, and salt. Beat into the creamed mixture. Pour the batter into the syrup-lined pan and, with a spatula, spread the batter to the pan edges.

5. Bake for 30 minutes or until golden.

6. While still hot, invert the cake onto a serving dish. Serve plain or with whipped cream.

MAKES 8 SERVINGS

1 cup maple syrup
3 tablespoons sugar
1 tablespoon butter
1 egg
½ cup milk
1 cup sifted all-purpose
  flour
2 teaspoons baking powder
½ teaspoon salt
Whipped cream, for
  serving (optional)

VERMONT MAPLE SYRUP

Each year, as the end of winter approaches, the farmers of Vermont begin the process of making maple syrup. It is a technique that was taught to them by Native Americans, who have been making maple syrup for thousands of years. In the process, trails are cleared to the sugar maples. Trees that are over forty years old have a hollow tap set into the bark. The temperature shift from the frosty nights to the warm days causes the sap to drip. It's collected in buckets and brought to the sugar house.

Some farmers collect the sap in tubes that connect the trees directly to the sugar house. If you use the buckets, you've got to go out and collect the sap by hand. The tubes look like they're a lot easier . . . until a frightened deer runs through your sugar trees and busts all the tubing. Maple syrup making is a difficult and chancy business.

Once the sap reaches the sugar house, it is set to boiling over wood fires. The sap thickens, the sugar concentrates, impurities which result in cloudiness are carefully filtered out . . . and you end up with the finest maple syrup. Great on pancakes, waffles, and ice cream, but also a fine cooking ingredient, maple syrup is used in making Vermont Maple Syrup Upside-Down Cake and Frosted Maple Gingerbread Cake.

FROSTED MAPLE GINGERBREAD CAKE
SHELBURNE FARMS ◆ VERMONT

TO MAKE THE CAKE:

1. Preheat the oven to 350° F.

2. In a bowl, combine the egg, maple syrup, sour cream, and melted butter; blend well.

3. In a second bowl, sift together the flour, ginger, baking soda, and salt and mix well. Combine the liquid and dry ingredients until they are well blended.

4. Pour the batter into a greased and lightly floured 8-×-8-inch baking pan and bake for 35 minutes or until the cake pulls away from the sides of the pan.

5. Transfer to a serving dish and let cool before frosting.

TO MAKE THE FROSTING:

6. In a bowl, combine all of the frosting ingredients. Mix until smooth. Spread over the cooled gingerbread.

MAKES 10 SERVINGS

CAKE

1 egg
1 cup maple syrup
1 cup sour cream
4 tablespoons (½ stick) butter, melted
2⅓ cups all-purpose flour
1½ teaspoons ground ginger
1 teaspoon baking soda
½ teaspoon salt

FROSTING

1½ cups confectioners sugar
1 tablespoon heavy cream
6 tablespoons maple syrup

YOGURT CAKE
THE RITZ-CARLTON ◆ MONTREAL, QUEBEC, CANADA

MAKES 8 SERVINGS

1 egg yolk
¼ cup sugar
2 cups plain low-fat yogurt
1½ cups cold skim milk
Two 1-ounce envelopes
   unflavored gelatin
2 tablespoons low-fat
   cream cheese, room
   temperature
Sponge cake, yellow cake,
   or lady fingers, to line
   bottom of 8- or 9-inch
   springform pan
4 to 6 cups assorted fresh
   fruit (berries, sliced
   bananas, kiwis, and
   pineapple)
1 cup apricot jam, heated
   and strained

1. In a mixing bowl, combine the egg yolk and sugar. Add the yogurt and whisk until well blended.

2. Place ¾ cup of the cold milk in a saucepan and sprinkle the gelatin over it. Allow to sit for 3 minutes while gelatin softens. Stir over low heat until the gelatin is dissolved, then cool to lukewarm.

3. Over a pan of simmering water, whisk the yogurt mixture until it is warm, not hot, to the touch. Whisk in the cream cheese and the remaining ¾ cup milk. Add the gelatin mixture and stir to blend.

4. Set this bowl into another, larger, bowl that contains about 2 cups of ice cubes mixed with 1 cup of cold water. Using an electric hand-held mixer or a whisk, whip the mixture at high speed until it thickens and increases in volume. When this occurs, stop whipping and allow the mixture to stand over the ice until you see it substantially thicken into a mousselike texture. Keep refrigerated.

5. Line the bottom of an 8- or 9-inch springform pan with your cake of choice.

6. Add half of the yogurt mixture, then half the fruit. Cover with the remaining yogurt mixture, tap the pan on the table to settle, and refrigerate at least 4 hours or overnight.

7. Unmold the cake onto a platter, decorate with remaining fruit, and glaze with the warm apricot jam. Return cake to refrigerator until glaze sets.

SHORTBREAD CAKE AND PRUNES
MURCHIE'S ◆ VANCOUVER ISLAND, BRITISH COLUMBIA, CANADA

1. In a bowl, beat the butter until soft. Gradually add the sugar, blending until very light and creamy.

2. Beat in the egg yolks, whole eggs, and sour cream. Sift the flour and the baking powder together and stir into the creamed mixture. Blend completely. Wrap this dough in plastic wrap and chill for several hours or overnight.

3. Preheat the oven to 325° F.

4. Roll out the dough on a floured surface. Cut the dough into 4 rounds 7 inches in diameter. Place the rounds on a cookie sheet. Bake 20 minutes until lightly colored.

5. Place 3 cups of the prunes, the orange zest, and the cup of water into a microwaveable container. Microwave for 10 to 20 minutes, until prunes have absorbed the water and have softened. (Alternately, you may do this in a covered, heavy saucepan, over low heat.) Cool slightly and use a food processor to puree. Cool to room temperature.

6. Place a disk of shortbread on a plate. Cover with a third of the prunes. Cover with a second disk and cover with another third of the prunes. Repeat once more and top with the fourth disk. Wrap in plastic wrap and refrigerate overnight.

7. Unwrap the shortbread and spread a layer of apricot jam over the top. Flatten the remaining 1 cup of prunes between two sheets of plastic wrap. Cover top layer of shortbread with the flattened prunes. Paint the apricot glaze over the prunes and allow to cool to room temperature.

MAKES 10 SERVINGS

1 cup (2 sticks) butter
1 cup granulated sugar, sifted
2 egg yolks
2 whole eggs
¼ cup sour cream
2½ cups all-purpose flour
1 teaspoon baking powder
4 cups pitted prunes
Grated zest of 2 oranges
1 cup water
½ cup apricot jam, heated, strained, and kept warm

PIES

OLD-FASHIONED BLUEBERRY PIE

MAKES 8 SERVINGS

4 cups fresh or frozen
  thawed, blueberries
⅔ cup sugar
2 tablespoons cornstarch
2 tablespoons fresh lemon
  juice
Prepared pie crust dough
  for one 9-inch double-
  crust pie
1 tablespoon butter
2 tablespoons cream or
  milk

1. Preheat the oven to 400° F.

2. Rinse and drain the fresh blueberries or drain the frozen blueberries. Set aside.

3. In a bowl, combine the sugar and cornstarch and mix well until all lumps disappear. Add the blueberries and lemon juice. Toss to combine.

4. Roll out half of the dough and fit it into a 9-inch pie pan. Fill with the blueberry mixture. Dot with the butter. Roll out the remaining dough. Moisten the edge of the bottom crust with water. Fit top crust over the filled pie. Trim and crimp edges. Make 2 or 3 vent holes in the top crust.

5. Brush the top crust with the cream or milk. Place the pie on a baking sheet with sides. Bake for 15 minutes. Reduce the heat to 350° F. and continue baking for 30 minutes or until the crust is golden and the filling is bubbling.

STAR-SPANGLED TART CHERRY PIE
HART, MICHIGAN

1. Preheat the oven to 400° F.

2. In a bowl, combine the 2 cups of flour and the salt. With a pastry blender or two forks, cut in the butter until the pieces are the size of peas.

3. Sprinkle the water over the flour mixture, 1 tablespoon at a time. Mix lightly with a fork. Continue adding water until the mixture forms a dough. Gather the dough into a ball, cover, and refrigerate for 30 minutes.

4. In a small bowl, combine the cherries, the 4 tablespoons flour, the sugar, and the almond extract. Set aside.

5. Divide the dough in half and roll it into two 10-inch circles. Line the bottom of a 9-inch pie or tart pan with 1 circle of the dough. Turn the cherry mixture into the pie pan. Cover the pie with the second circle of dough. Tuck the edges of the top crust under the edges of the bottom crust. Crimp to seal. Cut 6 to 8 vents in the top crust.

6. Brush the top crust with a light coating of milk. Bake the pie on the middle rack of the oven for 30 to 35 minutes until the crust is light brown.

MAKES ONE 9-INCH PIE

2 cups plus 4 tablespoons
   all-purpose flour
1 teaspoon salt
¾ cup (1½ sticks) butter
6 to 7 tablespoons cold
   water
4 cups pitted sour
   cherries, or three 16-
   ounce cans pitted sour
   (pie) cherries, drained
⅓ cup sugar
5 drops almond extract
¼ cup milk

CHERRIES

The cherry is a member of the rose family. It originated in Asia but became widely distributed throughout Europe and North America. The United States is the world's leading producer of cherries, with Michigan, California, and Oregon leading the way.

Cherries are either sweet or sour. Sour cherries can be eaten raw but they are better cooked with sugar and made into jams or pies. They are bright red. Sweet cherries tend to be larger and darker, sometimes even a mahogany red. They can be cooked but they are better raw. An excellent sweet cherry is the Bing cherry, named after the Chinese horticulturist who developed it in 1875. My personal favorite, however, is the Queen Anne cherry.

When buying fresh cherries always look for those that are firm, unblemished, and have a bright, clear color. Overripe cherries will deteriorate very quickly, which is fine if you are going to cook them. Slightly underripe cherries will ripen if kept at room temperature in a dark place.

TUDOR SURPRISE PIE

When most countries make a fruit pie, there's a crust on the bottom, then the fruit, and that's it. But in Tudor England, they developed a crust on top. That's where the surprise pie was invented. Remember the old nursery rhyme "Four and twenty blackbirds, baked in a pie . . . When the pie was opened, The birds began to sing . . ."? Well, that was a Tudor surprise pie, and they needed a crust on top to hide the surprise. So any time you see a fruit pie with a second crust on top, you're looking at a modern-day example of an old English food.

PEANUT BUTTER PIE
EMERIL'S ◆ NEW ORLEANS, LOUISIANA

Emeril Lagasse and his New Orleans restaurant are national gastronomic treasures. Inside his open kitchen, traditional Creole recipes are reborn in skilled hands.

FOR THE CRUST:

1. Preheat the oven to 300° F.

2. Combine the graham cracker crumbs with the butter or margarine, sugar, cocoa, and the peanut butter. Mix until completely blended. Press into an ungreased 8-inch pie pan and bake for 15 minutes. Cool completely.

TO MAKE THE FILLING:

3. Using an electric mixer, beat the cream cheese, peanut butter, and sugar together until light. Add the peanuts and vanilla and continue to beat until well blended.

4. In a separate bowl, with clean beaters, whip the heavy cream until stiff peaks form. Fold about a third of the whipped cream into the cream cheese mixture to lighten it, then add remaining cream and fold in carefully and quickly, so as not to deflate the whipped cream.

5. Fill the cooled pie shell with filling. Chill at least 2 hours in the refrigerator.

6. If desired, garnish each slice with whipped cream, chocolate syrup, mint leaves, and/or chopped peanuts.

MAKES ONE 8-INCH PIE

CRUST
1½ cups finely ground graham cracker crumbs
6 tablespoons melted butter or margarine
2 tablespoons superfine sugar
2 teaspoons unsweetened cocoa powder
2 tablespoons peanut butter

FILLING
8 ounces cream cheese
¼ cup peanut butter
½ cup granulated sugar
¼ cup chopped unsalted roasted peanuts
1 teaspoon vanilla extract
¾ cup heavy cream

OPTIONAL GARNISHES
Whipped cream
Chocolate syrup
Fresh mint leaves
Chopped peanuts

◆

SUGAR PIE
LOEWS LE CONCORDE HOTEL ◆ QUEBEC CITY, QUEBEC, CANADA

MAKES ONE 8-INCH PIE

¼ cup maple syrup
2 tablespoons butter
½ cup heavy cream
½ cup milk
1 cup maple or light brown
 sugar
½ cup all-purpose flour
Pie dough for an 8-inch
 pie, including lattice top

Tourism is a major activity for Quebec City, and its residents are tuned in to the needs of travelers. Nowhere is that attention to hospitality more apparent than at Loews Le Concorde Hotel. It's situated on a street called the Grand-Allée, which is the city's main boulevard. Many of the most important historic sites surround the base of the building. Atop Le Concorde is a revolving restaurant called L'Astral. It offers guests some of the more spectacular views of Quebec.

1. Preheat the oven to 375° F.

2. In a heavy saucepan, bring the syrup and butter to a boil, stirring constantly.

3. Add the cream and milk, stir, add the sugar and flour. Keep stirring and bring to a boil. Lower heat slightly so that the mixture does not boil over, but continue to simmer. Stir and cook until mixture thickens substantially, about 10 minutes.

4. On a lightly floured surface, roll out the pie dough. Line an 8-inch pie pan with dough. Pour the filling mixture into the pie shell. Cover with lattice strips. Crimp edges to seal. Bake for 30 minutes or until crust is golden brown, but do not overbake. Remove pie and cool to room temperature.

APPLE TART
HOTEL LE BRISTOL ◆ PARIS, FRANCE

1. Preheat the oven to 450° F.

2. Roll out the pastry into four 6-inch circles, ⅛-inch thick. Place on baking sheets.

3. In a small bowl, combine the cinnamon and sugar. Sprinkle the pastry with half the cinnamon-sugar mixture and dot with half the butter. Arrange the apple slices overlapping in a circular pattern and covering the entire surface of the pastry.

4. Sprinkle with the remaining cinnamon-sugar mixture and dot with the remaining butter. Bake for 15 minutes or until the apples are cooked through and browned on the edges.

5. Serve straight from the oven.

MAKES FOUR 6-INCH TARTS

1 pound pastry dough, chilled
1 teaspoon cinnamon
2 tablespoons sugar
2 tablespoons butter
3 apples, peeled, cored, and cut in thin half circles

WEIGHT-LOSS TIP

Wonder of wonders, there is a piece of scientific research that indicates that a sweet at the end of a meal can help weight-loss dieters. It looks like people who have grown up in Western societies have become conditioned to the taste of a sweet at the end of a meal. It works like a bell, telling us that the meal is over and we can stop eating. Without that signal, many people tend to overeat. So don't desert dessert, just try and make sure your torte is tiny.

OREGON PEAR TART
JACKSONVILLE INN ◆ JACKSONVILLE, OREGON

MAKES 12 SERVINGS

PEARS

2 cups white wine
¼ cup apple juice
  concentrate
½ cup brown sugar
2 teaspoons cinnamon
4 ripe pears, cored and
  thinly sliced

FILLING

6 tablespoons water
¾ cup granulated sugar
¼ teaspoon fresh lemon
  juice
¼ cup heavy cream
2 ounces cream cheese,
  room temperature
3 tablespoons unsalted
  butter, cut into pieces,
  room temperature
¾ teaspoon grated fresh
  ginger
2 cups ground hazelnuts,
  almonds, walnuts, or
  pecans

1. In a large sauté pan with a lid, mix the wine, apple juice, brown sugar, and cinnamon. Poach the pears in the liquid until soft. Remove the pears and set aside and continue simmering the liquid, uncovered, until it thickens.

2. To prepare the filling, in a medium saucepan, heat the water, sugar, and lemon juice over low heat until the sugar dissolves. Bring to a boil. Continue cooking until the sugar begins to caramelize, approximately 12 minutes. Remove from heat.

3. In a small bowl, whisk together the heavy cream and the cream cheese. Add to the caramelized sugar. Mixture will bubble vigorously. Add the butter, ginger, and the nuts and stir until well mixed.

4. Return the pears to the reduced poaching liquid and coat them with the liquid. Spread the nut mixture in the bottom of the tart shells. Arrange the pear slices in a decorative pattern on top.
  If topping is desired, whip the cream, sugar, and Frangelica in a cold metal bowl until it forms soft peaks and pipe it on top of the tarts in a decorative pattern.

PEARS

The pear is a member of the rose family, and it originated in southeastern Europe and western Asia. Sweet, luscious pears have a recipe history that dates back to Homer, the ancient Greek storyteller. The Romans were also great pear lovers and growers, and they spread the pear tree throughout their empire.

The French have been using pears since the Middle Ages. Today most of our popular pear varieties have French names such as Anjou, Bosc, Comice, and Forelle.

Except for Bartletts, which turn yellow when ripe, it is hard to judge a pear by its color. If the pears are still firm at your market, bring them home and place them under a bowl at room temperature. That will bring them to ripeness within a day or two. The pear is ripe and ready when it yields to gentle thumb pressure at the stem end.

◆

SHELLS
Twelve 3-inch prebaked
  tart shells

TOPPING (OPTIONAL)
1 cup heavy cream
1 tablespoon granulated
  sugar
1 tablespoon Frangelica

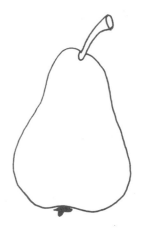

SPRING FRUIT TART
LE CIRQUE ◆ NEW YORK, NEW YORK

MAKES ONE 9-INCH TART

Prepared pie crust dough
 to line one 9-inch tart pan
½ cup currant jelly
½ cup apricot jam
1½ cups heavy cream,
 whipped
Fresh berries, such as
 strawberries, blueberries,
 and/or raspberries,
 washed and stemmed
Fresh fruit, such as
 apples, pears, and/or
 peaches, peeled, cored or
 pitted, and sliced

America's Queen of the Opera, Beverly Sills, is an extraordinary artist whose remarkable life both on and off the operatic stage has touched millions of people and whose glorious voice has been a vital force in musical history. Her prolific recording career has earned her many awards, including the prestigious Grammy Award. Her television performances have garnered her a total of five Emmy Awards. And if that weren't enough, her autobiography made her a best-selling author.

As general director of the New York City Opera, she has been credited with guiding many aspiring young singers along in their international careers. Her twenty years of work as national chairman of the March of Dimes has helped to raise over eighty million dollars to fight birth defects.

This fruit tart recipe was prepared for her at a lunch we had together at Le Cirque.

1. Preheat the oven to 350° F.

2. On a floured surface, roll out the pie dough and fit it into a 9-inch tart pan. Crimp the edges to make a pattern. Prick the shell with a fork.

3. Bake the tart shell for 10 minutes. Remove from the oven and let cool completely.

4. In two small saucepans, over medium-low heat, melt the currant jelly and apricot jam separately. Remove from the heat and set aside.

5. Cover the tart shell with the whipped cream. Arrange the berries on the whipped cream around the outer edge of the crust. Starting in the center, arrange the sliced fruit overlapping in a circular pattern until the whipped cream is completely covered.

6. Brush the berries with the melted currant jelly and brush the sliced fruit with the melted apricot jam. Refrigerate the tart until ready to serve.

◆

THE APPLE
AND GOOD HEALTH

Scientific research has shown that the potassium in fruits and vegetables may help people avoid heart disease. One of the fruits that meet the specifications of the research is the apple. Nice . . . an apple a day may actually help keep the doctor away. It appears that a single serving of fresh fruit each day may decrease the risk of stroke by forty percent.

The apple is also high in pectin, which appears to help move excess fat through your body and thereby reduce cholesterol levels. The apple itself has no cholesterol or fat. Reducing the fat and cholesterol in your diet is often a key to good health.

Not as significant as its anti-heart disease properties, but still quite valuable, is the apple's ability to act like a toothbrush. Dental studies have shown that the fibrous texture of the apple, the fact that apples don't stick to the surface of your teeth, and the apple's juice combine to act like a toothbrush. They help to clean your teeth and massage your gums, and that reduces your chance of getting cavities.

The apple is also an excellent food for babies. Unlike orange or pineapple juices, apple juice is so low in acid that it reduces the chance of an infant coming down with colic or body rashes such as are caused by high-acid juices.

◆

WALNUT TART
HALCYON HOTEL ◆ LONDON, ENGLAND

MAKES ONE 9-INCH TART

Prepared pie crust dough
  for one 9-inch tart
½ cup (1 stick) unsalted
  butter
½ cup dark brown sugar
4 egg yolks
¾ cup maple syrup
8 ounces walnuts
2 teaspoons fresh lemon
  juice
4 teaspoons lemon zest
½ teaspoon vanilla extract
Pinch of salt

The Holland Park district of London is one of the city's most handsome residential areas, and right in the middle of its tree-lined streets is the small, very beautiful Halcyon Hotel. The Halcyon has become famous for its private-home setting, its individually decorated rooms, and its excellent restaurant. The restaurant is called The Kingfisher, and it is directed by Chef James Robinson, who is responsible for the following tart. Rich and satisfying, a small slice of this delightful pastry makes a perfect ending to a meal.

1. Preheat the oven to 400° F. Line a 9-inch tart pan with the pie dough. Crimp edges.

2. In a mixing bowl, using an electric mixer, cream the butter and brown sugar until the mixture is smooth and light.

3. With the mixer running, slowly add the egg yolks and maple syrup.

4. Fold in the walnuts, lemon juice and zest, vanilla extract, and the salt. Pour into the tart shell.

5. Set the tart pan on the middle rack of the oven and bake 10 minutes. Reduce heat to 325° F. and bake 30 to 35 minutes longer or until set.

6. Remove from the oven and let cool before serving.

LINZERTORTE
GOLDENER HIRSCH HOTEL ◆ SALZBURG, AUSTRIA

1. Preheat the oven to 350° F.

2. Mix the flour, ground almonds, granulated sugar, cinnamon, cloves, and baking powder together in a bowl. Cut up the margarine or butter and add to the dry ingredients. Rub in by hand until the mixture looks sandy.

3. In a small bowl, beat 1 egg and stir into the dough with a fork. Stir only until smooth. Wrap dough in plastic wrap and refrigerate for 30 minutes.

4. Press half of the dough into the bottom of a buttered 9-inch springform pan. Spread the preserves over the dough, leaving a 1-inch margin around the outside.

5. By hand, roll the remaining dough into pencil-thin ropes and form a lattice pattern over the preserves. Pinch off excess at edges of pan. When lattice is complete, use remaining dough to roll more ropes and place 3 concentric rings around the outer rim of the torte.

6. Beat the second egg. Gently paint the lattice and the border with the beaten egg and sprinkle with the sliced almonds.

7. Bake about 40 minutes until dough is set and light gold.

8. Cool the torte in the pan on a rack. Remove the sides of the pan and loosen the bottom of the torte with a knife or a metal spatula. Slide the torte onto a platter. Dust with confectioners sugar.

MAKES 8 TO 12 SERVINGS

1½ cups unbleached all-purpose flour
1 cup finely ground almonds
¾ cup granulated sugar
1 teaspoon cinnamon
¼ teaspoon ground cloves
1 teaspoon baking powder
¾ cup (1½ sticks) margarine or butter
2 eggs
⅔ cup raspberry preserves
¼ cup sliced almonds
Confectioners sugar

NEVER-FAIL PASTRY

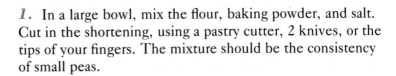

MAKES ENOUGH DOUGH
FOR TWO 10-INCH DOUBLE-
CRUST PIES

4 cups all-purpose flour
1 teaspoon baking powder
1 teaspoon salt
1 pound Crisco shortening
1 egg
1 tablespoon vinegar
Cold water

1. In a large bowl, mix the flour, baking powder, and salt. Cut in the shortening, using a pastry cutter, 2 knives, or the tips of your fingers. The mixture should be the consistency of small peas.

2. In a large measuring cup, place the egg and the vinegar. Then fill the measuring cup to the ¾ mark with very cold water.

3. Pour the liquid mixture into the dry ingredients and mix until the dough just pulls together.

4. Wrap the dough and store in the refrigerator if not using immediately.

ABOUT FAT

Fat is an important nutrient because it is a concentrated source of energy and carries important vitamins. It also helps make food taste good. However, too much saturated fat in your diet can increase your blood cholesterol level (even more than cholesterol itself does), increasing your risk of heart disease. In addition, diets high in total fat have been linked to other health problems, such as obesity and some forms of cancer. Therefore, most health experts recommend you restrict your total fat intake to no more than thirty percent of the total calories you eat over a period of several days, and saturated fat to no more than ten percent.

There are several simple things you can do to reduce the amount of saturated fat in your diet. Most of these measures will also help you reduce your consumption of total fat.

1. Since most of the saturated fat in our diets comes from animal fats, reduce the amount of red meats and full-fat dairy foods you eat. Then, choose lean cuts of meat and low-fat dairy products.

2. Substitute fruits, vegetables, and grains (pasta, bread, and cereal) for the fatty foods you eat now.

3. Choose your cooking oil carefully. All cooking oils are 100% fat, but some are lower in saturated fat than others. The Crisco® family of oils, which includes Puritan®, is always a good choice. Crisco oil is 90% unsaturated and Crisco-Puritan is 94% unsaturated—that's the lowest saturated fat of any oil.

◆

ABOUT SHORTENING

Shortening has been part of baking since Crisco was first introduced in 1914. The emulsifiers in all vegetable shortening create cakes that are higher and lighter and cookies that are softer and chewier than those baked with butter or margarine—and they contain fifty percent less saturated fat. If that's not enough, shortening also keeps fresh at room temperature, eliminating the need for refrigeration, so it's always soft and easy to mix.

◆

CLASSIC CRISCO FLAKY PIE CRUST

DOUBLE CRUST FOR
9-INCH PIE

2 level cups all-purpose
  flour
1 level teaspoon salt
¾ level cup Crisco
5 tablespoons cold water
  (some brands of flour may
  need more water)

1. Spoon flour into measuring cup and level. Mix flour and salt in bowl.

2. Cut in Crisco using pastry blender (or two knives) until all flour is just blended in to form pea-sized chunks.

3. Sprinkle with water, one tablespoon at a time, tossing lightly with a fork until dough will form a ball.

4. Divide dough into two parts. Press between hands to form two 5- to 6-inch "pancakes."

5. Flour rolling surface and pin lightly. Roll dough into a circle and trim 1 inch larger than upside-down pie plate.

6. Loosen dough carefully. Fold into quarters. Unfold and press into pie plate. Trim edge even with pie plate. Moisten edge.

7. Add filling.

8. Roll out top crust. Fold and lift onto filled pie. Fold top edge under bottom and flute with finger or fork.

9. Prick or slit top crust to allow steam to escape.

10. Bake according to filling directions.

1. Preheat oven to 425° F.

2. Follow mixing and rolling directions for double-crust recipe.

3. Thoroughly prick bottom and sides with a fork (50 times) to prevent shrinking.

4. Bake in preheated oven until edges become light brown (10 to 15 minutes).

SINGLE CRUST FOR
9-INCH PIE

1⅓ level cups all-purpose
  flour
½ level teaspoon salt
½ level cup Crisco
3 tablespoons cold water
  (some brands of flour may
  need more water)

ABOUT
PROCTER & GAMBLE

In the mid-1800s, Cincinnati was the most important pork-packing city in the world, and its sheer size led to the growth of industries associated with pork. When pork fat, called "lard," is produced, there are two byproducts: one is used to manufacture candles, the other to fabricate soap.

In 1837 there were two men married to sisters. One produced candles and the other produced soap, and they were always competing with each other to buy the pork fat they needed to make their products. One day their father-in-law suggested that they join together in one company. They did. One man's name was Procter and the other man was Gamble. As of April 2, 1837, they were a team. About fifty years later, Gamble's son, a trained chemist, developed a very fine soap, but he couldn't come up with a good name for it. One Sunday, Procter's son was sitting in church listening to a psalm about the purity of "the ivory palaces." As a result, he called the new soap IVORY—99 and $^{44}/_{100}$ % pure.

In 1911 Procter & Gamble came up with Crisco, the first all-vegetable shortening. Then they introduced Puritan, made of Canola oil, which is described by scientists as the most healthful cooking oil available. These days, they are working on Olestra, which cooks like any oil or fat, but is calorie free.

The story of Procter & Gamble is also the story of nutrition in terms of fats and oils in the United States. In the beginning we loved our animal-based fats and oils, but by the early part of this century we moved toward vegetable-based products. About mid-century, we started cooking with the oils that had the lowest levels of saturation, and now we look forward to a future of fats that are calorie free.

◆

COOKIES

ALMOND TILE COOKIES
RITZ-ESCOFFIER COOKING SCHOOL ◆ PARIS, FRANCE

MAKES ABOUT 15 COOKIES

2 egg whites
½ cup sugar
2½ tablespoons all-purpose
  flour
⅔ cup slivered almonds

The Ritz Hotel has built what is probably one of the most luxurious cooking schools in the world. The Ritz-Escoffier Cooking School attracts amateurs who want to learn to cook, as well as professionals who wish to improve their skills. The following recipe comes from the school's pastry class.

1. At least 2 hours before baking, mix all of the ingredients in a small mixing bowl until well combined. Cover and refrigerate until ready to bake.

2. Preheat the oven to 400° F.

3. For best results, use a cookie sheet with a nonstick finish. Drop tablespoons of the cookie dough onto the cookie sheet and gently flatten. Bake 4 to 6 minutes until the edges of the cookies are lightly browned, but the centers remain pale in color.

4. Remove the cookie sheet from the oven and immediately lift the cookies off the sheet and drape them over a rolling pin to form a gentle curved shape. Continue until all of the dough is used. Let cookies cool, then store in an airtight container.

CHOCOLATE CRINKLE COOKIES
CLYDE'S RESTAURANT ◆ TYSON'S CORNER, VIRGINIA

The following cookie recipe was developed by Clyde's pastry chef, Kathleen Stevens. As the cookies bake they spread out and develop a crinkly crust, and they are about the best tasting cookies it has ever been my pleasure to try and eat in moderation.

MAKES ABOUT 3 DOZEN COOKIES

½ cup vegetable oil
4 ounces unsweetened chocolate, melted
2⅓ cups granulated sugar
4 large eggs
3½ cups all-purpose flour
2¼ teaspoons baking powder
1½ teaspoons vanilla extract
1 cup chopped walnuts
1 cup chocolate chips
Confectioners sugar

1. In a large mixing bowl, combine the oil and unsweetened chocolate. Blend well with an electric mixer.

2. Add the granulated sugar and continue to mix. Add the eggs, one at a time, incorporating each egg into the mixture before adding the next.

3. Blend in the flour and baking powder.

4. Add the vanilla, nuts, and chocolate chips.

5. Cover the bowl with plastic wrap and refrigerate the mixture for at least 1 hour, or overnight.

6. Preheat the oven to 350° F.

7. Using your hands, roll the dough into golf ball-sized spheres, then roll them in the confectioners sugar. Place the cookies about 3 inches apart on a parchment paper-lined, ungreased cookie sheet.

8. Bake for 17 minutes. Cool on the cookie sheet for 2 minutes, then transfer to a rack to cool completely.

◆

AUSTRIAN JAM STRIPS

MAKES ABOUT 3 DOZEN
COOKIES

2 cups finely ground
  almonds
⅓ cup granulated sugar
1 egg white
¼ teaspoon almond extract
⅛ teaspoon salt
About ½ cup apricot or
  other jam, stirred until
  smooth
Confectioners sugar

*These are about as simple a filled cookie as one
could find, and yet they look festive and taste great.
The basic dough recipe is similar to that used for
macaroons.*

1. Preheat the oven to 350° F. Lightly grease 2 large baking
sheets.

2. In a bowl, combine all ingredients except the jam and
confectioners sugar. Mix the dough into a paste.

3. Lightly dust work surface with confectioners sugar.
Divide dough into 4 parts. Roll each part into a rope ¾ inch
in diameter and about 11 inches long. Place 2 ropes on each
baking sheet. Press a groove down the center of each rope,
leaving ¼ inch closed at each end.

4. Bake for 10 minutes. Remove from the oven; spoon jam
into the grooves. Return to the oven and bake for about
10 more minutes, or until golden brown. Cut cookie strips at
a 45-degree angle into 1-inch slices.

LEMON BARS
STAR'S RESTAURANT ♦ SAN FRANCISCO, CALIFORNIA

1. Preheat the oven to 350° F.

2. In a bowl, blend together the 1 cup of flour, the butter, and the ¼ cup confectioners sugar. Press this dough into a greased 8- × -8-inch pan. Bake for 15 minutes. Remove the pan from the oven, but leave the oven on.

3. While the dough base is baking, mix together the granulated sugar, the 2 tablespoons flour, the baking powder, eggs, and the lemon juice. When the base is removed from the oven, pour this lemon mixture over it and return the pan to the oven. Bake for another 20 to 25 minutes.

4. Cool in the pan. Cut into squares and sift confectioners sugar over all.

MAKES 16 TWO-BY-TWO-INCH SQUARES

1 cup plus 2 tablespoons
  all-purpose flour
½ cup (1 stick) butter or
  margarine, softened
¼ cup confectioners sugar
½ cup granulated sugar
½ teaspoon baking powder
2 eggs, beaten
4 tablespoons fresh lemon
  juice
Confectioners sugar, for
  dusting

BAKING POWDER SUBSTITUTES

Should you ever run short of baking powder, you can use this homemade substitute. For each cup of flour in the recipe, mix together 2 teaspoons cream of tartar, 1 teaspoon bicarbonate of soda, and ½ teaspoon salt. This mixture starts to work after it comes in contact with moisture, so the batter should be baked as soon as possible.

BORDEAUX ALMOND MACAROONS
ST.-EMILION, FRANCE

MAKES 2 DOZEN
MACAROONS

3 egg whites, room
  temperature
⅛ teaspoon salt
¼ teaspoon cream of tartar
¾ cup sugar
6 ounces blanched
  almonds, toasted and
  ground to a fine powder
2 tablespoons all-purpose
  flour

The town of St.-Emilion in Bordeaux, France, is world famous for its great wines. Locally, however, it has an equally significant reputation for its magnificent macaroons. Macaroons are small, round pastries produced mostly from ground almonds, sugar, and egg whites. There is no specific evidence as to when people first started baking macaroons, but by 1748 the kings of France were sending messengers to a particular convent because the nuns had become famous for their macaroons.

1. Preheat the oven to 325° F.

2. Line 2 baking sheets with aluminum foil. In a mixing bowl, beat together the egg whites, salt, and cream of tartar. Add the sugar a tablespoon at a time and continue beating until egg whites are glossy and form very stiff peaks. Gently fold in the ground almonds and flour. Drop tablespoons of batter about 1 inch apart on the prepared baking sheets.

3. Bake 15 to 20 minutes or until golden on the tips. Slide foil off baking sheets onto wire racks. Let stand 5 minutes. Gently peel foil away from backs of macaroons. Return macaroons to racks to cool.

4. The macaroons will store well in an airtight container at room temperature for 2 weeks; they will freeze well for about a month, not that I have ever seen anyone able to hold on to these tasty treats for more than 24 hours.

MAPLE NUT BROWNIES

1. Preheat the oven to 300° F.

2. In a small saucepan over low heat, or in a glass bowl in a microwave, melt the butter and chocolate.

3. In a bowl, using an electric hand mixer, combine the maple syrup, sugar, eggs, and vanilla. Add in the melted chocolate mixture. Beat until blended. Combine the flour, baking powder, and the salt and add to the batter. Stir in the nuts.

4. Pour the batter into a well-greased 8-×-8-inch pan. Bake for 1 hour, or until the center is cooked when tested with a wooden toothpick or a cake tester. Insert and then remove the toothpick from the center of the brownies. It should come out free of any moist batter. Cool and cut into 2-inch squares.

MAKES 16 BROWNIES

¼ cup (½ stick) butter
2 ounces unsweetened
  baking chocolate
½ cup maple syrup
½ cup sugar
2 eggs
1 teaspoon vanilla extract
½ cup sifted all-purpose
  flour
¼ teaspoon baking powder
¼ teaspoon salt
1 cup chopped nuts

ABOUT THE BAKER'S DOZEN

A baker's dozen is thirteen rather than twelve. The phrase comes from the time when butlers ordered all of the food for a household. When the butler chose a particular supplier for baked goods, they had a special deal. For every twelve the butler ordered for the family, he got a thirteenth free for himself.

PEANUT BUTTER COOKIES

MAKES 2 DOZEN COOKIES

1 cup (2 sticks) unsalted
  butter
¾ cup granulated sugar
¾ cup brown sugar
2 eggs
2¼ cups all-purpose flour
1 teaspoon salt
1 teaspoon baking soda
1 cup peanut butter
1 teaspoon vanilla extract

1. Preheat oven to 375° F.

2. Cream together the butter, granulated sugar, and the brown sugar until mixture is light and fluffy.

3. Add the eggs, one at a time, mixing well after each addition.

4. Sift together the flour, salt, and baking soda. Add to the butter-sugar mixture, a small amount at a time.

5. Stir in the peanut butter and vanilla; mix well. Drop teaspoonfuls of batter 2 inches apart on a greased baking sheet. Bake for 10 minutes or until cookies are done.

♦

SPICES THAT INCREASE THE SWEETNESS OF SUGAR

Until a German scientist figured out how to make sugar from the common European sugar beet, planters in the Caribbean amassed enormous fortunes from sugarcane. They also produced cinnamon, cloves, nutmeg, and allspice, which were known as the sweetening spices. They understood that by adding a little bit of any of those spices to their sugar, their sugar turned out to be much sweeter. They saved sugar and they saved money. You can use the same technique to save calories.

♦

CHRISTMAS TREE SPICE COOKIES

1. In a bowl, cream the butter and granulated sugar together until very light in color. Add the egg and honey and continue beating until the mixture is light and fluffy.

2. Sift the flour, baking powder, salt, ginger, and cinnamon together and stir into the butter-sugar mixture.

3. Wrap the cookie dough in wax paper and chill in the refrigerator for 1 hour.

4. Preheat the oven to 375° F.

5. Roll out the chilled dough until it is about ¼ inch thick and cut it with a 3- to 3½-inch cookie cutter. Place the cookies on a lightly greased baking sheet and sprinkle them with multicolored sugar.

6. Bake for about 12 minutes, or until the cookies are golden.

MAKES ABOUT 2 DOZEN COOKIES

1 cup (2 sticks) unsalted butter
1 cup granulated sugar
1 large egg
½ cup honey
4½ cups all-purpose flour
¾ teaspoon double-acting baking powder
½ teaspoon salt
2 teaspoons ground ginger
1 teaspoon cinnamon
Multicolored sugar for garnishing (optional)

CHERRY SUGAR COOKIES

MAKES 3 DOZEN COOKIES

DOUGH
1 cup confectioners sugar
1 cup granulated sugar
1 cup (2 sticks) butter or
  margarine
1 cup vegetable oil
2 eggs
1 tablespoon vanilla extract
4¼ cups all-purpose flour,
  sifted
1 teaspoon salt
1 teaspoon baking soda
1 teaspoon cream of tartar

CHERRY TOPPING
1½ cups cherry pie filling
½ cup chopped nuts
½ cup flaked coconut
3 tablespoons granulated
  sugar

TO MAKE THE COOKIE DOUGH:

1. In a mixing bowl, using an electric mixer, cream the sugars, butter, oil, eggs, and vanilla.

2. Add the flour, salt, baking soda, and cream of tartar. Mix to combine.

3. Divide the dough into 4 cylinder shapes, each about 1¼ inches in diameter. Wrap in plastic wrap and chill until firm, about 2 hours.

TO MAKE THE COOKIES:

4. Preheat the oven to 350° F.

5. Combine all the topping ingredients and set aside.

6. Slice the chilled dough about ¼ inch thick and place the slices on ungreased baking sheets about 1½-inches apart. Using the back of a teaspoon, make a small depression in the center of each cookie and fill with about 1 teaspoon of the cherry topping.

7. Bake for 8 to 10 minutes or until golden. Cool on the baking sheets, then remove the cookies, using a spatula.

COOKIE HISTORY

The word "cookie" comes from a Dutch word meaning "little cake." The first cookies were probably a festive form of bread made without a leavening agent. Historical evidence indicates that early cookies were used as ritual offerings to pagan gods by poorer members of a clan. The wealthy constituents of a society would sacrifice an animal to their gods; less affluent associates would take dough and form it into the shape of an animal for their offering.

During the baroque and rococo periods (seventeenth and eighteenth centuries), cookie molds reached their most elaborate forms. German and Slavic bakers produced ornamental cookies inspired by poems, stories, historic events, romantic legends, and religious symbols. This happened most often in northern Europe and evolved into the forerunners of the highly elaborate cookies that became a basic part of Christmas baking.

When precious spices reappeared in Europe after the Middle Ages, they were quickly incorporated into cookie recipes.

PETTICOAT TAILS
THE CITADEL ◆ HALIFAX, NOVA SCOTIA, CANADA

MAKES 16 PETTICOATS

½ cup confectioners sugar
¾ cup (1½ sticks) butter
1½ cups sifted all-purpose
  flour
½ teaspoon vanilla extract
¼ teaspoon salt
Confectioners sugar, for
  dusting

Nova Scotia is one of the Atlantic Provinces of Canada. Halifax, its capital, was founded by Lord Cornwallis in 1749. It was designed to be a military and naval base for the British colonies in their conflict with the French. The Citadel, constructed in the mid-1800s, formed a major element in the Halifax defense complex. Today it is a part of one of Canada's National Historic Parks. You can visit The Citadel and see how things looked and operated in a military fort of the period.

When The Citadel was built, the power of the British army was at a high point; the food of the British army, however, was the pits. There were no professional chefs. The men didn't know how to cook and the government wanted to spend as little as possible on food. The officers gave the troops just enough to keep them from mutiny. The French army, on the other hand, believed that the cook was the most valuable man in the unit. They'd never let a cook get near combat. The French felt that if the captain was killed, the lieutenant would take his place. But if the cook was killed, then dining was dead, and that was unacceptable.

The present kitchen at The Citadel reproduces a group of classic Scottish sweets for tourists to sample, including these Petticoat Tails.

1. In a bowl, using an electric mixer, cream together the ½ cup confectioners sugar and the butter.

2. Add the flour, vanilla, and the salt. Mix until thoroughly blended. Gather dough into a ball, wrap in plastic wrap or wax paper, and refrigerate for 2 hours.

3. Preheat the oven to 325° F.

4. On a greased baking sheet, press out the dough into a 10-inch circle. Using a knife blade, mark 8 wedges in the dough. Crimp the edge of the circle with a fork.

5. Bake for 25 to 30 minutes or until light golden brown and cooked through. Remove from the oven and cut along the wedge lines. Cool on the baking sheet, then separate the pieces.

6. Dust the petticoats with confectioners sugar.

SAFETY TIPS

AVOIDING FOOD POISONING

Extensive and thorough government inspections go a long way toward ensuring that the food you buy is wholesome and safe. Once you bring it home you should do a number of things to avoid the danger of food poisoning. Most of the two million cases of food poisoning reported each year in the United States are caused by improper food storage and handling in the home.

The first step to protecting yourself from food poisoning is to understand the difference between the organisms that cause food spoilage and those that cause food poisoning. Food spoiling organisms can grow at temperatures as low as 40° F. That's why food can spoil in the refrigerator. Most spoiled food smells bad, and you should discard it immediately.

Food poisoning organisms are harder to detect; their presence frequently cannot be detected by taste, smell, or appearance. They grow best at room temperatures and can continue to multiply at temperatures of up to 140° F., the internal temperature of rare meat.

- *To help avoid food poisoning, keep HOT FOOD HOT and COLD FOOD COLD. The 40° F.-to-140° F. range is what you want to avoid. Do not leave foods on the kitchen counter to defrost or cool down, keep them in the refrigerator.*

- *Cook all foods, especially pork, chicken, and eggs thoroughly. Internal temperatures for pork should be 165° F. and 190° F. for chicken. All eggs should be fully cooked throughout.*

- *Don't let the drippings from raw meat come in contact with other food. Don't use the same countertop or cutting board for both meat and other foods without thoroughly cleaning it first. That also goes for the knife you use and your hands.*

- *Report any cases of food poisoning resulting from restaurant meals or commercially prepared foods to your local poison control center.*

- *If you suspect that meat or poultry that you have purchased may be contaminated, you should follow this procedure:*

  1. *Refrigerate the food in its original container.*
  2. *Call the market where you purchased it and tell the manager.*
  3. *Call the USDA meat and poultry hot line Monday to Friday, 10 A.M. to 4 P.M. (Eastern Standard Time): (202) 447-3333 or toll-free (800) 535-4555.*

TREATMENT FOR POISONING

Because each type of poisoning is treated differently, you must call the poison control center to find out what to do. Keep the telephone number of your local poison control center near your kitchen telephone.

If the poison is not caustic, that is to say, it does not cause burns, the poison control center may tell you to induce vomiting. For this reason it is a good idea to keep a bottle of syrup of ipecac and activated charcoal tablets in your first aid kit. A teaspoonful of dry mustard dissolved in a glass of water can also be used to induce vomiting.

Other poisons are treated by diluting them with water. In any case, poisoning victims will need the prompt care of a doctor.

TREATMENT FOR POISONING

1. *Determine the type of poison ingested (get the container).*
2. *Call the poison control center.*
3. *Call an ambulance.*
4. *Follow any instructions received from the poison control center.*

◆

GENERAL KITCHEN SAFETY

- *Keep poisonous cleaners in a separate cabinet where they cannot be confused with foods. Don't keep them under the sink. Even if you lock the cabinet, a curious child can get into it while you have it open for your own use.*

- *Dangerous items should be kept above the reach of children but below the eye level of adults. Anything that would not ordinarily be eaten should be regarded as a potential poison.*

- *Don't drink or pour hot liquids when holding a child.*

- *Don't let knives or pot handles stick out over the edge of the stove or countertop —they can easily be knocked over or pulled off by a child.*

- *Wipe up spills immediately—before someone slips.*

- *If you wear loose-fitting clothes in the kitchen, be aware that they could easily catch fire.*

- *Don't set your water heater thermostat above 120° F. Water hotter than that can scald very quickly.*

- *Don't fight grease fires with water. Keep an all-purpose (ABC) fire extinguisher in the kitchen. When heating oil for frying, keep the pan's lid handy to smother any flare-ups.*

- *If you are fighting a fire and it doesn't immediately come under control, stop and get out of the house.*

◆

BURNS FROM HEAT

Most kitchen burns are caused by picking up hot pots without proper protection or by spilled hot liquids. They are mostly first- and second-degree burns, which are quite painful.

When heat is applied to the skin, it is conducted into the deeper tissues and can burn them too. Treat all burns with cold water as soon as possible. The area must be cooled all the way through to the deeper tissues to prevent deeper burning. This will take about five minutes. The cool water will also help numb the burn.

Next cover the burn with a dry sterile dressing. If you are not sure if a burn is serious, or if the burn is as large as your palm or involves the face, it should be seen by a doctor. If the burn does not need a doctor's care, apply an antiseptic cream or ointment, and change the dressing daily. Bacitracin is often used as the ointment for burns on and above the neck, Silvadene for burns below the neck. Burned skin is subject to infection, so watch for heat, redness and swelling, and fever. If there are signs of infection, see a doctor.

BURNS FROM HEAT

1. *Immerse burn in cold water for at least five minutes.*
2. *Cover with dry sterile gauze.*
3. *If not serious, treat with antiseptic ointment. If serious, see a doctor.*
4. *Watch for infection. If signs of infection are present, see a doctor.*

CHOKING

- *A choking person cannot talk or make many sounds. Coughing should be considered a good sign.*

- *Do not use the Heimlich maneuver on infants or small children.*

- *For choking infants, hold the child with his head down, supporting his head and body with your arm, and deliver four quick back blows between the shoulder blades with the heel of your hand. Adjust the force of the blow to the size of the baby.*

- *For small children over one year of age, place them on their backs and give them four rapid compressions of their abdomen, just below the breastbone. Adjust the force of your thrusts to the size of your child.*

- *Choking is tragically common among children under four. Their chewing action is not fully developed and food may shoot to the back of their mouths and become lodged in their windpipe. This is especially true of foods that have skins, like hot dogs and grapes.*

IF VICTIM IS CONSCIOUS:

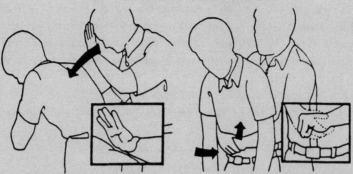

4 quick hard blows   then   4 abdominal thrusts
Repeat until food is forced out.

IF VICTIM IS UNCONSCIOUS:

4 back blows   then   4 abdominal thrusts   then   clear mouth

CUTS

Most kitchen cuts are caused by knives, tin cans, and skewers. All cuts are treated the same way. You stop the bleeding, then prevent further contamination. First apply direct pressure to the wound. If you have time, use a sterile pad, but for heavy bleeding use any cloth or your hand, whatever is faster. If you use a gauze or cloth and it becomes soaked, do not remove it—it has clotting factor on it. Just add more dressings on top of the first one.

If blood loss is severe or lasts more than six minutes, seek emergency medical treatment.

TO STOP BLEEDING

1. *Apply direct pressure to the wound.*
2. *Cover with a sterile dressing.*
3. *Clean and disinfect wound.*
4. *Get assistance for serious wounds.*
5. *Deep puncture wounds should be seen by a doctor.*

Cuts that can be easily treated at home should be bandaged after the bleeding is stopped. Wash the cut with water and an antibacterial such as Betadine. Then cover the wound with a sterile dressing secured with tape or roller gauze. The bandage should be changed daily. Watch for signs of infection.

Deep puncture wounds must be treated by a doctor because there may be internal damage, and because you cannot clean them properly. If an object such as a skewer is stuck in a person, it should be left in place and bandaged securely. It should only be removed by a doctor in an emergency room.

TO BANDAGE MINOR WOUNDS

1. *Wash wound with water, then Betadine, or other antibacterial.*
2. *Dry with sterile pads.*
3. *Apply Bacitracin, or other antiseptic.*
4. *Cover with a sterile dressing.*
5. *Secure dressing in place.*
6. *Change dressing daily and watch for infection.*

KEEP YOUR TETANUS IMMUNIZATION UP TO DATE

CHEMICAL BURNS—BODY

Chemical burns can be caused by strong acids and alkalies found in many of the cleansers used at home. Many of these burns can be avoided with the use of rubber gloves and protective eyewear.

Chemical burns should be rinsed with cool water for at least fifteen minutes. If you can't get all of the substance off your skin, a hospital will be able to help you in their emergency room.

CHEMICAL BURNS—BODY

1. *Remove contaminated clothing.*
2. *Flush burn with cool water for fifteen minutes.*
3. *Cover with sterile gauze.*
4. *Apply antiseptic, watch for signs of infection.*

CHEMICAL BURNS—EYES

Eyes are extremely vulnerable to chemical burns, which should be treated by flushing with water for at least fifteen minutes. Make sure that the eye with the chemical in it is lower than the other eye so that the chemical does not drain into the uninjured eye. After thorough rinsing, cover the eye with a dry sterile pad and go immediately to an emergency room. Do not rub the eye.

CHEMICAL BURNS—EYES

1. *Flush affected eye immediately with cool water for fifteen minutes. When you tilt your head to flush your eye, keep your injured eye below the uninjured eye so the runoff does not come in contact with the uninjured eye.*
2. *Cover with sterile gauze.*
3. *Go to emergency room.*

◆

INDEX

Agricultural fairs, 130
All-American Idaho Potato and
   Turkey Salad, 173
Almonds
   cookies
      Austrian jam strips, 298
      macaroons Bordeaux, 300
      tile, 296
   fish fillets with, 30
   fish with bananas and, 38–39
Appetite suppression, 93
Apple cider, chicken in, 92–93
Apples
   baked, Oregon, 245
   cake
      spiced, 264
      Swedish, 262
   carmelized, 92–93
   crisp, with oats, 249
   crumble, 244
   in Dialogue of Fruits, 239
   facts about, 231, 263, 287
   hot dessert, 242
   muffins, with cornmeal, 231
   pancakes, 217
   pork chops, currant, 112
   squash stuffed with, 163
   strudel, 246–47
   stuffing, with chestnuts, 233
   tart, 283
Artichokes
   chicken breasts and, 70
   facts about, 221
   hearts, pasta with, 141
   pizza with, 220
Asian-style Beef Fillets, 101
Asparagus
   facts about, 144
   with lemon-herb dressing, 146
   risotto with, 144
Austrian Jam Strips, 298
Avocadoes
   guacamole, 202
   in relish, 190

Baker's dozen, 301
Baking powder, substitutes for, 299

Bananas
   in Dialogue of Fruits, 239
   facts on, 40
   garnish, for fish, 38–39
   granola flan with, 248
   in lemony frozen yogurt, 257
   milkshake, 40
   muffins, 230
   in yogurt cake, 274
Barbecues
   chili basting sauce for, 206
   facts about, 206
   marinade for, 207
   techniques for flavoring, 208
   tips for, 204–5
Basil
   facts about, 15, 54
   as pizza topping, 227
   in tomato soup, 15
Basting sauces
   Carolina-style, 203
   chili barbecue wet, 206
   facts about, 208
Beans
   black, soup, 2
   facts about, 179
   navy, soup, 4
   navy or white, sauce, 137
   salad, five bean, 178
   salsa, salmon with, 49
   string, dry-fried, 164
   white, cassoulet with, 18–19
Beef
   boiled, beef broth and, 102–
      103
   curry, with rice, 104
   fillets, Asian-style, 101
   meatballs, Swedish, 124–25
   meatloaf, Clyde's, 126–27
   in meat pies, 128–29
   sauerbraten, 98
   steak
      chicken fried, 114
      facts about, 96
      salad, 185
      sesame, 97
      with three peppers, 96

   stew, 17
   See also Hamburgers; Veal
Berry Cobbler, 251
Black Bean Soup, 2–3
Blackberries, 256
Bleeding, stopping of, 316
Blenders, Waring, 198
Blueberries
   in cobbler, 250, 251
   in Dialogue of Fruits, 239
   facts about, 234
   pie, old-fashioned, 278
   scones, 235
   in summer pudding, 255
Bluefish, Omega 3 oil in, 43
Bordeaux Almond Macaroons, 30
Boysenberries, 256
Breads
   cherry tea, 210
   Jarlsberg twist, 212–13
Breakfast, IQ and, 235
Broccoli
   facts on, 134*n.*, 169
   with olives, 147
   rigatoni pasta with, 134
Brown-and-White Pound Cake, 270
Brownies, maple nut, 301
Brussels sprouts, 169
Burns, first aid for
   chemical, 317
   from heat, 313
Buttermilk stuffing, 74–75
Butternut Squash and Winter Pear
   Bake, 162

Cabbage
   coleslaw, low-calorie, 182
   facts about, 182
   leaves, salmon with, 48
   red, 151
      salad, 180
Caesar Salad, 182
Cakes, 261–75
   knowing when done, 264
Calcium, children and, 260
Caneberries, 256
Canola oil, 92, 294